Essays in Migratory Aestheti

Thamyris/

Intersecting: Place, Sex, and Race

Essays in Migratory Aesthetics: Cultural Practices Between Migration and Art-making

Editors

Sam Durrant

Catherine M. Lord

Rodopi

Colophon

Design

Mart. Warmerdam, Haarlem, The Netherlands
www.warmerdamdesign.nl

Printing

The paper on which this book is printed meets the requirements of "ISO 9706:1994, Information and documentation – Paper for documents – Requirements for permanence".

ISSN: 1381-1312
ISBN: 978-90-420-2236-2

Printed in The Netherlands

Mission Statement

Intersecting: Place, Sex, and Race

Intersecting is a new series of edited volumes with a critical, interdisciplinary focus.

Intersecting's mission is to rigorously bring into encounter the crucial insights of black and ethnic studies, gender studies, and queer studies, and facilitate dialogue and confrontations between them. Intersecting shares this focus with Thamyris, the socially committed international journal which was established by Jan Best en Nanny de Vries, in 1994, out of which Intersecting has evolved. The sharpness and urgency of these issues is our point of departure, and our title reflects our decision to work on the cutting edge.

We envision these confrontations and dialogues through three recurring categories: place, sex, and race. To us they are three of the most decisive categories that order society, locate power, and inflict pain and/or pleasure. Gender and class will necessarily figure prominently in our engagement with the above. Race, for we will keep analysing this ugly, much-debated concept, instead of turning to more civil concepts (ethnicity, culture) that do not address the full disgrace of racism. Sex, for sexuality has to be addressed as an always active social strategy of locating, controlling, and mobilizing people, and as an all-important, not necessarily obvious, cultural practice. And place, for we agree with other cultural analysts that this is a most productive framework for the analysis of situated identities and acts that allow us to move beyond narrow identitarian theories. The title of the new book series points at what we, its editors, want to do: think together. Our series will not satisfy itself with merely demonstrating the complexity of our times, or with analyzing the shaping factors of that complexity. We know how to theorize the intertwining of, for example, sexuality and race, but pushing these intersections one step further is what we aim for: How can this complexity be understood in practice? That is, in concrete forms of political agency, and the efforts of self-reflexive, contextualized interpretation. How can different socially and theoretically relevant issues be thought together? And: how can scholars (of different backgrounds) and activists think together, and realize productive alliances in a radical, transnational community?

We invite proposals for edited volumes that take the issues that Intersecting addresses seriously. These contributions should combine an activist-oriented perspective with intellectual rigor and theoretical insights, interdisciplinary and transnational perspectives. The editors seek cultural criticism that is daring, invigorating and self-reflexive; that shares our commitment to thinking together. Contact us at intersecting@let.leidenuniv.nl

Acknowledgements

The editors wish to acknowledge the financial assistance of the AHRC Centre for Cultural Analysis, Theory and History (CentreCATH), and the Amsterdam School for Cultural Analysis (ASCA) in the development of the project from which this volume of essays emerged.

Many thanks are due to Michael Katzberg for copy-editing the manuscript.

The editors are especially grateful to Lily Markiewicz for her generosity in providing us with a detail from her installation *Promise II* for the front cover of this volume.

Contents

which memory attempts to narrativise the disjunctions of both time and space to which migration gives rise. While not all migration is traumatic, trauma theory has a particular relevance to the attempt to produce a migratory aesthetics in so far as movement between cultures with different, even incommensurable world views almost inevitably gives rise to what Cathy Caruth would describe as a crisis of understanding. How does a migratory aesthetics deal with such crises? Is its function essentially compensatory or exploratory? Ought it move to secure a temporary psychic abode for the migratory subject, what we might describe as a space in time, or ought it teach us how to move beyond ourselves, beyond the need to belong? For those who have economic or affective ties to more than one country, aesthetics potentially offers a way of memorialising one's passage through the world or indeed the passage of one's ancestors (a passage explored by Joy Smith in her essay on the politics of memorialising Afro-Dutch slavery). For others, aesthetics becomes, as Lily Markiewicz suggests in her discussion of her own artistic practice, a way of accommodating oneself to one's not belonging.

In order to read aesthetics as itself migratory, it may be necessary to break with the traditional understanding of art as realism. The Platonic understanding of *mimesis*, in which the artwork is an (inferior) copy of the world, fails to account for the ways in which art making takes place in the world and is itself a worldly activity. Rather than being a representation of the world, art is an act of world making that alters, however subtly, the fabric of the cultures in which we live. The well-worn debate between Marxism and Postmodernism that has so fractured postcolonial studies (see Parry and Lazarus on the one hand and Bhabha, Spivak and their followers on the other) is often reduced to a privileging of realism and historical content on the one hand and an emphasis on aesthetics and experimentalism on the other. But within the Marxist tradition there is an anti-idealist understanding of mimesis that does not see art simply as a mode of recording the content (the events) of history but instead emphasises the historical content of form itself. For Marxists such as Walter Benjamin and Theodor Adorno the relationship between the artwork (form) and the world (content) is reciprocal; artwork and world are structured by the same relations of production and mimic one another in their construction. Thus the artwork need not be judged in terms of its verisimilitude, on the accuracy of its reproduction of, for instance, a particular history of migration, but rather on the degree to which the art work itself *becomes* migratory, the degree to which it mimics – at the level of form rather than content – that which it sets out to represent. A migratory aesthetics might therefore stand as both product and critique of a migratory world, and the uneven economic relations that give rise to the manifold "enforced" and "voluntary" modes of contemporary migration.[1]

The essays collected here, which cover art making in various fields, from literature and fine art to film and photography, are then broadly materialist in their assumption that art and politics are not simply interwoven, but also constitutive of one another.

In remaining mindful of this dialectical, two-way relation, we hope to avoid the twin pitfalls of postcolonial diaspora studies: on the one hand there is the danger of over-aestheticisation in which the experience of the migrant is generalised into a migrant aesthetic that is then universalised as a multicultural ideal; on the other lies the cynical dismissal of aesthetics that denies the migrant any agency in the process of cultural change.

Graham Huggan's essay offers a sustained critique of the aestheticisation of migrancy in the work of cultural theorists such as Iain Chambers and Paul Carter. However, the most influential instance of such "travelling theory" is Homi Bhabha's 1990 essay "DissemiNation," in which the migrant figures as the return of a repressed colonial history, a return that de-seminates or unmeans the nation and magically transforms it into a site of postcolonial hybridity. Although Bhabha touches on less positive experiences of migration, the cumulative movement of the essay turns his final example, the migrancy of Gibreel Farishta in Rushdie's *The Satanic Verses*, into *the* exemplary figure of dissemiNation, the "principle of avenging repetition" that will tropicalise London, grant English footballers close control and turn Cockneys into languid Latin lovers. Although Bhabha's understanding of (post)modernity as structured by the time-lag of colonial history is central to any understanding of the uneven temporalities of contemporary global experience, in choosing to conclude his essay by celebrating the performative dimensions of cultural translation, Bhabha inaugurates a tradition of romantic postcolonialism that tends to overestimate the liberatory effects of migration on the cultures of the host nation and underestimate the less liberatory effects of migration on both migrant and host nation: what Bhabha tellingly neglects to mention is the psychic cost of migration on Gibreel, namely a disabling schizophrenia that eventually leads him to commit suicide.

If Bhabha's essay, in its interweaving – even conflation – of fiction and reality, art and history overestimates the radical potential of the aesthetic without sufficient attention to the material constraints that attend the experience of migration, the opposite danger lies in the underestimation of the aesthetic, understood as a sphere of high culture that has nothing to do with the experience of the everyday, and the concurrent overestimation of political constraints. In such analyses, the migrant can only ever appear as tragic victim of a culture that either rejects or assimilates her without a trace. Such is the charge that has often been (unfairly) levelled against Gayatri Spivak, and her seemingly doom-laden insistence that the subaltern cannot speak.

In her latest work, *A Critique of Postcolonial Reason* (1999), Gayatri Spivak maintains her deconstructive vigilance, shifting her critical gaze from the subaltern to the ethnographic figure of the native informant. The "native" in the informant produces a paradoxical concept, in so far as, in today's global networks, to inhabit a culture untouched by diaspora or displacement is an impossibility. Spivak turns the native informant against itself, reading it as a "figure, a figuration, put forward to counter the unfortunate effects of contemporary flirtations with the universalized, idealized, and thereby offensively misused figures of the 'nomad' or the 'migrant'" (Bal, "Three Way Mis-Reading"). Thus, analysis of the position of the native informant informs us not of the lived experience of "natives" but rather of the shifting interactions between agency, migration and the aesthetic entanglements that join these dimensions, while simultaneously guarding against romanticised conflations.

If aesthetics is precisely how we experience the everyday, then its force need be neither romanticised nor dismissed; rather, in analysing the art work, we are taking the measure of cultures in transition, registering the impact of the migratory across different human environments and differently empowered subjects-in-process. As these subjects choose, fail or refuse to migrate, so they produce different benchmarks for the practice of the everyday across distinct social and cultural fields.

The first section, "Practices within Practices," opens with Bal's own meditation on the meanings associated with migratory aesthetics. Her essay "Lost in Space, Lost in the Library" raises the knotty problem of political correctness, identity politics and the paradoxes of locating either in a conceptual and literal space of migration. Bal explores her own video work to discover "what happens" between cultural analysis and its practice. Her concern is "provenance." Artistic work is site-specific yet globalisation involves the shifting of the contextually sensitive artefact into other arenas, in which the artwork's cultural and political currency requires translation, or indeed may not be open to such transformations, as there may no "original" to keep intact. Bal's own film acts as something which can problematise the very provenance label which has partly inspired the visual work. The film's main character, Daryush, speaks different languages in different registers and with different emotional nuances. Language and artistic medium become entwined in word-image stakes that help the viewer to reconsider the very migrations and losses involved in negotiating linguistic and aesthetic registers.

As a visual artist and scholar, Lily Markiewicz brings her aesthetic practice to bear on the question of the homeless, or "unaccommodated," dimension of artistic work. Her essay, "No Place – Like Home," explores how artists use their work to make dwellings, to move paradoxically into displacement to feel less displaced. Aesthetic experience is itself a perpetual migration between inner and outer, between the affective and cognitive dimensions of both making and experiencing art, between proximity and distance. Exploring her own artwork alongside Freud's concept of the uncanny, Markiewicz suggest the possibility of an aesthetics which is simultaneously housed and homeless.

Catherine M. Lord's response to the use of artistic work in the scholarly article is to produce a short story which offers a futuristic vision of migratory aesthetics, in part responding to Isabel Hoving's article on networking concepts and the concept of a "native informant." Lord's narrative explores the vicissitudes of being a woman writer in an eco-crisis set in a London of the not too distant future. "In the Cooler" is a story that considers how aesthetic products will themselves migrate to survive.

Ecological disasters are but one force that leave the sense of any home desolate and turn the uncanny into the condition for the emergence of new worlds.

In the second section, "Pasts in the Present," Judith Tucker's essay "Painting Places: A Postmemorial Landscape?" argues that landscape painting is a not a stationary object of contemplation; rather, it is a movement towards and away from the object of its research. Deploying Marianne Hirsh's concept of postmemory and Leo Spitzer's analysis of nostalgia, Judith Tucker explores her own artistic practice as a second generation German immigrant. Inspired by photographs of the beach resorts of pre-War Germany taken from a pre-war family album, Tucker's latest work both returns to and moves away from the longed for spaces of the past, paradoxically producing new landscapes through an aesthetics of nostalgia.

Like Tucker, Joy Smith explores the dialectic between remembrance and amnesia in "Diasporic Slavery Memorials and Dutch Moral Geographies." Smith situates Cynthia McLeod's novel *Hoe duur was de suiker?* (*How Expensive was the Sugar?*) between the registers of historical slavery and the contemporary global context of identity politics and self-protectionism. Smith reads the reception of McLeod's best-selling novel alongside the controversy surrounding the design and location of the 2002 Dutch National Slavery Memorial. Both novel and monument raise difficult questions about the ways in which histories of forced migration are consumed. The words on the monument, "Shared Past Common Future," invite an analysis of the oxymoron at stake. While there is a certain acknowledgement of the past, the problems inherent in Holland's so-called "multicultural society" are simultaneously underestimated.

Migratory aesthetics as the traveller's attempt to negotiate herself between spaces referential and imaginary finds further exploration in Sarah de Mul's "Travelling to the Colonial Past as Migratory Aesthetics: Aya Zikken's *Terug naar de atlasvlinder*" Mul develops her analysis of the narrator's travelogue of a return to Sumatra: migratory aesthetics should not be reduced to the notion of a migrant's aesthetics. Instead, as Mul's reading suggests, identity categories should not conflate the migrant with some mythologized notion of an aesthetic agent.

In the third section, "Displaced Aesthetics/The Aesthetics of Displacement," homelessness as a result of the trauma of Middle Eastern history and politics finds exploration in Ihab Saloul's "Exilic Narrativity": The Invisibility of Home in Palestinian Exile." The catastrophe of Palestinian displacement in 1948 (*al-nakba*) has produced a "cinema of exile" which analyses home as longed for, invisible and diasporically unavailable. Saloul develops a specific but multivalent concept, "exilic narrativity" which draws out the complex strategies by which cinema can call on voices and grammars of place, self and other. Such cinema can aesthetically locate itself beyond the fiction-documentary divide, and the notion of a migratory aesthetics joins with that other term that Saloul poetically imbricates into his discussion, that of "drifting storytelling." His case study is the 1972 film *Al Makhdu'un* (translated as *The Dupes*) that he reads not as a direct representation of migrant experience (Palestinian exile), but rather as a migratory aesthetic which theorizes and gives shape to such an exilic experience. Within the film's multiple stories, the migrant is not just a teller of inter-spatial journeys, but also an index of an exilic Palestinian identity in transition.

Migrating people are, in certain texts of cultural theory, accounted for and conceptualised through poststructuralist theories of displacement. In his essay "Unsettled Settlers: Postcolonialism, Travelling Theory and the New Migrant Aesthetics," Graham Huggan invites reflection on the way in which diverse experiences of migration are homogenised by "travelling" cultural theories which in turn mask the material inequalities that govern migration and the often racist immigration policies of the First World – Australia's historical privileging of Anglo-Celtic migrants is a particularly salutary case in point. Huggan alerts us to the ways in which the discourses of migrant and postcolonial studies encapsulate the "metaphorisation of migration," and it is this process of metaphorisation which can, if not properly critiqued, act as alibi for a worldly elite.

While Huggan calls into question the ease with which the experience of migration is accommodated within poststructuralist vocabularies, Sam Durrant's "Storytellers, Novelists, and Postcolonial Melancholia: Displaced Aesthetics in Chinua Achebe's *Things Fall Apart*" suggest historical reasons for this common ground in tracing the impact of modernity across both Europe and its colonies. Postcolonial attempts to come to terms with multiple histories of displacement and migration are in many ways continuous with modernism's agonistic relation to tradition and its concomitant understanding of art as "the shock of the new." His analysis of Chinua Achebe's *Things Fall Apart,* traditionally understood as a realist novel that ethnographically informs us of pre-colonial native culture, is inextricably linked to the ruptured aesthetics of modernism as it attempts to register the trauma of cultural displacement.

By contrast, Wim Staat's essay on "Transgression of Everydayness in Heddy Honigmann's P®IVÉ: A Dutch Case Study in Stanley Cavell's Film Ethics" focuses on the displacements that occur within metropolitan culture. Statt situates P®IVÉ as an oblique response to contemporary Dutch anxiety about Muslim fundamentalism that retrains the lens on home-grown Christian fundamentalism. The film reveals how the aesthetics of the everyday can be shifted by "internal" others who disturb the restrictive traditions of their own native community in order to express hitherto repressed histories of loss. Here, then, it is the Western native who "migrates" the everyday aesthetics of his own community.

In Section four, "Relations, Conflations and Traumas," the slippery and difficult connection between agency and culturally, globally layered spaces finds fresh scrutiny in Isabel Hoving's "Between Relation and the Bare Facts: The Migratory Imagination and Relationality." Her approach enables migration to be followed as a political, economic and social dynamic that encounters migrant writing and an "imagination of space." Her analysis is centred around the concept of "Relation," first set out in the anti-identitarian approach of Martinican writer Edouard Glissant, which releases the notion of migrant identity from its moorings in essentialism. Like other discourses inspired by post-structuralism (Glissant takes his cue in part from the work of Deleuze and Guattari), Glissant's approach might initially seem productive for an analysis of migratory aesthetics, but its tendency to universalise leaves it vulnerable to materialist critique. Hoving considers both literary and philosophical critiques of his approach, and illuminatingly places his work alongside various environmentalist approaches.

Sudeep Dasgupta pulls no punches in his views on the appropriation of the term migration. In "Running A(g)round: Migratory Aesthetics and the Politics of Translation," Dasgupta challenges the value of turning migratory aesthetics into a workable term. If "migration" is treated as the aesthetic framework within which to analyse the migrant's subjectivity, the aesthetic as a category may suffer the vicissitudes of being depoliticised. Dasgupta suggests strategies for a non-conflationary reading of migration and aesthetics in an analysis of *Before Night Falls*, directed by the Cuban filmmaker, Julian Schabels, and inspired by the life of the Cuban émigré Reinaldo Arenas, who died of AIDS in New York in 1990. Dasgupta points out that the praise accorded to the filmmaker's talents privileged his artistic and political status as neither entirely inside nor outside mainstream society. This manoeuvre says much about the valorisation of the migrancy of texts and the manner in which the migrant becomes placed in an aesthetic category which can smooth over the singularity of particular experiences of migrancy.

While the conflation of lived realities and aesthetic representation needs to be avoided, there is an equally pressing need to explore the interface between different realms of theory and practice and their impact on one another. In "Daydreaming Before History: The Last Works of Sigmund Freud and Charlotte Salomon," Griselda Pollock offers a meditation on the function of the archive that is equally inspired by deconstruction and psychoanalysis. She begins with Freud's *Moses and Monotheism* and Said's rereading of Freud's last work as an anti-identitarian parable of Moses as Egyptian migrant, and goes on to juxtapose Freud's last work with the paintings of Charlotte Salomon, both of which were traumatically marked by the anti-Semitism of the 1930s and early 1940s. Here again migratory aesthetics is not simply the representation or archival depository of migrant histories but work which itself "remembers," not only bearing the traces of its traumatic passage through history but also recovering agency precisely at the moment of its seeming negation: Salomon's attempt to make creative work an act of migrant exit from a murderous history affirms a certain aesthetic freedom even in the face of her transportation to Auschwitz in October 1943.

Pollock's essay is thus a fitting conclusion to *Essays in Migratory Aesthetics*. In a bid to take the measure of a world both in transit and transition, a bid that is, by the very nature of its task, always doomed to failure, the essays that follow attempt to sustain that necessary tension between romanticism and cynicism, affirmation and critique, the determinism of history and the radical force of aesthetic creativity.

Endnotes

1. For a comprehensive historical survey of the concept of mimesis, including Adorno and Benjamin's materialist revision of the term, see Gebauer and Wulf.

Works Cited

Achebe, Chinua. 1959. *Things Fall Apart*. New York: Ballantine, 1991.

Bal, Mieke. "Three-Way Mis-Reading," *Diacritics*. 30.1 (2000), 2–24.

Bhabha, Homi. "DissemiNation: Time, Narrative and the Margins of the Modern Nation." In *Nation and Narration*, ed. Homi Bhabha. London: Routledge, 1990.

Caruth, Cathy. *Unclaimed Experience: Trauma, Narrative and History*. Baltimore and London: Johns Hopkins UP, 1996.

Gebauer, Gunter, and Christoph Wulf. *Mimesis: Culture/Art/Society*. Trans. Don Reneau. Berkeley: University of California Press, 1995.

Gilroy, Paul. *After Empire*. London: Routledge, 2004.

Hardt, Michael and Antonio Negri. *Empire*. London and Cambridge MA: Harvard University Press, 2000.

———. *Multitude*. London: Penguin, 2004.

Lazarus, Neil. *Nationalism and Cultural Practice in the Postcolonial World*. Cambridge: Cambridge University Press, 2003.

Parry, Benita. *Postcolonial Studies: A Materialist Critique*. London: Routledge, 2004.

Rushdie, Salman. *The Satanic Verses*. 1988. Dover, Delaware: The Consortium, 1992.

Spivak, Gayatri. *A Critique of Postcolonial Reason: Toward a History of The Vanishing Present*. London and Cambridge MA: Harvard, 1999.

I. Practices within Practices

Lost in Space, Lost in Library

Mieke Bal

As the one who initially came up with the term "migratory aesthetics" I feel compelled to begin this reflection with a brief exploration of what it can possibly mean. A "travelling concept" (see Bal 2002) if ever there was one, on the one hand it falls back on the notion of aesthetics, and on the other it coins a modifier for that notion, truly modifying it. This modifier indicates that migratory aesthetic is an aesthetic, but takes the latter concept literally, as *a condition of sentient engagement*. Thus, it is part and parcel of those concepts that attempt to establish an active interface between viewer and artwork. Examples are "relational aesthetics" (Bourriaud), "empathic aesthetics," (Bennett) or simply "political art." These attempts consider the artwork to be empty as long as the act of viewing is not inherent to it, and that act is called upon to do political work.

The modifier "migratory" does not refer to migrants or actual migration of people, nor would I, as user of the concept, presume to be qualified to do so. What the modifier means instead, how it relates to the three concepts above, and how it can help us understand possibilities for art to be politically effective, is the subject of this paper. "Migratory aesthetics," then, is a non-concept, a ground for experimentation that opens up possible relations with "the migratory," rather than pinpointing such relations. As a provisional circumscription of the modifier, let me call it a feature, or a quality of the world in which mobility is not the exception but on its way to becoming the standard, the means rather than the minority.

Migratory, in this sense, does foreground the fact that migrants (as subjects) and migration (as an act to perform as well as a state to be or live in) are part of any society today, and that their presence is an incontestable source of cultural transformation. I would like to present the modifier as a constructive focus of an aesthetics that does not leave the viewer, spectator, or user of art aloof and shielded, autonomous and in charge of the aesthetic experience. If aesthetics is primarily an encounter in which the subject, body included, is engaged, that aesthetic encounter is migratory if it takes place in the space of, on the basis of, and on the interface with, the mobility

s a given, as central, and as at the heart of what matters in the contem-
hat is, "globalized" world.

s I am pondering the meaning of migratory aesthetics, I am drawn to those questions that have preoccupied the progressive sections of the western academy for the last two decades. These include issues of cultural identity, of regional specificity, of under-studied provenances, of affirmative action, all housed in environments of politically-aware scholars: feminist studies, gender and queer studies, postcolonial and anti-racist studies. The issues that informed these environments have not gone away. Instead, they have been recuperated by movements of regressive politics, also called back-lash, orchestrated by those who possess the skill of picking out the critical problem of each of the concepts we used to believe in and of turning these against those who attempt to engage with the world and resist the usual, banal exploitative attitude toward others. For example, the term "politically correct" was a positive notion, indicating a more sensitive and caring attitude to those mainstream cultures construed as its "others." From the perspective of back-lash, it has been abducted to become a negative, for friend and foe alike. Such abduction has had consequences for the terrains of interdisciplinary research.

As it happens, during the same two decades, interdisciplinary movements have produced unrest in the established disciplines. It is, of course, no coincidence that the two developments are related, although they do not overlap. Having been involved in both movements, I am interested in exploring how "migratory aesthetics" can be of help in attempts to safeguard what was valuable in those movements, both academically and socially. I will discuss this double issue of the meaning of migratory aesthetics and the interdisciplinarity inherent in what is variably called cultural studies or cultural analysis – through a small experimental artefact. As an example of a cultural study or analysis for which the library is not of easy access, perhaps not even equipped well enough, I will present a short video, called *Lost in Space*. This video was an experiment, and it concerns migrants. It is also an aesthetic object and as such it is anchored in movement, not just of people, but also of media, of images, and of voices.

The video was to help me get more of a grip on a question I wanted to address but that remained too vague. Firstly, I wanted to consider how to proceed from a vague notion of dealing with an artefact I felt passionately about, to something that was an object of study. How to go from a vague notion of something that you passionately feel is very important to something that can actually be studied? Secondly, I am also interested in preserving the ethical imperative that made me raise the question in the first place. The question to which this film was meant to suggest a partial and provisional answer was one of methodology: how can we be culturally specific in our analyses of cultural processes and artefacts, without nailing people or artworks to a provenance they no longer feel comfortable claiming as theirs? Obviously, this topic concerns cultural studies or, as I prefer to call it, cultural analysis, in the present, at a time of what is called "globalization," but where that term hinders rather than helps my project. Globalization is better documented in sociological studies such as those by Saskia Sassen, or in economic studies. Cultural studies tends to focus on a more comprehensive approach, on being more inclusive of non-mainstream cultural production, but I have not found much to help me with my question. Yet, it seems an important one.

Globalization sounds very much like the opposite of old terms such as "provenance," "cultural location of background," even "context." As it happens, the contextualists in art history and literary studies – also called new historicists – who revolutionized their respective fields in the 1980s, are presently more established than they once were, and with that established condition, more closed to the issues they once found so important. The problem is that they remained loyal to their once-revolutionary positions; they failed to endorse mobility. I am not suggesting one is to abandon positions in the wake of intellectual fashion, but to modify them in engagement with other views, in turn generated by transformations of the world. Such a commitment to stay engaged with the present seems to me to be the only responsible way to be historical.

Globalization appears to suggest that the centre is no longer in the West; the centre is nowhere. Yet, it is in the name of globalization that Western institutions now exhibit artworks from regions hitherto kept at bay, buried in regional museums or considered folklore. At best, the masterpieces from a particularly sophisticated culture such as east-Asian Buddhism either get their own museum – in Paris, the Musée Guimet – or their own, somewhat separated section in national museums such as the Louvre. It will take a lot of serious and creative reflection before works from cultures such as Bénin can be meaningfully displayed among the masterpieces of Western art, although many agree that masterpieces they are. Precisely because they are masterpieces they are considered to require their own context – at least, this is why their separate exhibition remains the only mode of showing them.

Provenance makes a lot of sense in terms of identity politics. The added advantage of disciplinary decorum is that provenance has always been a staple of art history. This, however, is where disciplinarity and continued dominance of those in the mainstream who consider it unnecessary to take inequality into consideration as an intellectual issue, threaten to join forces. For, at the same time, bringing together art from a region or country on the simple basis of the "made in" label, in shows like "Indian Summer," Fall 2005 in the Ecole des Beaux Arts, smacks a bit of exploitation, of the new colonization after de-colonization.[1]

But globalization as an issue, a problematic, is also at stake in other ways, in art practices where the provenance can no longer be taxonomically identified. This would be, then, the "migratory" of aesthetics. Globalized art – what would such a term mean? This is not an art from nowhere, for such an art, I contend, does not exist. Since art making is a material practice, there is no such thing as site-unspecific art.

What I would like to discuss is a practice of art-making that addresses globalization, as a problematic, that takes it on, so to speak, and that derives its "provenance label" from that problematic; *that* is what anchors it.

In particular, the medium of video lends itself to such art; at least, that is what I have experienced in my attempts at participating in such a video-based art form. I would like to present a short, 15-minute film that I made with an Iranian artist living in Berlin. This collaboration – which, unfortunately, has presently ended – was an attempt to be responsive to Arjun Appadurai's 2001 appeal to "grassroots globalization" and the important concept of "research imagination." As a team, we felt, we had enough experience with cultural difference to be able to reflect on the twin issue of over-specifying, in an ill-directed identity politics, and erasing difference, in an equally ill-conceived pressure to assimilation under the label of globalization. What I would like to argue through this presentation – of the film itself and my thoughts about it – is the cultural specificity of the film's aesthetic. But this specificity, without denying cultural difference – on the contrary, it foregrounds it – is localized in the globalizing movement of people itself.

This aesthetic was no *a priori* decision, a starting point from which we set out to make this work. Instead, this aesthetic happened. Leaving the aesthetic open to what would happen was the only a priori decision we took. It happened when I was interviewing people for what was meant to be a series of short films as part of an installation, on the triple notion of *home, security, and borders*. In the course of a few months the projected installation changed and became a short, 15-minute film that is meant to stand on its own. It has experimentation with sound at its heart. The medium that dominates it is the human voice. The way the sonoric quality of the voices was both made and performed through the work of sound, came as a result of their struggle with globalised languages. Let me tell you why.

The subject matter, theme, or topic of the film is displacement, dislocation, the subjectively experienced consequences of migration. Hence, the theme focuses on globalization through an intimate approach with actual migrants. But this thematic centring is emphatically not the point of the aesthetic. We conducted interviews with people who were themselves familiar with experiences of displacement or who worked with people in comparable situations of displacement. This could be because they had moved to another country, or because their country was taken away from under them. Or simply because they left home to start college. But a topic does not make an aesthetic. What does make an aesthetic is the sentient encounter with subjects involved. In this case, one of the people, a man from Iran who had been an asylum seeker for no less than sixteen years, triggered the experience and the aesthetic of the subsequent film; an aesthetic I consider a good example of a *migratory* aesthetic. In the remainder of this paper I will explain why, and what it means to call the aesthetic migratory – what kind of sentient binding it performs, and why that matters.

This man, called Daryush, spoke very limited English, and clearly suffered from his difficulty in saying things that mattered to him. Yet, he had volunteered for the project and even insisted, when we were hesitant, to be included. So, both his desire to speak and the difficulty he experienced when speaking both became relevant factors. The difficulty of speaking was important. First, I tried to solve the problem by seeing if we had another language in common. We did not, for I did not understand the languages he was fluent in, Farsi and Greek, while he did not speak French. Hence, out of practical necessity we continued to wrestle with English. This is a situation that any non-native speaker of English will recognize, whereas native speakers of English may need a leap of the research imagination to get the point of the difficulty.

The conversation was slow and painful, and I was wondering if we would actually be able to use the footage. Then something happened that made his speech absolutely central to the project; it determined the aesthetic style of it. At one point, when I asked him what he most missed about his home, he fell into a frantic expression of the incapacity to speak. He was most desirous to speak, but most incapacitated by the foreignness of the language we were using. I told him he could speak in Farsi. While I was unable to respond to his answer, I would be able to understand it later, since my partner in the project is also from Iran. After a few seconds of total silence – I was beginning to wonder if he had understood my proposal – words, sounds that I did not understand at all tumbled out of his mouth, for me only musical, with a distinct melody and rhythm, while his face had also changed: previously cramped with pain, now more relaxed. The differences – his fluidity of speech and his animated face – were the more striking as his speech so far had shown the typical a-melodic flatness of depressed speech. I asked him what he had said but he only smiled and didn't say. Some time later I got the words translated. To my surprise as well as delight it turned out he had said that what he most missed was speaking *his own language*.

As I could only acknowledge belatedly, this was the crucial, performative moment of the production. I was unable to respond to his words when I heard them, and yet something in his voice told me he was indeed saying something that was crucially important to him. I took his hand, and he hugged me, with tearful eyes. When, later, I did understand his words, he was no longer there to interact with my understanding. Of course, I felt terribly inadequate; the least I could have given him in turn for his collaboration was some comfort, however momentaneous. This double discrepancy – between speech and understanding, and between meaningful sound and senseless sound – then, became the basis of the film. The migratory aesthetics took the form of a work *on* and *with* discrepancy. In practice, the result was the following. We decided to sever sound from vision, as in Daryush's interview, and to place sound *in competition* with noise. The hope was that something radical would happen to the sound, here, especially that part of the sound that consists of the voices, of the speakers.

I would like to talk about what kind of aesthetic, as I phrased it earlier, *happened*, and what that meant, first, for the relation between art and politics, and second, for me as a scholar making art as a laboratory for migratory aesthetics. Here, the issue of interdisciplinarity joins forces with migratory aesthetics. In what I call, for lack of a better term, art making, I have experienced, learned and understood aspects of social life that all the books and journals in the world couldn't teach me. I want to propose this experiment as a reflection on the importance, the meaningfulness, and the impossibility of, what the title of the panel of a conference in Paris in which I participated called the designation of a cultural area in the organization of artistic production.[2]

What I learned in the laboratory of art was that making *Lost in Space* had direct resonances with the shortcomings of the discipline of art history as I know it, not because there is anything inherently wrong with that discipline, but simply because it is one: a form of disciplining, of limiting what can be said or written about art. What I learned was, firstly, an experience of perception in its irreducible bond with duration. Duration pertains to temporality, the domain of literature and theatre, film and music, and has only recently and reluctantly been accepted as an issue of art history. That acceptance is due to the increasing importance of video-related art forms, and not because the discipline recognises the crucial importance of duration in the encounter with any artwork.

Secondly, I learned the importance and consequences of the unity of perception and sensation that undermines the distinction between subject and object. Yet, it is on this distinction that visual art has always based its specificity, its "nature." To sum up: what I realized through the interview with Daryush is this: the world as we knew it, art as we knew it, the limits and concepts and distinctions by which we lived, were all transformed by the brief sensation of *losing clarity*. Including the clarity of where this bit of art production comes from. The sentient encounter that is the aesthetic event became migratory in this sense: detached from the self-evident certainty of who and where we are, and tumbling inside the experience of someone else caught in a state of mobility which curiously imprisons him. Mobility as, paradoxically, a prison.

One point of discussion emerged right away that is bound up with the position of English in the world today: the problem of linguistic imperialism – the advantage English speakers invariably have over others – versus the need to communicate across boundaries. With Daryush, as with some others, I felt, almost physically, the violence I was doing to the interviewees by imposing a generalized English as the language of communication. Yet, there was no question that his contribution was important, and his eagerness to participate was a clear indication of that felt importance.

One of the consequences of this double bind was the aesthetics of the accent. Making the film the way we did was an attempt to use the "accented" English of the speakers. Not only did accented English become the standard, compared to which the "perfect" English of native speakers was also heavily accented, and the German – or

Farsi, for that matter – of some others, just another accent. Also, we tried to probe the accented speeches in the effort of translation, to make them speak with their double tongue: English, and more, not less.

Losing clarity, then, leads to a gain in insight. One of the many insights that the difficulty of clear communication provided, was, for example, the insight that we all need technological supplementation to sharpen our senses. We may not realize it, but wearing glasses or contact lenses is just one instance of such supplementation. Needing a foreign language to speak, on an everyday basis, is another. This example leads us to the most foregrounded element of the film's aesthetic: the separation of language as it is visible – in mouths, in gestures, in bodies – from language that is audible. Language, in the film, then, is at first made to disintegrate. First you *see* it, then you *hear* it. And while you hear it, you are almost being distracted from it by the written word.

This written word you need, and the realization of that need is a confrontation with your own inadequacy. You see language first when, in the extensive credit sequence that opens the film, the speakers are shown, saying what they turn out to be saying in the film, but without voice. This is frustrating; at first, one assumes the sound is defective. Later, some of the gestures seen earlier fall into place. For example, one woman says that politics is like changing pants (trousers): every so often you put on a new pair of pants while your body remains the same, and similarly, politics forces us to "put on" a new enemy every so often. Just think of the way the misnomer "Arab" currently replaces the equally problematic qualifier "communist." You see that strange gesture of simulating putting on pants, but it doesn't make sense. Not yet. Only later do you realize, if your memory is capable of putting that gesture together with that speech, why she was making the gesture. This appeal to a memory that cannot hold all is, in turn, a reminder of the durational aspect of film.

Instead of hearing the voices, during those first few minutes of the film, you hear a sound track of street noise. Nothing special, nothing to understand, just noise, in the physical as well in the informational sense of the term. This noise competes with the sense that language is being spoken. The point of this competition was to bring out in the open a realization that underlies the project, to protect it from a false division. It puts the speeches in the street, so to speak; it puts private, personal language out in the political domain. This merging of private and public, undermining a long-standing false opposition that no one really believes in, is somehow difficult to give up. Making street noise the first thing you hear, while seeing people speaking that you cannot hear, was like a preface that qualifies everything else.

After this sequence, the reverse happens, when the film "proper" begins. Now, we hear the voices but no longer see the speakers. The focus is now entirely on the speeches. Yet, this is not a reversal between visual and auditory sensation. For, instead of seeing the speakers speak, we see their words while we hear them, translated into an English that never quite exactly matches what they say, written large over the screen.

Like the street noise competing with the mouths and the bodies of the speakers, this written English is put in competition with the voices. It is written in such a large print over the images that these, as a consequence, become background, a form of visual noise, in turn comparable to the street noise of the opening sequence.

At this point I wish to add a few remarks to keep the discussion focused on the issue of how to develop a research project in cultural analysis: interdisciplinary, and "migratory" at the same time. A first issue concerns narrative, which is my first theoretical specialization. To the frustration of viewer – at least, I speculate that this is frustrating – the images that accompany the speeches and the written transcriptions or translations of these, go nowhere, narratively speaking. That doesn't mean that the film is devoid of narrative. On the contrary, the lack of a satisfying narrative direction and ending only foregrounds narrativity, as a problem, denaturalizing it from its self-evident cultural domination. Narrativity is inevitably part of film, if only due to the workings of characters, sequentiality and duration.

But here there is more to the problem of narrativity. Changing positions, the speeches, sometimes evoking memories in brief narrative fragments, do not in themselves constitute a narrative. In the film, the speeches are short statements, spoken directly and hence, addressing the viewer as a second person. The credit sequence has already shown this, and visually, the viewer remembers the modes of address. When hearing the voices and reading what they say one remembers their body language: the body-speak was sometimes frontal, as though the act of talking took the viewer's position, sometimes obliquely sideways and clearly in conversation with one of the filmmakers. Instead of being elements toward one narrative, the speeches make a narrative out of the encounter with the addressee – the viewer.

But the narrativity goes farther than this. In turn, the visual background consists of four sequences, perhaps four potential stories, thus appropriating through viewers' expectations the most common linguistic or literary cultural form, or mode as I prefer to call it. But as much as implying narrative, these four sequences are blasting it out of the water. These are sequences of images with a narrativity, even some suspense, and slightly unsettling. But these narratives can only abort; they lead nowhere. This seemed important to me, and again, the visual narratives "just happened" during the editing process. We found ourselves editing not only failed, aborted narratives, but also narratives of (state) failure. These narratives of failure turned out to coincide with the failure of narrative that informs the film as a whole.

In order of appearance, first punk youngsters are just sitting, whiling away time, thickening duration while their dog is the only figure trying to do something. Then a futile but coerced effort to clean the public park after the Love Parade in Berlin occupies the time of the unemployed. In the third visual sequence, the safety measures of the police are inadequate. Policemen protect the US and UK embassies, but are unable to prevent bike riders from transgressing into the blocked-off territory. In the fourth, fire fighters are unable to do more than smash a window; the water from their hoses leaks out and sprays the passers-by, not the fire. They only manage to destroy, not protect the house on fire. By means of the failure of the actions shown, the four sequences show the inadequacy of narrative to account for the state of mobility and displacement, as well as the inadequacy of security measures. Mobility here does not produce gripping tales of travel; it produces cultural stagnation, a stagnation for which the so-called host cultures must be held accountable. This is a four-chapter narrative of inadequacy, of impotence to deal with change.

This conclusion about the inadequacy of what is, in fact, a very traditional answer to danger, seemed important. What we see in these visual sequences is a kind of social stagnation where what visual non-stories have in common is that they inflect, gloss, and further "accent" the speeches we hear. Thus, they foreground, we can conclude, the impossibility of narrativity to flourish under conditions of social stagnation. This is where culture and politics inevitably intersect. They also distract us, in a way symmetrical to what noise tends to do when we are concentrating on vision. But there is also sound, noise, street sound, in these background sequences. When the sounds produced in these narratives of futility become louder, threatening to compete with the voices, we realize that the written word, itself a further "accent," offers only a tenuous hold. This can be seen as a connotative statement – if such a thing is logically possible – on the inadequacy of the library, the primary tool of disciplinary, disciplined research.

Meanwhile, this also brings me back to sound, made so central, in this film, to foreground the migratory aesthetic. Sound, in this project, is a tool, perhaps a weapon, against some of the dominant tendencies in viewing, in a culture saturated by cinema and television and its standard modes of identificatory absorption. Sound, not as support of but displaced from the image, pushed rigorously out of sync, thus counters, for example, the voyeuristic tendencies built into a cinema of individual story-telling, including witnessing. It counters a documentary tradition of telling the story of one to stand for the adventure of many. This is where, ordinarily, visual and linguistic narrativity join forces – a force we have sought to withstand in this experimental film. I am not saying that this tradition is inherently politically wrong, or unethical. It is just a mode, a very efficient and adequate one, but perhaps for that very reason, one that should not have a monopoly.

What alternative to the logic of synchronic sound and image can be suitable for an aesthetics that is migratory – that is, one that endorses and explores the mobility of the current social world? If we believe – as I firmly believe we must – the asylum seeker who considers being deprived of his tongue the essence of being severed from his home, then we must reconsider the importance of this *acoustic mirror* – to invoke Kaja Silverman's brilliant account of voice in cinema (1988). This term felicitously captures the non-reflective acoustic surroundings that contribute to shaping the identity of the subject – from the infant's mother's voice, Silverman's primary topic in her study, to what I am pointing to here, when that primary acoustic surrounding is lacking, and replaced by the voices and sounds, both languages, accents, and tone of friendliness or hostility, reassurance or threat. I have not found any scholarship on this particular problem, that the mother tongue is out of reach, in some cases even forgotten, but not replaced with anything of the same identity-shaping force.

For this reason alone, identity politics, important as it remains in some situations, cannot be the sole answer to the problem posed by "the migratory." This tool for self-realization that has been taken from people in displacement is a key component of what it is to be human. It turned out – I discovered, while making this film – that this acoustic mirror must be taken very seriously, and perhaps be considered an area where we can all contribute, socially, to the further and better shaping of the kind of society that globalization has produced. This is a huge step from the initial problem, which I repeat:

How can we be culturally specific in our analyses of cultural processes and artefacts, without nailing people or artworks to a provenance they no longer feel comfortable claiming as theirs?

Let's say, to cut a long story short, that through making this film in which listening was an enormously important part, I have learned to understand an aspect of my vague question I didn't know existed, namely, that in the absence of a clear cultural identity for so many, the "culturally specific" has to be redefined as, say, the "multiculturally specific."

Such specificity is conducive neither to a melting pot nor to separate spheres, nor to assimilation nor to cultural essentialism. Instead, by that redefinition the cultural remains in sight even where no central culture can be detected. Now, when I say "listening," I am using a verb that has both an intellectual and an affective, even an ethical dimension. This is also important in itself. For, through that realization I learned that an intellectual, academic project does not stay in its isolated place. It spills over into a world where other values than intellectual achievement are important. This brings me to the relevance of the practice of *making* as a form of research – as a deployment of Appadurai's research imagination.

Let me wind up by connecting the key terms of this research: culture, human existence, art, video, practice. Having, or being in, a culture is a fundamental human feature, even, one could claim, a human right. Yet, a number of the migrants speaking in this film have no such thing. If art is one of the means we have to explore and address fundamental questions of what it is to be human, then the current condition of displacement – including displacement "at home" where the home has been taken away, as in Palestine, for example – is a relevant, indeed, central place to start for innovative practices of analysing that domain of "culture." Video art, which disposes of technological tools to produce experiences one would not ordinarily be able to have, is an efficient, indeed powerful means to raise such questions and bring us a step closer to a tentative and provisional answer.

The practice of video making can raise these questions on the sensorial level, not, or not exclusively, intellectually. When making this short film, we found that questions not easily addressed in text form emerged and imposed themselves when voice and noise were put on the same level of importance. The different means we deployed to wrench sound away from its facile synchronicity with images were our attempt to cope with these persistent questions. These decisions, aesthetic, ethical, as well as intellectual, also "just happened" in the sense that they were responses to what happened during the making of the film rather decisions taken prior to the making of the film. This happening is the performative aspect of the situation we put ourselves in when we go out of the library organized by disciplines, into the messy world.

The culture of displacement we found there is not "globalized" in the way westerners tend to conceive of globalization. The steady stream of migrants moves mainly in one direction only; the direction indicated by the fundamental lack of justice in the economic divisions that are called "globalization." The centre is nowhere, for the displaced in the first place. But where does that put them, in terms of a cultural realm they can live in as "theirs"? In a culture of displacement, the insight that the acoustic mirror is the cultural home of individuals gives settled people a specific ethical task. "We" – if I may be forgiven for using, albeit ironically, this problematic pronoun, qualifying it as people who do live in a more or less continuous acoustic environment – we, then, to be sure, cannot return to Daryush, or any of the other speakers who might crave it, their mother tongue; nor can we make up for that loss.

But we can produce a substitute, poor as it may be, to that primary acoustic mirror. We can produce, that is, an acoustic, indeed an integrated sentient mirror that would be not a mother tongue but a friendly tongue: a linguistic, sonoric environment of friendliness and welcome, interest and collaboration. There is a narrative aspect to this proposition. This environment of friendly voices as a culturally multiple sonic space will be a form a *retroversion*. This narratological term refers to the technique, in story-telling, of referring back to earlier events that happened before the primary storyline. A friendly acoustic mirror, in this sense, can recast the reassuring quality of the home soundscape in the new environment. That is, an acoustic mirror that can engage with, and in the end, help substitute for, the soundscape of displacement. This is a cultural provenance as well. This would be the ethical counterpart of migratory aesthetics: the ethical imperative to provide a congenial, friendly soundscape in which mobility – the migratory – is not the despised exception but the valued norm.

Why would art that is ordinarily categorized as visual help to explore this possibility? *Lost in Space*, as I mentioned before, has been a laboratory of experiment, including in this sense. Vision, when on the side of the viewer doing the looking, responds, on the side of the image, to an *appearance*. This word, I suggest, must be given its full weight, not in the metaphysical sense of appearances in miracles, but almost as strongly and powerfully. It was our hope that the mix of rhythm in duration, of linearity interrupted, of technology as a tool to acknowledge fragmentation and supplementation, of sounds competing with other sounds and with images, can suggest a form in which people are encouraged to *appear*, not as *images* to be voyeuristically captured, nor in the name of a cultural provenance that keeps them imprisoned as "different," but in a synaesthetic fullness that only becomes possible after the collapse of the effect of the real, that greatest lie of all. The centre is *nowhere* – but it only takes one space, a small, graphic gap, to turn that half-way statement into something more liveable: the centre is *now-here*.

Endnotes

1. Gayatri Spivak's famous phrase "the neocolonialism in postcoloniality" has far from run its course. See, of many places, her 1999 critique.

2. "History of Art, Cultural Studies and the Understanding of Contemporary Art in Globalization." Film screening and discussion in the INHA European Symposium "Contemporary Art and Globalization: Issues, research, resources and networks in Europe," Paris, 1 December 2005.

Works Cited

Appadurai, Arjun. "Grassroot Globalization and the Research Imagination." *Globalization*. Durham, NC: Duke University Press, 2001. 1–21.

Bennett, Jill. *Empathic Vision: Affect, Trauma, and Contemporary Art*. Cultural Memory in the Present. Stanford, Calif.: Stanford University Press, 2005.

Bourriaud, Nicolas. *Postproduction: Culture as Screenplay: How Art Reprograms the World*. New York: Lukas & Sternberg, 2000.

Sassen, Saskia. *Cities in a World Economy*. Thousand Oaks, London, New Delhi: Pine Forge Press, 1994.

———. *The Global City: New York, London, Tokyo*. Princeton, New Jersey: Princeton University Press, 1991.

———. *Globalization and Its Discontents*. New York: The New Press, 1998.

Silverman, Kaja. *The Acoustic Mirror: The Female Voice in Psychoanalysis and Cinema*. Bloomington: Indiana University Press, 1988.

Spivak, Gayatri Chakravorty. *A Critique of Postcolonial Reason: Toward a History of the Vanishing Present*. Cambridge: Harvard University Press, 1999.

Thamyris/Intersecting No. 17 (2007) 37-48

No Place – Like Home

Lily Markiewicz

The framework for the following discussion is based on my artistic practice and certain ideas about trauma and the uncanny. I look at the concept of artistic practice as dwelling, which here is understood as synonymous with both a making of place and feeling at home. What I want to problematize is not the notion of artistic practice as a way of being in place, but rather that this implies housing oneself or feeling at home. I will consider artistic practice and the viewing of artwork as a possible instance of losing oneself, of becoming what I would like to call unaccommodated. The term "dwelling" has most closely been associated with the writings of Martin Heidegger.[1] Like many philosophical models it has migrated to the realm of the arts where the concept of artistic practice as dwelling is often understood as synonymous with being in place or as a making of place and even feeling at home. In my own artistic practice, which revolves around film, video and photography, largely in the context of installation, I have extensively explored this notion of a making of place. For me, this was, and still is, largely about ideas of "home" in general and "belonging" in particular; with both concepts referencing Judaic teachings about memory, redemption and individual responsibility and belonging in community, rather than territorial conditions or national affiliations. It is from here that the following ideas about feeling at home in the context of art making, and by extension, the viewing of it, have emerged.

In popular parlance, being at home is often associated or conflated with feeling good, feeling safe and comfortable. Yet, to feel at home could signify a simple being used to something, having become familiar. That this familiarity is not necessarily also a comfortable one may well be known to many of us who have tried to shift out of habitual circumstances or patterns of behaviour. If unsuccessful, we often end up feeling uncomfortably comfortable. In an ironic turn, Edmond Jabès inverts this to what could be called feeling comfortably uncomfortable. For him, existence after the Holocaust is a placeless one, and it is this placelessness that provides the condition from which to write: "It [this absence of place] confirms that the book is my only habitat, the first and also the final. Place of a vaster non-place where I live." ("Jewish Writing" 26) For him, there are no certainties, except maybe that there are none, that "every question [is answered] with another question" (*Book of Questions* 116). Jabès, one could say, talks about being at home in homelessness.[2] He proposes, in line with Jewish tradition, that a Jew is at home only in the text. Words, or more specifically, the book, provide the place that is home.[3] Others have extended such a construction beyond the confines of this grouping to encompass everyone under the so-called post-modern condition of fragmented decentredness. Unlike them, I am not proposing we all have become wandering, questioning Jews. For me, the term Jew is a complex one, too closely associated with a set of historical circumstances and my individual experiences, especially of anti-Semitism, to use it as a metaphor for a generalised sense of displacement, up-rootedness or marginalisation.[4] Jabès' writings speak to me about the impossibility of answers in a world filled with questions. He asserts that there is: "no place for the question which is not also a question of place" ("Jewish Writing" 30). Such questions may then relate to (the creation of) a specific place, or to an experience of placelessness, or to the notion of being at home as a version of being in place. They may also point to an *unmaking* of sorts.

Given my own experience of growing up in Germany as the daughter of non-German Jewish Holocaust survivors, and as someone who has migrated subsequently to another country and culture, thinking about artistic practice as a version of being in place has for a long time provided, along with many other historical and post-structuralist arguments, a persuasive and adequate structure from which to think about questions of place and space, belonging and identity in general. Feeling much like a "wandering Jew," I have thought of a work of art, and even artistic practice, as a place to dwell. For me, this has always been in the first instance an opportunity to engage in speculations about the conditions of and possibilities for being.[5] Furthermore, I understood art and artistic practice as a temporary construction of place that could answer, if not to a wish for a certain belonging or at-homeness, then at least to a sense of *housing oneself*. In this context, I have come to the phrase "housing oneself" in an attempt to find an adequate translation for the German *wohnen*, which has been variably translated as dwelling, living, residing or inhabiting. In German, it suggests both an at-homeness and a feeling comfortable. In what follows, I have deliberately stayed clear of using the word dwelling so as to differentiate the concept of housing oneself from being, or being in place. What I want to problematize here is not the notion of artistic practice as a way of being in place, but rather, the notion that this implies housing oneself. Or, to return to Jabès for a moment, that it offers "a refuge" (*Book of Questions* 13).[6]

Having come to make a distinction between dwelling and housing oneself as a direct outcome of my own artistic and critically reflexive practice, I now consider art-making and viewing as an activity that is neither bound to a specific geography, nor

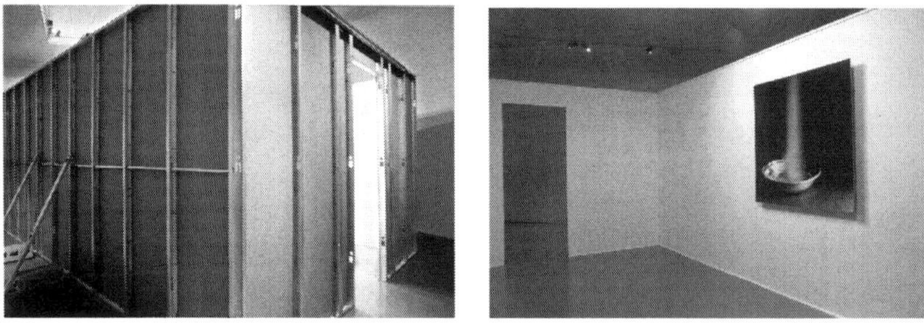

Figure 1 *Places to Remember I*. 1995. Installation detail.

to a sense of home or belonging. Though I still think of artistic practice as a space to dwell in the sense of allowing for speculation, I no longer understand art making, or the viewing of it, in terms of providing a way to house oneself, or a place to feel at-home. Rather, I have come to consider these activities as a possible instance of losing oneself, of becoming *unaccommodated*. I can also say, with hindsight and without going into much detail that the places I have created, even if I thought of them initially as places-to-be, have always also been places to be or become unaccommodated in. Furthermore, I have realised that the contradiction the two approaches apparently suggest, may rather be another, even complementary way to think about dwelling and the activities of making and viewing art.

For example, in *Places to Remember* (1995),[7] I built a temporary construction situated within an already enclosed space, a walk-through shelter open to both sides, the rough makeshift outside revealing a pristine inside.

Slightly further away from the temporary walls, four speakers are suspended from the ceiling, circumscribing the material boundary with yet another invisible border. At regular intervals a female voice encircles the temporary shelter, moving from one speaker to the next, her voice's echo filling the entire room with speculations about belonging, perception, history and the imperative to remember.

Sound 1 (extract)[8]

(...)

If I lived for long enough in one place, would I become part of it, like those having always lived there, or like those who came to it without hesitation to make it theirs? Would I, like them, be tied to this place and become associated with it, become part of it, and it part of me?

(...)

Would I then also be one with them, or would I, with no external sign to distinguish me, be readily pointed out, with everything earmarking my difference, my intrusion?

(...)

But tell me, how does one pronounce a hyphen, or listen to the promise of a land?
(…)
Tacitly I watch them gathering their years and plant them into grounds fertile with bone-meal, prayers, dreams. Their palms, stretched out, turned up, are soiled with fear. How do you build a home with hands like these?
(…)

One possible question to start with is to ask about what happens when we think of the process of making and viewing work as an event which I'm defining here simply as a moment in time and as an incident that *takes place*. More specifically, one can say that there is the making of place in place of one left behind, or no longer wanted, or available, and there is also the making of place which is not a substitute. Both describe a deliberate action towards *becoming accommodated*: literally, the making of a place to inhabit, as dwelling-place[9] and, by extension, the making of a home. Home alludes to both the positive values of comfort and safety along with their more negatively inflected counterparts of complacency and habituation. In turn, the notion of becoming accommodated also references a dimension of already inscribed "unbelonging."[10] For one can say that we know something simply by its counter-part; that we know night through day, light through dark, presence through absence, remembering through forgetting and, I would argue, involvement through disengagement. Binary constructions work not just as pairs but also as signposts for a dialectical approach. And though I don't mean to propose that such a process should guide the making or viewing of art, I do find it a useful framework with which to approach certain questions of reception, perception and re/cognition.

Each of my installations consists of several elements, denying the viewer a command of the space from a single point of view. It forces them to manoeuvre differently in relation to each element.

For example, it is difficult to view the triptych from within the construction without a sense of being overwhelmed and dislocated.[11] As feedback from visitors to the installation at various venues attests to, the size of the triptych pushes the viewer to the very edge of this place, so they often find themselves, in their attempts to gain a measure of control over the image in front of them, backing into the other image at its opposite wall. It is as easy to overwhelm an audience with over-sized images as it is difficult to engage and include them in the fragile relationship between the images and their spatial holding configuration. To then use the self-same configurations to manipulate the viewer, often into apprehension, carries its own set of problems.[12] Furthermore, to become accommodated we may need to accommodate, a process that vacates and refills as much as it simply shifts. To become habituated, accustomed to, adapted to, to become familiar and even familial, we may need to accommodate what may be unwanted, unfamiliar, frightening even. That such a shift may not be entirely voluntary is another matter, though relevant to my argument and the context of this book. One

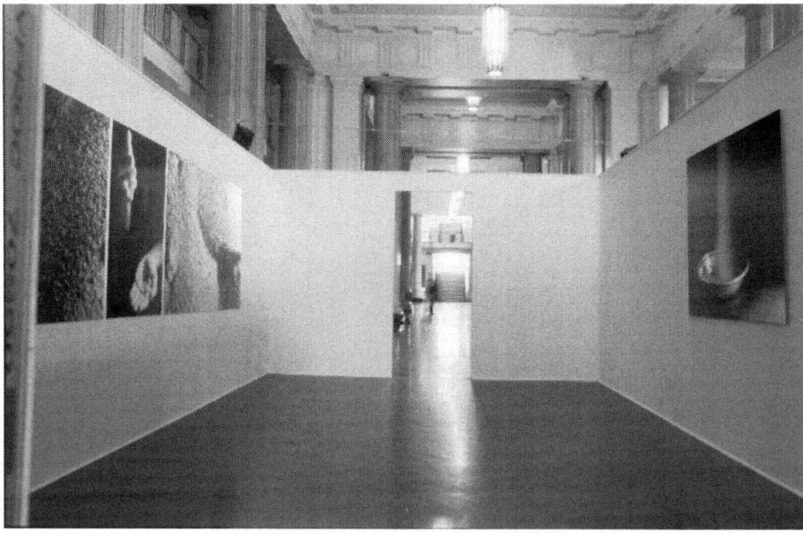

Figure 2 *Places to Remember II*. 1995. Installation detail.

context to which the concept of the familiar is often linked is the uncanny, *das Unheimliche*, which brings us back to the place it originates from: the home, the familiar, the Heim. "*Unheimlich*," as Freud writes, "is what was once *heimisch*, homelike, familiar; the prefix 'un' is the token of repression" (*SE XVII*, 245).[13] Repression, by definition, is what makes something familiar both inaccessible and curiously resonant.

In *Places to Remember* I used the image of sand with its attendant associations of time, building material and earth/desert. In another series of installations entitled *Promise*, the evident materiality of sand and cibachrome photography has been replaced by the fluid uncertainty of water and the unstable, continuous development of the dyeline print.[14]

What connects both is the use of sound, although the indexical nature and speculations of the human voice in *Places to Remember II* has been replaced by a more abstract evocation of time and space in *Promise II*.

Sound 2

[Loop which alternates the sounds of a lone figure swimming laps, later joined by splashing, shouting children and general pool noise, with the muted configurations of an underwater soundscape that drowns out everything above the water surface.]

Promise II suggests the environment of a public pool, where the potential for paradoxical experiences of pleasure and distress, release and confinement, isolation and communality exist side by side. As well as defining the limits of our earthbound, air-breathing existence, water also offers us a set of peculiar pleasures: a vicarious sensory world of semi-weightlessness which we usually enter in a state of near-nakedness, a world of

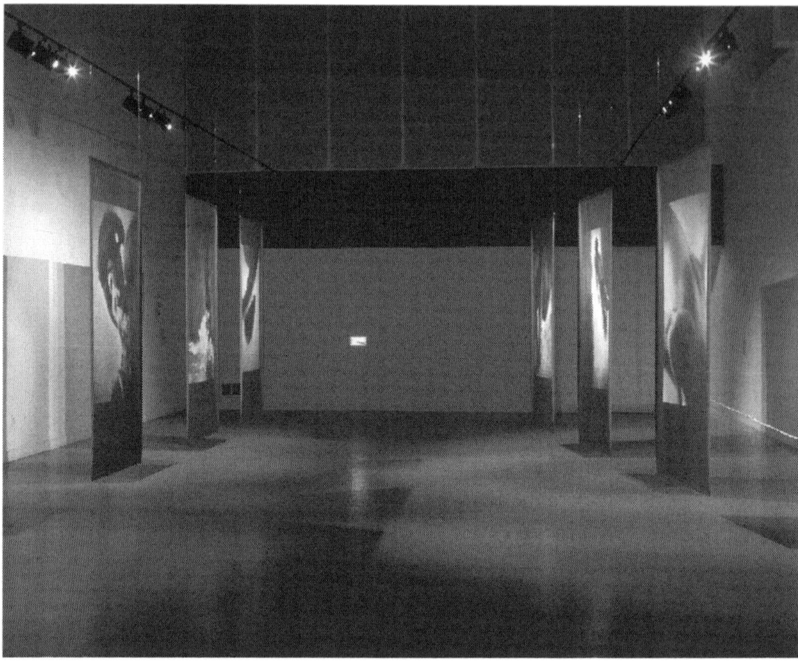

Figure 3 *Promise II*. 1997. Installation view.

isolation and intense physical sensation that can be thrilling and erotic, alienating and terrifying in equal measure. Water poses an existential paradox to humans – it is something we cannot live in, but also cannot live without. As in most of my work, I intended the piece to function on a primarily sensory level, offering the viewer a version of the experience encapsulated in the images themselves. In this sense, the work holds a dual and paradoxical function. On the one hand, it could be seen to provide a link between our fantasies of and yearnings for a primal sense of "belonging" or self-possession. On the other hand it may simulate our terror of dispersal and loss of control which is often provoked by the increasingly complex set of interlocking roles we play and by the circumstances we encounter in everyday life. Each panel, suspended from the ceiling by fishing tackle, silently and gently sways in the space. Arranged so that they form a kind of passage, narrowing towards the rear, a flicker is visible in the far distance. On closer inspection it reveals itself as a video-loop of a goldfish, eyeing the viewer's every move.

What is not immediately apparent though is that each individual photographic panel will gradually shift in colour and eventually turn white.

What makes this possible is a technique that uses old-fashioned architectural paper and reprographic processes allowing the dye, once it has been exposed to light, to continually develop.

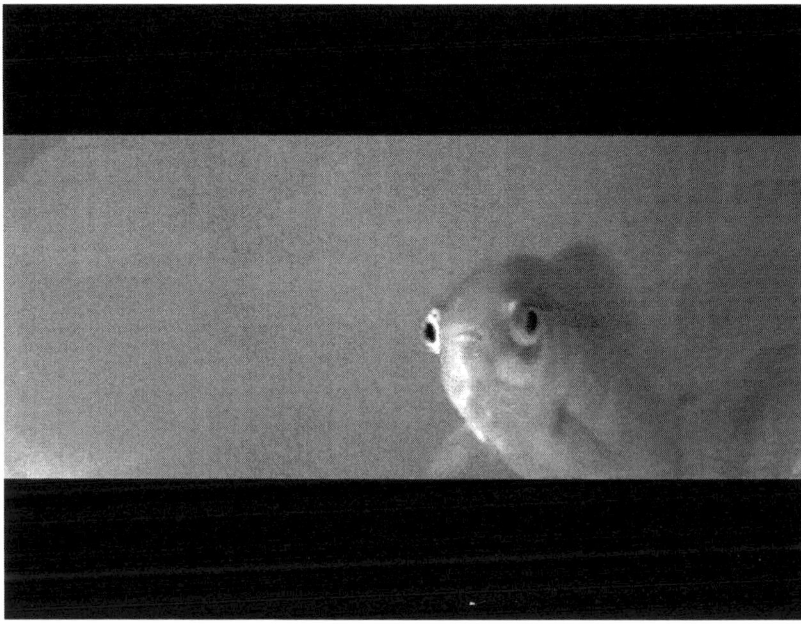

Figure 4 *Promise II*. 1997. Installation detail.

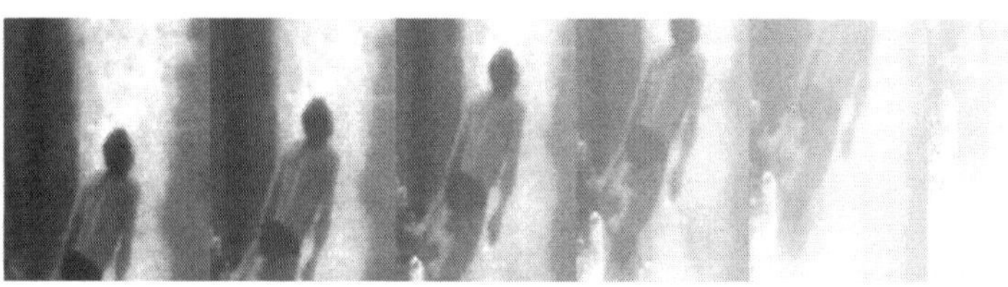

Figure 5 *Promise II*. 1997. Installation, second detail.

Like *Places, Promise* also explores aspects of remembering and forgetting. It has been suggested that one is the condition of and for the other that they are in interdependent relation. Yet there are instances in which such separations seem suspended altogether and a curious simultaneity occurs. In psychoanalysis and recent work in other fields concerned with questions of place and memory, traumatic memory is defined as an occurrence that is not located in a past but is experienced non-chronologically and non-topographically as of and in the present. Consequently boundaries between a then/now and a there/here are dissolved and what has taken place in the past is not experienced as separate from the present. The distinction between something remembered and something happening/experienced in the present moment is not possible, and compulsion allows no rational approach.[15] At the heart of this experience is a fundamental contradiction, which is also a further simultaneity: what is experienced is both present and absent, continuous and disrupted.

In my own encounters with making/viewing art, I have occasionally experienced time in such a non-linear fashion. Yet I am not necessarily suggesting that this amounts to a traumatic experience.[16] Ernst van Alphen (1997) has suggested that a distinction can be made between work that simply re-presents and work which creates a space of affect, in which the viewer is drawn into a direct experience of a condition which is merely pictured (illustrated) in its representational counterpart. Writing in particular about work that engages with WWII and to a certain degree its aftermath, he has called it the "Holocaust-effect," though it is clear that this concept is far more wide-reaching than such a name suggests. I think of the realm of affect as a kind of quasi-traumatic configuration, which is also reminiscent of an archaic level of early subjectivity, into which we are displaced when the familiar becomes strange and we are forced to negotiate often contradictory meanings, working primarily on a sensory level. Such experiences can be disorienting because we are suddenly, if momentarily, left helpless. This helplessness, I believe, is further compounded by the necessity to come to terms with our regression. A number of scholars have written about the complex interlinking of trauma, affect, witnessing, mediation, embodiment and their implications on notions of place,[17] to which I cannot do justice here, but which I would like to link to my notion of becoming unaccommodated. Furthermore, drawing on van Alphen's categorisation, I would like to make a distinction between two approaches to viewing work: one is to seek an experience and the other is to prioritise understanding (cognition).[18] Nevertheless, I think that there are instances beyond such a choice. For example, one of my first encounters with an installation that affected me immediately and beyond my control was when I entered tentatively into the darkness of a corridor, which suddenly opened out to an equally dark space filled by a revolving screen and a booming voice. I felt physically assaulted by the voice and afraid that the screen would hit me. Although, at the time, my preferred approach was "understanding" rather than "experience," none of my attempts to cognitively master my experience helped to retrieve what the voice said or what the images on the screen actually consisted of. All I remember is that I left feeling disturbed and shaken.

To understand that there is an experience creates a distance to that experience. Experience happens in the now whilst understanding necessitates a delay, a stepping away and distancing from the actual experience. But is it possible, at the moment of encounter, to maintain a choice between experience and understanding? The recognition that something has occurred, never mind the desire to examine, review or rework it, constitutes a shift, requires some adjustment. Maybe one could argue that the moment of affect, whether precipitated by an unexpected encounter or triggered in the process of seemingly controlled spectatorship, is beyond control, reason and simple aesthetic contemplation. Although different models offer differing speculations as to the processes at work, most understand affect as prior to the constitution of signification.[19] One may even argue, prior to the experience of emotion as emotion, which can itself be thought of as a complex state, itself consistent of several interlocking sets of affects, which function over time, and crucially include possibilities of ideation. According to this proposition, in the realm of affect complexities collapse, and in this state of reduced perception, only one place, one time exists. To conceptualise what one has seen, however, is to return to a complexly structured and differentiated time/space. Furthermore, Freud reminds us that: "[I]n psycho-analysis there is no choice for us but to assert that mental processes are in themselves unconscious," and warns us: "not to equate perceptions by means of consciousness with the unconscious mental processes which are their object" (*SE XIV*, 171). To conceptualise one's experience, then, testifies primarily to certain cognitive processes. If the initial experience has placed us in the space of affect, is the recognition that something has happened not a stepping out if this place?[20] Put differently: if we enter into the realm of affect, through encountering a work of art, and thus become dislodged in an instance of regression, could both the "turning towards" and a "turning away from" what just happened (respectively: coming to consciousness and repressing) be guided equally by an ordering impulse that directs us out of the disorienting state of affect towards a more familiar, boundaried place? Could this be thought of as an impulse that motions us towards becoming accommodated again?

I have already referred to the usefulness of a dialectical approach, and I want here to revisit a conception of pairings that understands them as neither mutually exclusive nor contradictory. Freud, writing on the uncanny, notes that "... *heimlich* is a word the meaning of which develops in the direction of ambivalence, until it finally coincides with its opposite, *unheimlich*" (*SE XVII*, 226). Most of my works are grounded in the ordinary everyday and use domestic, low-resolution production methods (non-professional camera-formats and one-chip video); my images are of the most basic familiars (sand, water, naked bodies), located in local familiars (parks, pools, homes). I often build enclosed or enclosing spaces for them. Yet they resonate something more unfamiliar, gesture towards something unknown, hidden. What I present may potentially be recognised, yet it is also quite foreign; something one may be drawn to, yet is also frightened of. As much as I create spaces the viewer can enter into, I also deny access to the very space that is created – thus inviting hesitation, doubt and ambivalence. What seems certain in this context, is that uncertainty can be very "unheimlich" and we can easily become unaccommodated. Describing her viewing experience of *Promise II*, Dorota Glowaka writes: "The large size of the images washes away the contours of the human body: I struggle to bring them into focus, tensely waiting for the familiar shape to emerge from the inchoate mass of blueness. The discord between the swift movement of the diver and the perfect stillness of its image tenses my muscles. Vertigo: the uncanny sensation of being ungrounded, submerged, left breathless by the indistinct figures of the swimmers suspended in the aqueous void. Feelings of sensory deprivation and sensory abundance envelope me with crescendoing intensity. The dread of being dispossessed of light, of air, of life-giving warmth – my body registers the cold temperature in the room with a shiver. Suddenly bereft of foundations, robbed of memory, I yield to the sublime fear of ultimate privation, “the strongest emotion the mind is capable of feeling” (49).[21]

Expressed in simple terms, the uncanny is constituted in a turning away (forgetting, repressing) from an occurrence too difficult to accommodate in our conscious construction of reality. Yet the turning away is not entirely complete. It leaves traces behind that facilitate some kind of recognition or resonance, or return even. Freud thought it a specifically mild form of anxiety (*SE XVII*, 217–56), and we think of it as different to a traumatic experience. However, in both instances, remembering and forgetting[22] are central to a construction and experience of reality. Generally speaking, remembering and forgetting are associated with negotiating personal history and experience, as well as with the forming of communities or collectives (Rehan 1990). Remembering and forgetting are also deeply embedded in our psychic capacity to house ourselves, to negotiate a being with others and self. Assuming that the making of work, and in some instances the viewing it, is a process that incorporates some of the above mentioned aspects, could it also be thought about as a kind of journey, a to-ing and fro-ing between what is known and what is unknown, remembered and forgotten, discovered and dismissed, clear and unclear? Could it be a process whereby none of these categories are consistent or simple, and all are bound into paradoxical relationships, where one can come “to coincide with its opposite”? Not all creative or viewing processes function on this level. However, when they do, they challenge what we “know,” disturb us and, if only for an instance, unhouse us, dislodge us, loosen us from what has kept us in place, housed us, accommodated us, provided a home.[23]

Endnotes

1. I am thinking here particularly about *Being and Time*, 1962.

2. Even though homelessness could also be understood as the condition of uncertainty, I would not want to reduce it to that, as I have argued below.

3. In traditional Jewish belief the word/book is the word of God (Torah) and home therefore is belief in and engagement with the word.

4. Furthermore, there are increasing pointers to a deep scarring left by a continued marginalisation, persecution and oppression, which is transmitted from generation to generation as explored not only in the context of recent studies in trauma (Caruth 1995, and in the same volume van der Kolk and van der Hart).

5. Being Jewish, but also more generally being alive, being human etc.

6. (...) I wrote you. I write you. I take refuge in my words. (...).

7. Like most of my works, *Places to Remember* is a series of independent, yet inter-related installations. Each of the works investigates different aspects of our present sense of being; focussing variably on the inter-connectedness of past, present and future, expressions of belonging, conditions of uncertainty, ambivalence and transition and how to affectively engage with an audience.

8. All extracts from Markiewicz, 1992.

9. Note that the *Concise Oxford English Dictionary* offers "dwelling-place" as its first definition of "home". 513.

10. See also Irit Rogoff, 2000.

11. Although the dimensions for this installation vary according to the proportions of the external space, the inside of the internal construction is never wider than 3.50 m. The overall length of the triptych is 4.70 m.

12. I'm thinking here of certain architectural formations that are designed to overwhelm, especially ones identified with fascist ideologies, though over/life-sized sculptures and images/projections especially in small spaces may function similarly.

13. All Freud quotes are from the Standard Edition, henceforth abbreviated as SE. Also, on the fundamental difference in the understanding of the uncanny between Freud and Heidegger see Michael Sipiora, <www.janushead.org. 3-1/msipiora.cfm> (accessed 11.12.05).

14. Dyeline describes a reprographic process where a print is exposed but not fixed and thus keeps "developing". This means that the colour of the original, which starts out as a dark blue turns, via purple and various lighter shades of blue, to white.

15. See van der Kolk/van der Hart in Caruth 1995 who specifically refer to Janet's distinction between narrative memory as the ability to remember something that is clearly located in the past and understood as such and traumatic memory, which triggers an experience in the present that re-enacts an unresolved past occurrence with no capacity to conceptualise (narrate) it and which is often accompanied by original affective and motoric elements (Caruth 1995/163).

16. Though I am certainly not excluding such a possibility either.

17. See also Felman and Laub, 1992; Hirsch in Suleiman (Ed.) 1998; and in Miller and Tougaw (Ed.) 2002.

18. Both approaches will inevitably include elements of the other. The distinction I seek here is one of a "first instance."

19. Felmann and Laub are particularly interesting for their linking of affect, memory and witnessing. I am also referring here to a differentiation Christopher Bollas made in conversation with Griselda Pollock in the closing session of Congress CATH 2005, Bradford Film and Television Museum,

which can be accessed via the centre CATH website, where he clearly distinguished between the realm of affect and emotion.

20. In this instance I use recognition as distinct from understanding and as preceding it. Obviously, all of this is based on the assumption that an artwork can facilitate in equal measure a re/configuration, recognition and understanding of experience (as separate yet interrelated).

21. Glowoka's quote is from Edmund Burke, 39.

22. The linking of repression with forgetting and remembering with consciousness is tentative and in this instance specific to the framework of this particular argument.

23. Home as simply that which is most familiar to us and thus "safe," comfortable.

Works Cited

Burke, Edmund. *A Philosophical Enquiry Into the Origin of Our Ideas of the Sublime and Beautiful*. Notre Dame: University Press, 1986.

Caruth, Cathy, Ed. *Trauma, Explorations in Memory*. Baltimore and London: John Hopkins University Press, 1995.

Felman, Shoshana and Laub, Dori. *Testimony: Crisis of Witnessing in Literature, Psychoanalysis and History*. London and New York: Routledge, 1992.

Freud, Sigmund. *The Complete Psychological Works of Sigmund Freud*. The Standard Edition, General Editorship: James Strachey, in collaboration with Anna Freud. London: Hogarth Press and the Institute of Psycho-Analysis, 1962.

Glowaka, Dorota. "Lily Markiewicz's visual (po)ethics." *Lily Markiewicz, Promise II*. Mount Saint Vincent University, Halifax: Canada, 2002.

Gould, Eric, Ed, *The Sin of the Book*. Lincoln and London: University of Nebraska Press, 1985.

Heidegger, Martin. *Being and Time*. Oxford: Blackwell, 1962.

Hirsch, Marianne. "Past Lives: Postmemories in Exile". *Exile and Creativity*. Ed. Susan Suleiman. London: Duke University Press, 1998.

——— "Marked by Memory: Feminist Reflections on Trauma and Transmission." *Extremities; Trauma, Testimony and Community*. Eds. Nancy K. Miller and Jason Tougaw. Urbana and Chicago: University of Illinois Press, 2002.

Jabès, Edmund. "There is such a thing as Jewish writing." Ed. Eric Gould. *The Sin of the Book*. Lincoln and London: University of Nebraska Press, 1985.

——— *The Book of Questions, Vol. 1* (Trans. Rosemary Waldrop). Middletown, Connecticut: Wesleyan University Press, 1987.

Markiewicz, Lily. *The Price of Words*. London: Bookworks, 1992.

Sykes, J.B. Ed *Concise Oxford English Dictionary*. Oxford: Oxford University Press, 1977.

Rehan, Ernest. "What is a Nation" (Trans. Martin Thom). Ed. Homi K. Bhabha, *Nations and Narration*. London and New York: Routledge, 1990.

Rogoff, Irit. *Terra Infirma*. London and New York: Routledge, 2000.

van Alphen, *Ernst. Caught by History: Holocaust Effects in Contemporary Art, Literature and Theory*. Stanford, CA: Stanford University Press, 1997.

van der Kolk, Bessel A. and van der Hart, Onno. "The Intrusive Past: Flexibility of memory and the Engraving of Trauma." Ed. Cathy Caruth. *Trauma, Explorations in Memory*. Baltimore and London: John Hopkins University Press, 1995.

Thamyris/Intersecting No. 17 (2007) 49-56

In the Cooler

Catherine M. Lord

In a not too faraway time.

April had become a crueller month. Mabel Arden's bottle of water was close to her pencil and paper. Her greying, blonde hair branched over her hemp cardigan. She removed the wires from the X-pod that fed into her ears. Then she followed her instincts and analysed the scene around her. She sniffed the air for its kaleidoscope of synthetic deodorants and unwashed bodies. She listened. In the Kings Cross café, *Harry's Hide-out*, she registered the counterpoints of Chinese, Indian, Arabic, Spanish, African, and Dutch. There was a British family in front of her. They were smoothing down the greased hair of their children. The three-year old girl had lifted a bottle of water into the air and was trying to pour the contents over her head. The mother grabbed the bottle and secured back the top.

"Do that again" hissed the mother "and no more bedtime stories for you." Under the pressure of this threat, the child exploded. She was then walloped and hauled outside.

Mabel scribbled down this moment of *zeitgeist* on a brown paper bag. She placed this in one of her own novels, which she kept as a file. It was a professional heirloom, which she always left in Harry's safe. She turned the book over on a piece of protective plastic. Gel and an old scarf wiped off the irritation of sweetener that cemented the café table. On her novel's back cover was a younger picture of Mabel, specifying the *Crime Writer of the Year* award. She covered this over with a copy of the LCD menu.

Harry's Rehydrate Specials
KojoJel Delight:
Jelly served with medically weak tea in Korean sized cups.

Isotone Pickup:
Treated April Shower with Electrolytes to Delight.

Space Shuttle Truffles:
Moist Candy for Dryness Blues

She counted her ration tags. Her lower back pain had never been worse. Adjusting her posture, she massaged the burning point of her sciatic nerve. Writing was agony, as was standing or walking. Her options were limited. Paracetemol based substances were diuretics. Drugs such as "tenderzapem," the painkillers that left the body's fluids unaffected, were not covered by her health insurance. And given the recent flooding and hospital toll, she knew that the cost of a visit to the clinic for an injection could leave her without food for days. She could not afford to get weak and deal with another attack of mosquito fever. To afford the injection for her back, she would have to be shortlisted in that evening's contest. Then at least the "Society for On-Site Narrative" would remunerate her. For that to happen, the story she told that evening at the Camden Lock Motivational Event would have to garner sufficient votes. She would have to be in the top three to earn payment.

She stared at the blank page and drank her weak Earl Grey. Another story about events in the wake of the failure of the Thames barrier would simply not do. She picked up her pencil and wrote between the lines of the used, music sheet paper. At least another gale would come and blow some refuse from the recycling machines of the rich. On the winds of bricolage, Mabel might have the luxury of an everyday miracle: one piece of paper, blank.

A twinge at the back of her sacrum sent pains shooting down to her knee. Now she felt nauseous. Harry re-tied his dreadlocks behind his neck as he sat next to Mabel; her tears soaked the back of her large hands.

"Mabel" he said in polished south of the River, "Take the health badge."
"Can't."
"Shelia wants you to 'ave it. She hasn't used her credits. Just go down to the health centre."
"Too many uniforms. If they do a retinal ID, I'm screwed."
"They got better things to do."
"Really?"
"Get over it. They were only doing their job."
"I was saving people's lives and they treated me like an animal."
"Police get stressed too, just like everyone else."
"It wasn't me who was brandishing a Kalashnikov. It was the drowning man."
"Do you know what those are bringing on the market now?"

No. Nor did she care. Mabel reminded herself that tears cost fluid. She took action, putting everything in her backpack and wiring her boots to a set of green-battery roller skates.

She headed cautiously through the crowds towards Camden town. She had but one option left. It was her only chance of surviving the day, of being able to write and perform her story. And she needed inspiration. Past the old tube lived Sun Xiaoging, her acupuncturist. Mabel replayed an old conversation in the theatre of her backpain.

> "It's a question of brain chemistry" Sun had explained.
> "Please don't tell me it's all about positive thinking."
> "I didn't say that" said Sun in her hybrid of mid-Atlantic and London. "Its about networks," she continued, "and not just the ones in the body."

Sun's words radiated through Mabel's hopes as she considered one option – begging Sun for a free session. But Sun was not answering her mobile. Mabel arrived at Sun's flat building, its water dishes poking from the walls, waiting for the next down pour. There was sufficient rain in England. But money and water had interacted to produce baffling states of emergency. A country that had water resources could not necessarily distribute them.

Nothing would be the same again, Mabel reminded herself, as she gazed at the cornice of the front door with its nostalgia of a Georgian window frame. The chipped blue door roared open. A naked man in socks, covered from top to toe in acupuncture needles, flew down the street, carrying a brief-case. Police brandishing stun darts, plastic handcuffs and a white hood pursued him. Some minutes later, colliding between tenants entering and leaving, Sun emerged.

"Black marketers. They get wind of when they'll get arrested and think a session is a safe house." Sun yelled to the disappearing bodies: "Make sure you get me back my bloody needles!" She packed some *Galaxy Wars* pod-games into her parachute trousers.

> "I don't suppose, ..." enquired Mabel.
> "I've got to make a statement at the police cross-point and then do a shift on Accident and Emergency."
> "I don't know what to do."
> "Mabel, I don't think your sciatica is just a question of your accident."
> "Sorry?"
> "Do you have a place in which you feel you can be present?"
> "Who the hell does?"
> "In Chinese medicine, we think that certain back complaints are about being in the wrong place."
> "I don't get it. You're flood displaced – do you have back pains?"
> "Not physical. I've no easy answers. It's about finding a place to be present, in the here and the now."

"But all I ever wanted to do was make a decent living as a storyteller. Make my mark, however modest."

"You are, just do it here and today."

Sun shot into London's smog and azure haze.

Whimsically, Mabel considered Sun's paradigm; the young healer laid claimed to an old soul. But from Mabel's days of studying forensic medicine for crime fiction, she wanted the empirical solution. Her pain escalated.

As she approached Camden Lock, she saw a group of engineers. Two men and a woman spoke Dutch, and a woman and man with helmets spoke in Spanish. English was an osmotic ally between the combatants. She saw Shelia attempting to interpret. They were working on a water barrier construction made of metal and a new form of plastic that could filter water before being treated. But they were arguing over the height at which the filters should be put. Shelia waived.

"Mabel – I'm looking forward to your story for tonight."

"Storm comes tonight" interrupted a Dutch accent.

"If there is an event tonight" ventured Mabel "what sort of story would you want to hear?"

The responses were rapid. No stories about environmental disaster. How about *The Tempest* in 10 minutes? A Chinese tale about Dragons becoming fresh water glaciers had won a prize. Mabel had particularly liked the Dutch story about rowing your floating house across the Channel to catch the health-food store. What about a version of *Dinosaur Crèche* meets the *Book of Naked Revelations*? The epic poem of rap dimensions, culled from Cuban and Arabic folklores, had indeed pushed the envelope. Hearts swooned over the poem about growing one flower in the Sahara desert. Someone adored the idea of a Mongolian Jane Austen adaptation, in instalments, running through the season. No more reality event stories. And anyone who told an oral history about decorating their one million pound studio flat would be canal-ducked. Everyone had loved the instalments of *Sex, Hurricanes and Pigeon Flu*.

The rebirth of oral storytelling was the only artistic improvement Mabel could identify in a time now dubbed, the "post-tipping point." Given the constant crises on the power grid, televisions and cinema screens were to be watched in groups and for selected hours of the day. At least this made the experience more of an event. For Mabel, the downside was that celebrities were festooned with no less attention than decades before. One American émigré to the UK declared that she was no longer going to invest money in designer cleansing oils, but put the capital into school fees. People loved to hear these stories on the *Celebrity Channel*. Ostriches and sand, thought Mabel. She considered how, over and over, she had paid her dues. And yet, here she was, in her mid-fifties, without even a small boat mortgage, no decent health insurance, and all this after years of writing hard copy novels and their Internet inheritors, P-Podplays and telescripts. And she had won awards. But writers had gradually lost even their limited celebrity status. Actors and producers, who ruled the Internet and had bought up the realms of prose writing, had even further hijacked the power-base of the storyteller. Mabel was a rare entity: a fiction writer who had not multi-tasked into further careers in media. To be a writer pure and simple was to be part of a dying breed. Writers were no longer even unacknowledged legislators. The leftovers of the old certainties had melted with Siberia. There was little distinction between corporate capitalists, media producers and the mafia. There was neither world enough nor time.

Mabel skated up Haverstock Hill and took a right turn. Then she saw the line of barbwire; behind were multimillion-pound terrace houses. At each end of the street was a police guard. She had to show her identity strip just to skate the street. And as usual, when quizzed about her business, she declared it to be cleaning. Her synthetic and hemp clothing declared her fit for the caste. She took the street slowly, before coming to an unobtrusive stop. She leant against a power-pole, to ease the pain. Then across the street, she did notice a minor miracle. A man with a cleaning mop and bucket, cursing in Italian, was hurrying out to put the mop into the recycle machine at the end of the street. In a moment of carelessness, he had left the silicone crystal keys hanging in the barbwire guard. All she needed was sanctuary, for a couple of hours. She needed water, some food and a place to rest.

Mabel saw the moment like someone in the midst of a violent asthma attack beholding an oxygen tank. She skated through the opening in the barbwire. Once in the kitchen at the back of the house, Mabel removed her skates and placed them into a stationary spinning contraption, the water-saving dishwasher. Before the cleaner could return, she had rapidly hobbled up the stairs and found the bedroom. She opened a wall panel, and hid. Sequestered in the midst of a man's wardrobe, she heard the cleaner return. The sounds indicated that he was hitting the buttons of the burglar alarm. He closed the door behind him and the digital locking device made its music. Mabel knew from the X-Pod adverts that these houses had emergency locks on the inside, so she could leave when necessary. It was still 11 am in the morning. Her "on-site" narration performance would begin at 9 pm. If she were lucky, she might have five hours before someone returned home from his corporate kingdom.

When she looked up from the air-conditioned, Japanese bed, she saw a wall studded with photographs. And each one had the same protagonist, in different parts of the world, surrounded by the virtual natives and diasporas. "Virtual" was an admission that in these times, "native" was a problematic term. And someone who wanted to claim that loud and clear was the star actor in each of the photographs.

She examined a wall full of the one and only, media celebrity, Hollywood film star and our next global politician, Leo di Beckheim: blonde Leo in Africa, punished by the sun, his arms around the smiling emaciated; Leo in Siberia, floating around with a team of multicultural scientists, defusing the unstoppable methane; Leo patting a drop-jawed polar bear; Leo in Mexico, everyone in transparent gasmasks. Was the owner of the house a di Beckheim disciple? She went back down the narrow stairs and decided to get ethnographic in the living room. Over the fake fireplace were the awards. She knew their looks and definitions by heart. She spotted two SAGs, a SWAG, a NYCCA, three LACCAs, an Emmy, two Golden Globes, an Orange BAFTA, an Easy Set EUFTA, a Macrosoft IFA, and the exquisite, Katherine Blanche Achievement Award. But at the centre of them all, strategically positioned under a laser light, were two Oscars. Now her sciatica snarled. She went over to the computer. She needn't have worried about hacking into the email, for the ultimate sin had been committed. Leo had left his machine *on*, and that was exactly the sort of electricity-wasting crime that would be scandalous on the news. She saw one open mail – "Hi Leo!" Nauseated by the waste, she shut down the machine herself.

If she was not mistaken, she had heard on the *Celebrity Channel* that Leo was filming in Scotland. Perhaps she had all day, all week or world enough and time before the cleaner ever returned. She hadn't eaten properly for days. When she went into the kitchen, she found that rarity, a fridge. They were only supposed to be switched on at certain times. And most foods were supposed to be bought on a daily basis. But then, who would do police raids on the rich and check their thermometers? A rich man could hire a computer specialist to forge the digital readings. But when she opened the fridge, it was empty. Then she spotted a special drawer, and next to it rubber gloves. What she pulled out from the smoke of helium condensation was an illegal and hyper-expensive toy, the "Book of Life" game. It had a special case to take to parties. She had heard that Leo loved to attend parties and throw them in venues in central London; but he never invited people back, except a privileged few. He often talked about the "crowd/life divide." Clearly, Leo took his kit out of the house and acquired blood samples. He would bring them home and hence their DNAs could be preserved. Then one day, perhaps on the day of Judgement, mused Mabel, after Yellowstone super-volcano had blown up and most had died, the few surviving scientists might resurrect these tissue of tissues. She wanted to be cloned, despite her distaste at the thought of her secret sharer being stuck in a theme park.

Mabel took a needle and a clean phial and made her DNA mark. She looked at the other labels. The archive of the kit contained a number of phials with the same name. Obviously, Leo had been making back-ups. This helped her strategy. She found one phial that had a single name, and using a diamond pen attached inside the fridge, she forged Leo's handwriting, repeated that name on the phial containing her own DNA.

Mabel wondered what lay ahead. "Be present, in the here and now" she intoned as each of her feet made their way up the Amazonian wood stairs, with what looked like their carpet of tiger-skins. Then she came to a door. The doorknob felt suspiciously as though it were covered in crocodile skin. She opened the door on what she supposed was the "body cleaning" space. And there she found the unholy of all unholies. Bound in the nutshell of a chapel-like rectangle, lit with stain-glass windows, which were fitted with air-conditioning, was the ultimate illegal possession – a bath. After the tipping point, they had been made illegal. Tanks for water collection had to be monitored. A bath with gold hot and cold water taps could land someone in prison.

Mabel had watched too many films not to know what to do. She watched the water fill, she felt the glow of the air conditioning; she filled the contents with the antique soaps of Channel and Axe. Steaming into action, she raided the medicine cupboard, and found "tenderzepam," "triaxepam" and "libriumfume." She knew the trixepam was the strongest and the best. Mabel had brought three half-litre bottles of water from the hoards in the fridge and was downing two pills. She drank the water until her kidneys underwent orgasms. She immersed her gladiator's body in this baptism of the present moment.

There was a lot to do before total submission. She cut off all the rattails from her hair and illegally expunged them down the toilet. She washed her hair until all available conditioner was exhausted. She combed her strands until not one knot was left. She must have filled the bath for a third time before she noticed, that in the cool air from the air-conditioning stained glass, anxiety was an illusion.

Perhaps Leo would not be back for weeks.
Life was here.
Perhaps the earth could be saved.
Survival was possible.
Happiness was here.
Here and now.
The clouds, the air, and no pain.
White.
Plastic.
"You have the right to remain silent," said the voice.
A pity she was not covered in acupuncture needles.

Four male officers forced her clothes on. The plastic cuffs yanked her hands behind her back. The white hood and its stains of old blood covered her face. She could smell the residues.

"You really think there aren't hidden cameras?"
"Did Leo like the movie?" she asked. She said no more after the punch in her stomach.

The overland train to the police holding-centre bridled with bodies, in all positions. Prisoners vomited and defecated over each other. She was reminded of the time she had saved the African man with his antique Kalashnikov, his only family heirloom, and been accused of attempting to fire on police. That was when the sciatica had started.

They took her into solitary confinement. This cooler had no mattress, but only a bucket, and she was granted one bottle of water. The heat was ruthless.

"I can go and tell the press about Leo's bath" she tried weakly. They ignored her. Eventually, a man in an expensive suit appeared, and presented her with the paper work. She was to sign a document saying that she would never reveal what occurred in Leo di Beckheim's house; failure to sign could result in internment. These days, the time period was indefinite.

She signed.

The storm came that night and further eroded the arrogances of human endeavour. After one month in the cooler she was sent to a women's prison for one year. With good behaviour it might be 7 months. For days, she would empty her mind, breathing in and out. She recalled the textures of the water and the depth of the bath. She repeated the words again: "here and now." Harry and Shelia appeared at visiting hours with some "Space Shuttle Truffles." Inside she found the triaxepam.

She wondered about getting work when she left jail. She had signed a document saying she would say nothing about Leo di Beckheim's house. But perhaps she could change the names, improvise the city, change the street names and imagine entirely different houses. But at least she knew that somewhere in Leo's house, her act of idiosyncrasy bore chances of survival in the here and now that never sleeps. She thought of her DNA. She thought of her story that one day might speak its name. Her sciatica eased. This time she had found a way to make her mark.

II. Pasts in the Present

Thamyris/Intersecting No. 17 (2007) 59-80

Painting Places: A Postmemorial Landscape?

Judith Tucker

What follows below is an alignment of the practice/discipline of landscape painting with theoretical research into second-generation memory. I investigate the implications of the dialogue between the materiality of both paint and landscape, the practice of painting and these theoretical concerns. Through this realignment I attempt a more integrated perspective on different aspects of second-generation memory that may have become separated academically as objects of different disciplines. The issues have developed out of the painting/objects and the painting/processes, and I hope to demonstrate how a very particular relationship with and understanding of "landscape" might lie in the creative process itself. This chapter is cumulative and accretive as I present and re-present my practice for (re)interpretation by the viewer/reader in the light of the preceding sections.

My current research concerns landscape, place and geographic metaphor in contemporary painting. Painting, both as practice and as art object, becomes a site for the investigation of current concerns of loss, un/belonging, dis/connection and home. My project has been to explore these issues through sight and touch and to mediate these experiences in and through paint. In this chapter I explore the way in which I came to consider issues of so-called second-generation memory through examining my painting practice. Then in turn how an awareness of these issues has influenced that practice. I am going to begin by locating my own practice in terms of contemporary notions of place. Next I explore how paint and landscape might interrelate, how one can be the interface for the other, and what possibilities there are in the place that is created at this interface. This leads to a consideration of distance from the site of experience and second-generation memory or "postmemory" drawing on the work of Marianne Hirsch. As I explore these issues I will demonstrate how, for me, visual art as place making and the notion of "postmemory" interrelate. Finally, I will introduce my new project Re/visiting, Re/visioning, Re/placing. This project is in process and has involved visiting sites from my pre-war family album. I am going to provide a few examples of artists whose work provides a critical framework for my own. What I glean from my own painting practice is painting as a model for reflection and for making connections and so I am going to begin by making some connections.

Here and There

The phenomenologist Edward Casey opens his book *Representing Place: Landscape Painting and Maps* by asking the apparently simple question: why represent landscape at all?

> *Why move to representation when the experience of landscape is dense enough, and frequently pleasing enough in its own way. Why seek* other *ways, particularly representational ways that appear to signify a secondary status and that only complicate matters further? Why represent what is already presented so effectively and thoroughly in ordinary, direct experience?* (viii)

While he goes on to discuss whether there is indeed any landscape that is not already a represented landscape, and, although I acknowledge that it is crucial to engage with considerations of whether "landscape" and its mediated forms are mutually determining, what is important here for me is precisely this very question of the difference between direct experience in the landscape and that sort of experience which might be considered to have a secondary status. It is through considering this very question in relation to my own practice that my most recent work has developed. This notion of a secondary status or perhaps a belated experiencing at second hand is not only pertinent to but is now driving my work.

It is certainly no longer necessary to travel in order to image the landscape. Indeed, many painters make landscape imagery without necessarily experiencing an encounter in a "real" landscape or place, never leaving their studio. Choosing rather to reference images of landscape, which have already been mediated in some way, through photography, video or the internet, their concerns might be with the nature of representation. Their practice may well be concerned with detaching themselves from the landscape they image, perhaps in an overt acknowledgement of an intense dislocation. I am thinking here of painters such as Peter Doig, many of whose richly textured paintings derive from the notion of a film still where the action might just have happened – one instance of a sense of belated experiencing; of Masakatsu Kondo, whose photorealist methodology when imaging the "wilderness" appears to welcome us into a "real" landscape whilst paradoxically simultaneously distancing us; and of Carol Rhodes' compelling aerial views, which recreate for me a sense of the land that one receives on a flight, where, dislocated from the environment by height and speed, one unknown landscape blurs into the next. This distancing is enhanced not only by the lack of a sense of a specific location but also by the lack of any focused detail in what at first glance seem to be naturalistic images. Many of these paintings appear to be intangible, as if experienced in dreams or as memories.

There is great interest for me in the way in which these paintings make imagined or invented places for our minds and eyes to wander. I find in these places, sometimes complete artifice, certain parallels to the sorts of places which I seek to create.

For at least the past four hundred years landscape painting and travel have been inextricably linked, from imaging the grand tour onwards, and many other contemporary artists continue to travel as part of their practice, Ian Mckeever considers that it is through travel that he finds time as well as place. He writes of Emil Nolde: To travel is to find time, another time, just as much as it is to arrive at a place (19). This idea of finding another time, possibly a "time out" of the ordinary is, of course, one of the reasons any of us might travel on holiday. Many artists including myself deliberately reference an encounter elsewhere. For me the travelling to and from the location is a crucial part of the practice; the work begins long before making any mark. Thus my paintings make reference to a distant, and importantly, an *embodied* encounter in the landscape.

Caesura

This paradox of distancing and then attempting to connect across that distance opens up the opportunity to consider the work in terms of belonging, longing, sensuality and desire and, in doing so, creates a tension that becomes the subject of the work. The painted folds appear to conceal. Layers of paint actually conceal what lies underneath. What is visually absent, what is not there, is integral.

Lucy Lippard explains that while she derives a lot of pleasure from looking at landscape paintings she gains more from looking at the landscape itself. She considers that:

... a painting, no matter how wonderful, is an object in itself, separate from the place it depicts. It frames and distances through the eyes of the artist. (19–20)

In one sense it not is part of my project to create an object completely "separate" from the landscape which was the catalyst, nor am I attempting to recreate the precise experience of being in the landscape – even if this were possible, I'm not sure that it would it be desirable. Unlike Lippard, pleasure might not be the only sensation that I would be seeking. I consider my paintings to be both connected and separate

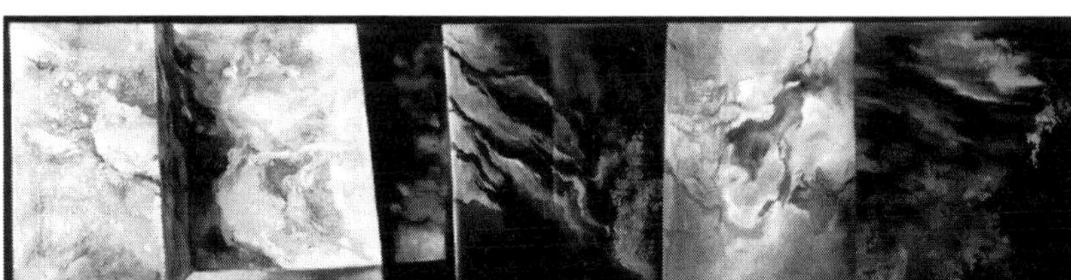

Figure 1 *Unfold*. 3 18″ × 72″.

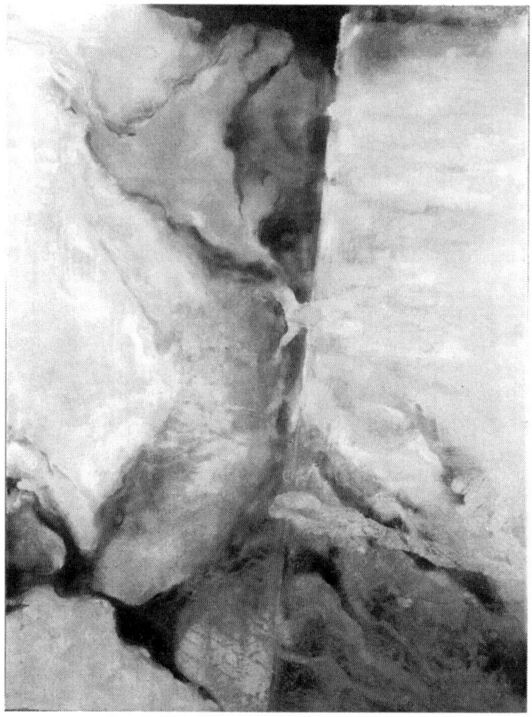

Figure 2 *Caesura 7.* 48″ × 36″.

objects. Framing and distancing are critical to my work, yet so too is a sense of attempted connection, a sense of "having been there." These works are not only mediations of landscapes; they are also mediations of a sense of absence and of longing. Certainly longing and desire have long been associated with landscape painting. When I visited the National Gallery's exhibition of German paintings, *Spirit of an Age*, in 2001, I was reminded forcefully of that Romantic desire in Caspar David Friedrich's *oeuvre* for the idea of a German nation. The desires and longings of the present are rather different:

> *The themes of exile, separation and return have provided a powerful means of exploring the self as an ongoing process of construction in time and place through the operation of memory as well as in the present, and in the articulations of loss and desire.* (Betterton 162)

To image landscape, and then to interpret and view these images in the light of such contemporary articulations of loss and desire and of dispossession could not be in starker contrast to projecting notions of nationality, ownership or even Romanticism onto such images.

This work exploits the metaphor of the border between land and sea, offering as it does the possibilities of passage, displacement, arrivals and departures: change.

I want above all to convey this sense of impermanence within a static image. This calls for a paradoxical combination of the meditative with the transitory. To this end I have produced work in series. An important strategy for conveying this sense of impermanence is the notion of a break, interruption or pause, which is why I called my most recent exhibitions *Caesura*.

Distant Dwelling

I have been considering the activity of imaging/painting "landscape" in relation to metaphors of displacement and through this I shall explore notions of inhabiting. Here, Caren Kaplan usefully considers how various different contemporary metaphors of displacement relate to ideas of location, suggesting that each metaphor is imbued with a sense of distance from a concept of position, placement or dwelling:

Thus exile is always already a mode of dwelling at a distance from a point of origin. Tourism is travel between points of origins and destinations. Diaspora disperses the locations of dwelling into a interstitial habitus. Nomadism is the most attenuated concept in relation to location. Yet even theories of nomadic rhizomes include "nodes" – those sites of intersecting movements or "lines of flight". (143)

"Landscape" painting, if considered as travel between conception and realisation, could perhaps be viewed as a type of "artistic tourism." This realisation that I did not want to make work about that which is nearby, but rather about somewhere that is distant, is what has opened up this line of thinking. As Caplan demonstrates, implicit in notions of displacement are, of course, the opposite notions that there must be a relationship between the landscape and ideas of home. In relation to this "at home/not-at-homeness" Irit Rogoff considers the possibility of an uncanny geography:

An uncanny geography, uncanny in Freud's sense of 'That sense of frightening which leads back to what is known of old and long familiar.' We have to remember that Freud's uncanny is actually the 'unheimlich', the unhomed or that which is not at home. Both its frightening and its familiar qualities come from its awkward relation to not being at home. (7)

I wonder if my paintings might be considered to express such an uncanny geography, if they might be considered to chart the awkwardness of not being at home?

Standing in Place

Griselda Pollock has both described the way in which painting might engage with both the intellect and affectivity of the viewer – who Pollock terms an "Other" – one who perceives and then interprets the painting as sign and also responds to the painting's material existence.

In a word painting oscillates between the emptiness of material substance, demanding a discrete understanding of its own properties and performance, and the metaphoric fullness of a material sign that stands for something other than itself. (Pollock 34–35)

What I found in Griselda Pollock's observations concerning the relation of the material to the metaphoric in relation to paint helps to describe my own project both in terms of the fabric of the landscape itself and the medium through which I have chosen to mediate it. Edward Casey suggests that place is what takes place between body and landscape. These paintings themselves might be considered to take place between my body and landscape; I would contend that these painted places are more than traces of an encounter: they become in turn a site of encounter for any viewer; they become other – or more – than a substitute for the experience in the location. The paint/ing becomes a metaphor for place, and a place in itself. No viewers of my work in the gallery have direct access to what I have experienced making work in the landscape. They can experience the *painting*, and, they in turn may create their own imagined place from this. Edward Casey might describe this occurrence as both standing for and standing in for:

In painting as in photography, a representation of a given landscape stands in the place of that landscape, *standing in for it in a new material form (being itself a material representation) and standing for it (as a sign for it). In both instances as well, landscape may be said to advance its position, to be* promoted *by taking up new residence in the artwork.* (23)

The very vocabulary that Casey uses – "stands in the place of" and "takes up new residence" – invites not only further consideration of distance from the site of experience but encourages a move to my second, related concern: that of the second-generation, transposition or postmemory.

I now believe that I unconsciously repeated a ritual of dislocation that goes back at least a generation. My mother and grandmother were refugees from Hitler's Germany arriving in Britain in 1939 after *Kristallnacht*. I do not know what it is to be a refugee, but I do know what it is to be the child of a refugee, and thus to inherit the insecurities of the rootless and some sense of what permanent exclusion from the land of one's birth can mean. The creative arts are considered by many to be one way of dealing with these transgenerational issues. Indeed, Ernst van Alphen considers that perhaps it is only through what he calls the imaginative discourses of art and literature that certain historical functions might take place (33–38). We understand that it is only afterwards, in repetition, that trauma becomes an experienced event. It could be argued that through my practice I re-enacted separation and recreated the experience of a sense of distance and loss for myself.

Marianne Hirsch draws a distinction between the memory of immediate survivors of the Holocaust and second-generation memory which she calls "postmemory" *(Past Lives 418–44)*. She distinguishes postmemory from memory through its generational break and from history by a profound personal link. She not only employs this concept to try to understand the experiences of individuals who grew up dominated by narratives that preceded their birth but also views it more extensively as a move towards an understanding of the formation of cultural memory. She considers that postmemory seeks connection emphasising the imaginative investment of the subject:

It creates where it cannot recover. It imagines where it cannot recall. It mourns a loss that cannot be repaired. And because even the act of mourning is secondary, the lost object can never be incorporated and mourning can never be overcome (422).

Since these disruptions are a part of my own history I would consider it inevitable that they have impacted on my practice; Hirsch proposes an aesthetics of "postmemory," drawing the comparison between art-making and wandering. She considers it a diasporic aesthetics of temporal and spatial exile that needs simultaneously to rebuild and to mourn, consistent with my practice. Through her work I reach *one* way of understanding my reiterative painterly activities. This series of paintings might not be postmemorial precisely in the sense that Hirsch defines it but they are informed by it and analogous to it. The building blocks of my postmemory have not been things but rather actions, some conscious, some unconscious.

However, having made these connections explicit, I no longer feel able to paint the North Devon coast. I now deal much more directly with these issues. I did not want to go to the more obvious and well trodden so-called landscapes of trauma, the sites of atrocities, concentration camps and so on. This is an area well explored by Ulrich Baer amongst others. One of the pitfalls that I want to avoid is the making of the subject matter into a fetish; it is perhaps at this point that certain ethical principles become important. I wish to work on an affective level and in any case I am not making work that is in any way directly referencing those events but deals with them tangentially and this would concur with some ideas inherent in Van Alphen's notion of the "holocaust effect," namely that it is perhaps precisely through an *indirect* reference to the Holocaust trauma that the impact might be felt.

Nostalgia?

Having recently read Hirsch's *Family Frames: Photography, Narrative, and Postmemory* in which she explores the ways that family photographs have been a means for determining both personal and cultural memory, one obvious place to start was by looking through my mother's photograph album. Thinking it unlikely to find many images of landscape in this album belonging to thoroughly assimilated and completely urban Berliners I was intrigued to find these snapshots of happy times in Ahlbeck in the 1930s, one of the three Baltic resorts known as the Kaiserbade, at the height of their popularity at the period of these photographs, apparently nicknamed the "bathtub of Berlin," and resolved to visit and work there.

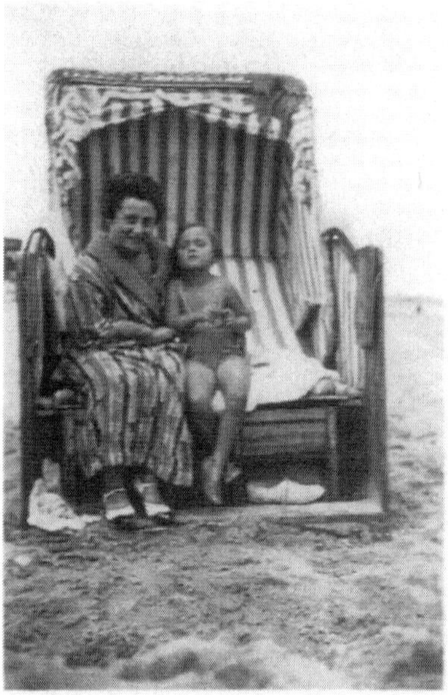

Figure 3 *Ahlbeck*. 1932.

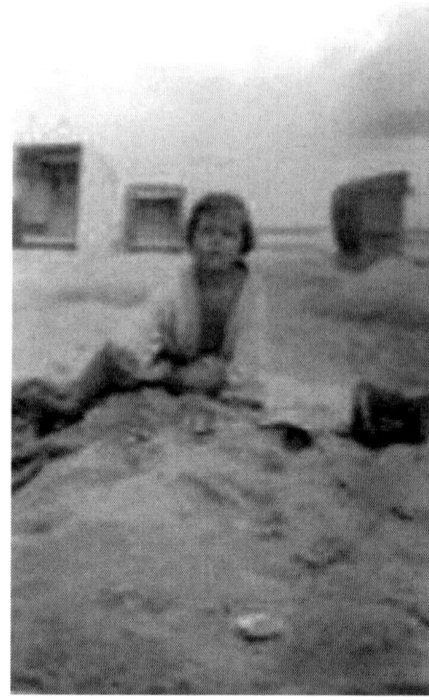

Figure 4 *Ahlbeck*. 1932.

Above are some photographs taken in 1932; of course, the next year they would not have been able to holiday there. This is a new way of working for me: in the past I have always worked from a visual stimulus, now I was going somewhere and I would have to make work from whatever I found there. So this new work is an adventure into unknown territory, both literally and metaphorically. The first of these new territories is that I began to make work from already mediated representations of this landscape, namely, maps and the original photographs. I have shown these in proximity to pieces that are derived from a direct encounter in the landscape.

The difficulty for me has been to find a balance between an over literal approach and one that is so far removed or tangential that it is impossible for any viewer to unravel the thought process. As I signalled earlier the choice to make work in a holiday resort was not only a very deliberate one but also, I would go so far as to argue, might even be considered an ethical one. In this context issues of home or belonging become problematised; after all, apart for those relatively few who actually live in holiday resorts these are places that people go to deliberately and safely to be not at home. Thus an aspect that has emerged is this landscape as a space for projection. What function might an encounter in landscape have for those of us for whom it is not necessarily a permanent part of our daily existence? How might we use it to relax and escape from the stresses and strains of our hectic urban lives? We might

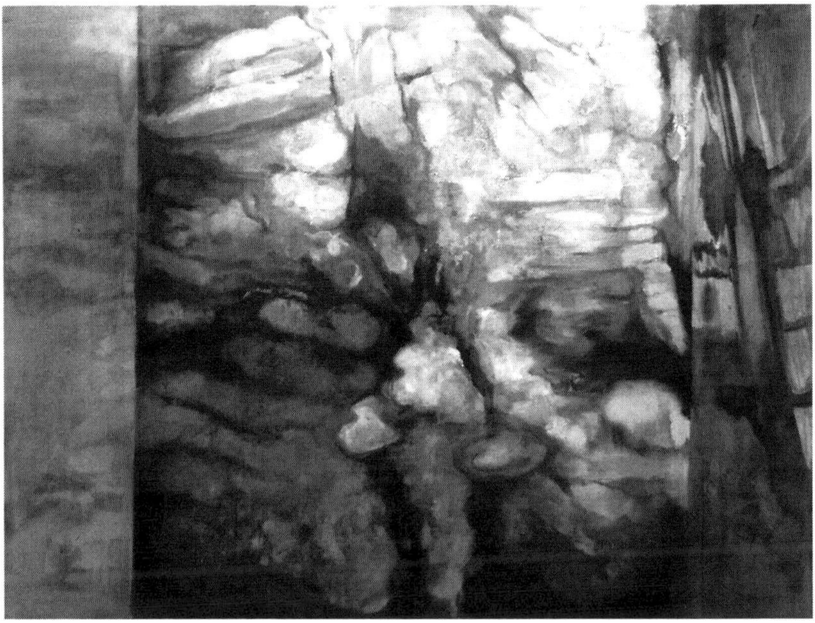

Figure 5 *Ahlbeck 1932/2003*. Oil on canvas, 36″ × 48″.

use it to enliven and invigorate us or to imbue us with wonder: perhaps to come into just enough contact with "wild" nature in order to contemplate the "spiritual" and then to return to what might be termed a "material" life. What might this vast, relatively empty space, this completely flat, featureless beach have meant for the German imaginary in the 1930s and what might it mean now? Ahlbeck is actually currently being marketed as nostalgic and the sumptuous restorations might represent a longing perhaps for a return to an innocent time, a Germany before either the DDR or the Third Reich.

In what follows I have selected and contrasted various authors' notions of nostalgia. These ideas have inflected my project, casting my landscape paintings in a different light. In relation to his considerations of Central European refugees fleeing Nazi persecution to Bolivia, Leo Spitzer explores how the meaning of the word has transmuted from its original etymology – Greek *nostos*, to return home, and *algia*, a painful feeling – to a more generalised meaning:

... nostalgia now also defined 'loss' in a more generalised and abstracted way, including the yearning for a 'lost childhood', for 'irretrievable youth,' for a 'world of yesterday' from whose ideals and values one had become distanced and detached. In this usage nostalgia became an incurable state of mind – a signifier of 'absence' and 'loss' that

could never be made into 'presence' and 'gain' except through memory and the creativity of reconstruction. (376)

I will consider how my paintings could be seen as signifiers of absence made into presence informed by nostalgia but (re)constructing and (trans)forming these experiences into something new. Donald Kuspit talks of a nostalgia in Laszlo Feher's work:

There is an aura of nostalgia to the scene, and nostalgia always means we are in the presence of something dead, if not yet emotionally over with something that endures in memory, and, while it no longer shapes the living moment, unconsciously influences the sense of life as a whole. Nostalgia is a way of processing the past without ever letting go of it. (129)

I am not sure that nostalgia always necessarily means that we are in the presence of something dead, but by introducing the notion of death, he foregrounds a connection between nostalgia, homesickness and mourning. Freud himself also believed that one could mourn one's country:

Mourning is regularly the reaction to the loss of a loved person, or to the loss of some abstraction which has taken the place of one, such as one's country, liberty, and ideal, and so on. (243)

In *On the Beaten Track* Lucy Lippard makes a distinction between good and bad nostalgia. She disagrees with Susan Stewart's view of nostalgia as a "social disease" of utopian inauthenticity:

Nostalgia is sadness without an object, a sadness which creates a longing that of necessity is inauthentic because it does not take part in lived experience ... nostalgia is the desire for desire. (Lippard 164)[1]

This expression of nostalgia as desire for desire has resonances for me in so far as I have a hunch that my paintings are not so much concerning a longing for home but concern a longing for desire. However, I question the notion of the inauthentic. I do not see this longing for desire as necessarily the result of inauthentic experiences. I believe that inherited experience is valid, that the present is activated by the past:

In a process labelled 'transposition' survivors' children were described as living simultaneously in the present and the past, transposing themselves to their parents' past, and attempting to compensate for their parents' losses. (Karpf 231)

Through my practice I seek to find a way of processing the past through creating something new which not only acknowledges what went before but is also equally concerned with the present and the future. What meaning can homesickness or nostalgia, a pain for home, have for the second-generation? I would propose that it might be relevant to consider the likelihood that mourning for the loss of the homeland is transmuted into melancholia/depression for the second generation, in that it is hard to feel a *conscious* sadness for a home that one never knew. Rather there might be an intangible feeling of restlessness and of not belonging. Freud writes of certain cases of melancholia that the patient cannot consciously perceive what has been lost:

This would suggest that melancholia is in some way related to object-loss which is withdrawn from consciousness, in contradistinction to mourning in which there is nothing about the loss which is unconscious. (245)

What sense, if any, could the binary of home/exile make to those of the second generation? Perhaps for this generation, the relational notions need to be reworked: one is at home/not at home, there is this longing but no place to situate the longing, the wandering itself becomes a home and a good deal of time is spent returning without a home to return to. Perhaps my painting practice is a form of this wandering itself becoming a home; the restless nature of my practice would suggest this. I appreciate Lippard's distinction between good and bad nostalgia: the latter is escapism, the former is a way of confirming continuity, perhaps a way of making sense of the present:

I would say that "Bad" nostalgia ... disrupting past and present, creat[es] a past that is merely a refuge from the present rather than inherited significance. (164)

What does it mean, then, that nostalgia is part of my lived experience, that it is desire removed from the senses, that I consider it a seamless and positive part of life, a reminder of breadth and depth, a confirmation of continuity? (164)

My paintings are infused with a sense of elsewhere, a sense of being "not there" in the site of direct experience; they themselves have become alternative sites of separation and longing. However, I feel that what I do by implication when using paint to remake/create a landscape/place is to say that it is not possible, let alone desirable, to wish to return to it, to that original experience. Rather we are here clearly in the present with the painting/place which has been shaped by the past. There is no sense that I am trying to recapture what is past; what I acknowledge in my paintings is that nostalgia/homesickness is a necessary component of my current lived experience. Rosemary Betterton writes that a reworking of what has happened in order is a way of creating current meaning:

The stories we tell ourselves about who we are – the half remembered events and places which shape our lives – are the foundations on which we build up a sense of self. Re-working what has already happened, we also give it current meaning, for history always represents the present as much as the past (173).

As Peter Fuller writes of the contrast of Poussin's stasis with Cézanne's promise of becoming:

It revives the emotions of his individual past, to speak of a possible transformed future. (156)

I hope that in my own reworkings through paint I not only make a possibility for current meaning but potential future meanings.

Resort

Since I am taking into account the rise of the cult of the resort in relation to the rise of the "modern" city and I am considering this in comparison to a contemporary urban relation with this coastal landscape. I decided to start my stay in Berlin, to go by train from there to the Baltic. In Berlin I stayed near the site of the Friedrichstrasse flat. In Ahlbeck I had arranged to stay in a Gruenderzeit villa which would have been around in the 1930s. I walked down a tree-lined road with contrasting remains of decayed DDR buildings and post-Wende lavish restoration, down to the beach and suddenly was on the sand, and felt for just a moment transported back. Little seemed to have changed since the '30s, there was the sea, the sand, the Seebrücke, the Strandkörbe.

Working on this flat, empty beach was difficult on a number of counts including working from what might be seen as a cliché. I wished my grandparents had the foresight to go to Rügen where Caspar David Friedrich had gone. There would have been a starting point with which I was a familiar: cliffs with the folds and invagin-ations. How was I going to make this appear any different from a beach in Norfolk? However, I had no choice but to stay with what I had in front of me. I feel that the challenge of trying to paint what at first sight was far from what I would have chosen instinctively has already taken my work forward in ways I could not have predicted.

Working from this sort of coast has inevitably opened up issues of my relation to German Romanticism and so to the Sublime. Iain Biggs has written about this aspect of my work foregrounding and clarifying these issues in a way that I had not. I found his writing very useful when thinking of how to approach this new project.

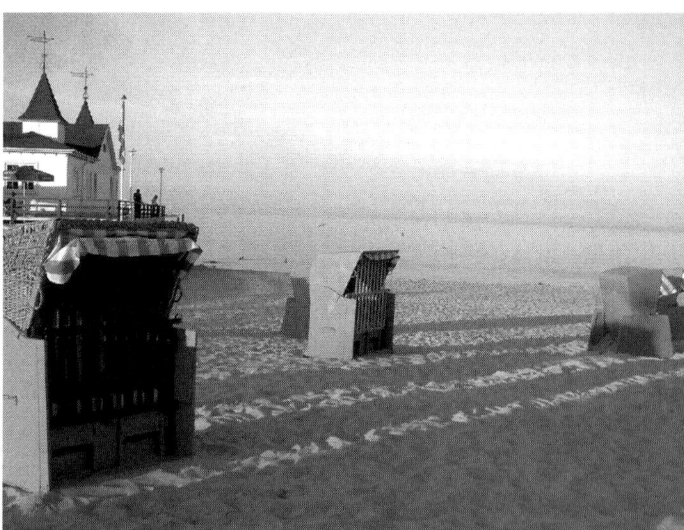

Figure 6 *Ahlbeck*. 2004.

For Tucker the solution has been to produce what I can only describe as images which offer us a sense of the sublime that is both present and, simultaneously, cancelled out. (7–8)

I began to realise that the particular physical aspects of this shoreline that I was intrigued with offer an opportunity to deal further with this paradoxical "cancelled out sublime." I am now looking at temporary structures in relation to the landscape, such as the pier or Seebrücke. I enjoy the literal translation: "sea bridge," a bridge that offers the promise of escape but goes nowhere. Another daily reminder of history: the Polish border, built at an apparently random place on the beach. This border is a surprisingly frail looking structure at an apparently random point along this flat beach. However, above all I have become fascinated by the ubiquitous strandkörbe.

They appear as an accessory or *parergon* of the pre-war photographs; their image is synonymous with the beaches of North Germany. Although they do not set out any formal boundaries of their own, in being situated on a beach they are located on the boundary between land and sea. These hybrids between beach hut and deck chair offer the possibility of a momentary shelter, yet standing empty on the beach they have a melancholy timbre. These structures fluctuate between offering a sense of being places of protection and in their very deficiency becoming almost mawkish ciphers of vulnerability.

My new work explores the risk of an intimate space within the basket contiguous with the open expanse beyond. Huddled together in groups they taken on an almost

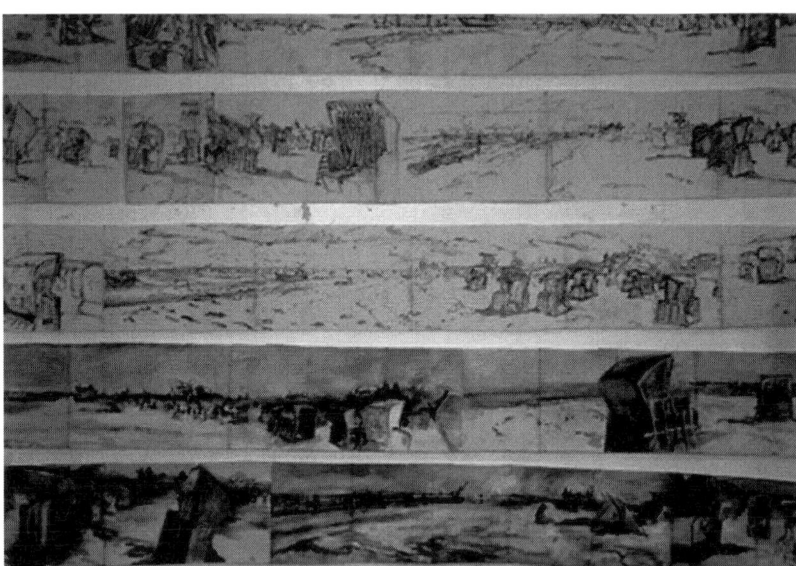

Figure 7 *Sketchbooks*. 2004.

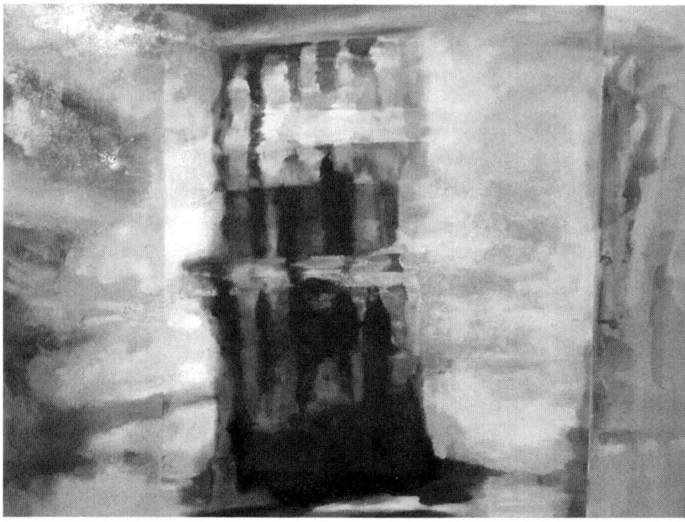

Figure 8 *Strandkorb*. Oil on canvas, 36″ × 48″.

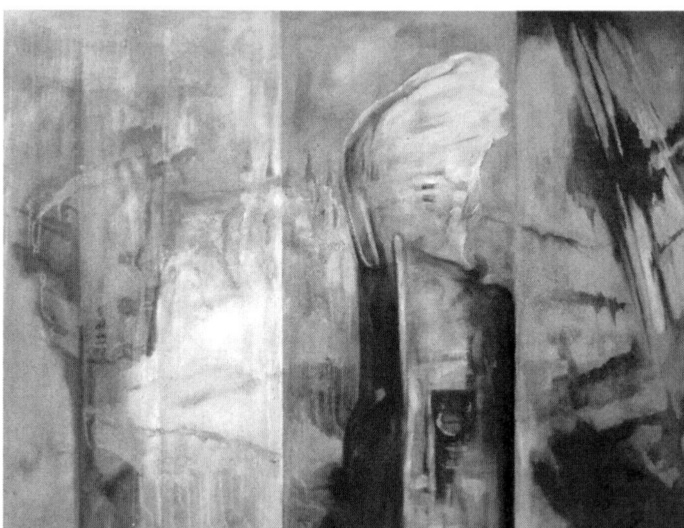

Figure 9 *Resort 1*. Oil on canvas, 36″ × 48″.

anthropomorphic quality, providing me with a resonant motif for my work. They could be thought of as objects of ridicule: a combination of kitsch, camp and nostalgia, comfortable chairs from which to experience the "sublime." They might almost be considered to have a satirical take on the concept of the necessity of a safe haven, to become a ludicrous version of a tent for the voluntary nomads from Berlin and,

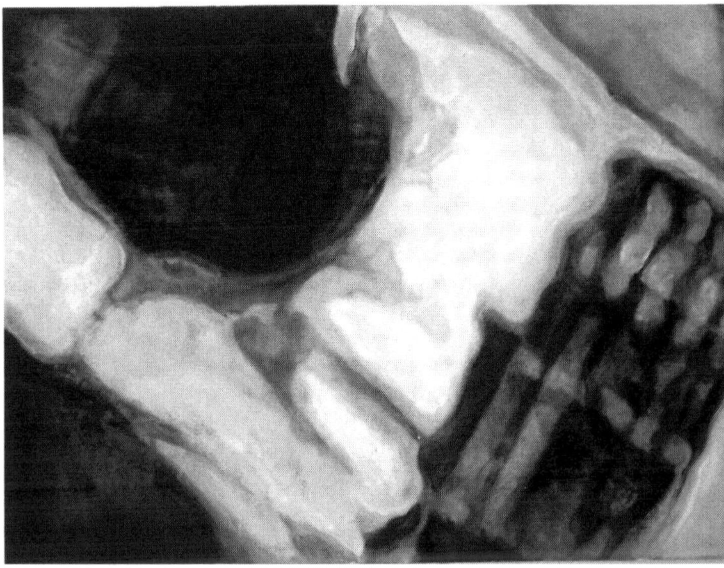

Figure 10 *Beach Shadows 3*. Oil on canvas, 36″ × 48″.

when gathered in their rows, looking for all the world a kind of parody of a transit camp.

It will not have escaped any reader's notice that much of the visual research into postmemory has been lens-based. I am asking the following question: what might it mean to represent this sort of place/landscape in a *painted* form? For me what is particular to painting as a practice (for example, the time taken, the layering, the evidence of the body which made the marks) mediates the external world and makes possible some sort of fusion between the internal and the external. This point resonates with the contiguous internal/external space of the strandkörbe. I think and discover through the process of making. I need to develop out of the materiality and processes in my practice. One aspect of this work is that I have had to rethink the language of paint that I am using; there is a re-evaluation of the vocabulary I use towards the figural, and a much more strategic use of the pearlescent and iridescent pigments. All paintings appear different according to the light but mine are very, very different: different aspects of the image become visible at different times according to the light and the position of the viewer, echoing the structures of memory.

Last year there was a large Philip Guston show on in London and, although he was painting in a very different context from me, I found his transition from what appeared to be abstraction to figuration very appropriate for my dilemma: how to include enough information about the content of the painting so that the viewer would be able to grasp the content while still exploiting all that he had gleaned from his earlier works? His answer, to combine a graphic idiom with a painterly motif, was not my solution, but to introduce an element of figuration has been. In consideration of any possible viewer of my work I should like to return briefly to Griselda Pollock's notion of painting as oscillating between both materiality and metaphorical fullness (34). While there is some slippage or shift required of the viewer to experience these two modes, it seems to me it is possible they act almost simultaneously. Perhaps the latter acts through the former via the subjectivity of the viewer; more of a hover, perhaps, than a true oscillation. The one reading does not seem to me to necessarily cancel out the other as it does in Wittgenstein's duck/rabbit where it is either the duck or the rabbit and to read the figure as one, destroys the illusion of the other (Wittgenstein 16–17). How might materiality become metaphorically full and how might it engage the intellect or affectivity of another?

My relation to my own paintings has altered in the light of this project. One-way in which this process of considering how materiality becomes metaphorically full may be evidenced within this text. While the descriptions and reproductions of my work remain more or less consistent throughout (in a sense one might consider they represent the *materiality* of paint) the emphasis, the meaning of those descriptions seems to change, to resonate differently in relation to the various discourses introduced. This (re)interpretation, (re)evaluation, of course, is even more potent in front of the material paintings themselves. I am reminded of Arnold Berleant's description of "landscape," and the same could apply to paintings:

A landscape is like a suit of clothes, empty and meaningless apart from its wearer. Without a human presence, it possesses only possibilities. (18)

I would hope that my paintings or drawings, once hung/exhibited/encountered, might transform at least one other, but, of course, this possibility cannot be foreseen. However, every technology has its own distinct way of making time tangible, each offers possibilities for different speculations concerning the relation of past, present and future. The choice of oil paint as my medium not only predicates the way in which I, the maker, mediate land but also the way it might be viewed. In the encounter with the painted surface, while any viewer brings her own history to bear on what she is looking at, she might also become aware of the deictic quality of the marks that refer back to the body of the painter: might it be possible that in the *viewing* of paintings past and present might become conflated?

I should like to conclude this paper with some further considerations of my practice in relation to Marianne Hirsch's writings. Drawing on the post-Freudian literature on trauma, she reminds us of the distinctions between two modalities of remembering, for example: "acting out" and "working through" (LaCapra) "perception" and "memory" (Mitchell) "traumatic memory" and "narrative memory" (van der Klok and

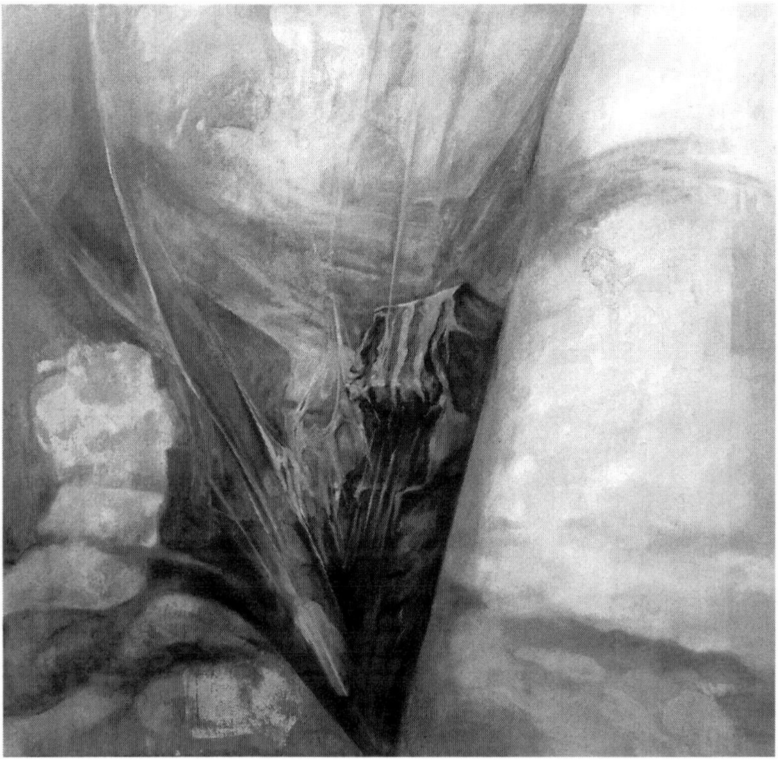

Figure 11 *Strandkorb II*. Oil on canvas, 65″ × 72.5″.

van der Hart). She suggests that these modes are neither oppositional nor mutually exclusive.

> *But the second generation – those who are deeply affected by events they themselves did not experience but whose memory they inherited – are also subject to different, if always overlapping modes of "remembering" ... I see a range between what Morrison has called "re-memory" and what I have termed "postmemory" between on the one hand, a memory that, communicated through bodily symptoms, becomes a form of repetition and re-enactment, and on the other hand one that works through indirection and multiple mediation.* (Marked by Memory 75)

The most important point that I would like to make here is that I feel that I am engaged in a process, a kind of transitional phase or movement, from the Caesura series which might be considered in a way a Toni Morrison "re-memory" position, or rather "transposition," a kind of unconscious repetition, a making it happen again, even "an acting out," to the Resort series which might be considered to be becoming closer to or analogous to Hirsch's postmemorial position or, perhaps, working towards a "working through." John Berger writes of Lisa Appignanesi's latest novel *The Memory Man* that what gives the book its particular tension are the "clashes between two movements, the movement backwards of memory, and the movement forwards of consequences."[2] This paradoxical dual movement is inherent in my new work but needs foregrounding. Another question is how to relate the "embodied" position taken in the first section of this paper to the "second generation" position outlined in the latter section. Hirsch argues that for postmemorial artists, the challenge is to describe an aesthetic founded on a mode of identification and projection that might include the transmission of the bodily memory of trauma without leading to the self-wounding and retraumatisation that is re-memory. She stresses the importance of

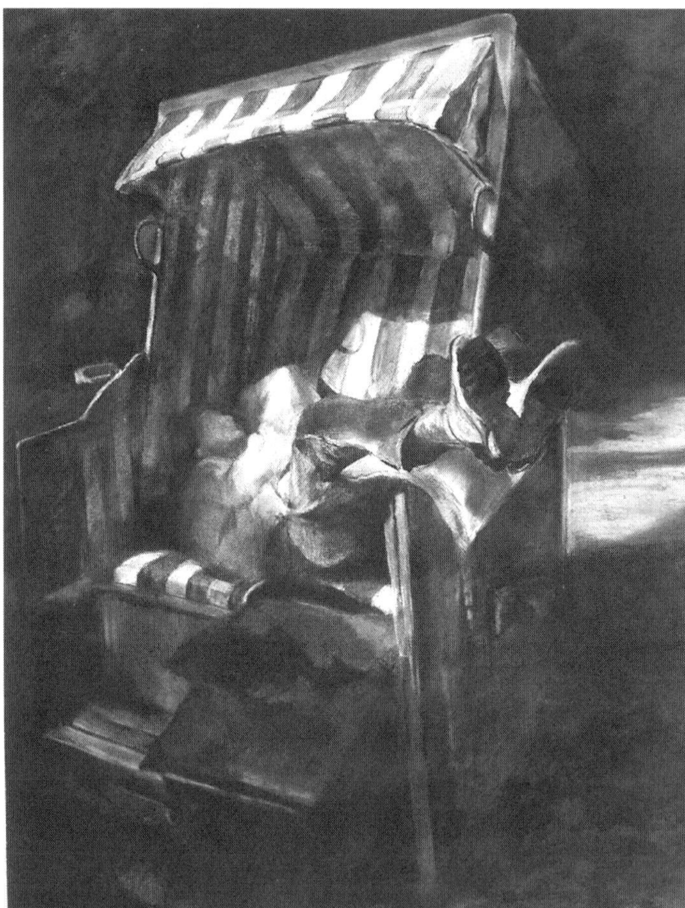

Figure 12 *Strandborb*. Charcoal drawing, 48″ × 60″.

awareness, and ultimately perhaps I would suggest an acceptance, of the unbridgeable distance separating the two generations. A multitude of distantiation techniques are currently in play in my paintings, even those pieces which appear at first sight to offer the viewer's eye and body a way in to the work. This apparent welcome is then subverted through other means: whether the hard brittle reflective surfaces, or the use of blurred photography, or the incorporation of images of my hands in front of the landscape. While this whole project has been triggered by photographs, I should like to emphasise that while the images I am currently engaged in making might ultimately appear similar to each other, it is crucial for me to consider that they stem from this variety of sources: some already mediated representations of landscape (the photographs and the maps); some from the notebooks, referencing an encounter on the beach in Germany; yet others directly from observation from the *strandkorb* I imported to Yorkshire, dislocated and stranded as far from the coast as is possible. This new work might be considered to have several strands. The one I have focussed on here is that of in some way contributing to an affective reading of history, a mediation of memory, but there are subtexts which are only touched on or pointed to in this paper, such as the relation between leisure and landscape, seen through the trope of the resort, both in the '30s and now. Through that relationship another set of very complex interrelations are emerging including the relation of pain to leisure, contemplation, escapism and visual pleasure. The challenge for me now is to reveal to a viewer something of this so as to encourage different viewing responses without resorting to being over literal.

Endnotes

1. Susan Stewart as used by Lucy R. Lippard, *On the Beaten Track* (1999).

2. This remark is attributed to John Berger on the dust-jacket of Lisa Appignanesi, *The Memory Man* London: Arcadia Books 2004.

Works Cited

Baer, Ulrich. *Spectral Evidence: The Photography of Trauma*. Cambridge Mass. The MIT Press, 2002.

Berleant, Arnold. *Living in the Landscape: Toward an Aesthetics of Environment*. Kansas: University Press of Kansas, 1997.

Betterton, Rosemary. *An Intimate Distance: Women, Artists and the Body*. London: Routledge, 1996.

Biggs Iain. "Re/visiting, Re/visioning, Re/placing" in *Judith Tucker, Resort at Only Atelier*. Wein, Austria and Leeds UK: Wild Pansy Press, 2003.

Casey, Edward S. *Representing Place: Landscape Painting and Maps* Minneapolis: University of Minneapolis Press, 2002.

Freud, Sigmund. *Mourning and Melancholia*. Vol. xiv (1914–1916). London: Strachey, 1957.

Fuller, Peter. *Art and Psychoanalysis*. London: Writers and Readers Cooperative Ltd., 1980.

Hirsch, Marriane. *Family Frames: Photography, Narrative, and Postmemory*. Cambridge, MA: Harvard University Press, 1997.

———. "Marked by Memory: Feminist Reflections on Trauma and Transmission" in *Extremities; Trauma, Testimony and Community* Eds. Nancy K. Miller and Jason Tougaw. Urbana and Chicago: University of Illinois Press, 2002.

———. "Past Lives: Postmemories in Exile" in *Exile and Creativity*, Ed. Susan Suleiman. Durham NC, Duke University Press, 1998. pp. 418–446.

LaCapra, Dominick. *History and Memory after Auchwitz* New York: Cornell University Press, 1998

Kaplan, Caren. *Questions of Travel. Postmodern Discourses of Displacement*. London and Durham: Duke University Press, 1996.

Karpf, Anne. *The War After, Living with the Holocaust*. London: Heinemann, 1996.

Kuspit, Donald. *The Rebirth of Painting in the Late Twentieth Century*. Cambridge: Cambridge University Press, 2000.

Lippard, Lucy R. *The Lure of the Local: Senses of Place in a Multicentered Society*. New York: The New Press, 1997.

Mckeever, Ian, "Thoughts on Nolde" in *Emil Nolde*. London: Whitechapel Art Gallery, 1995.

Pollock, Griselda. "Lydia Bauman: The Poetic Image in the Field of the Uncanny" in *Lydia Bauman, Landscapes*. Warsaw: Zacheta gallery, 1997.

Rogoff, Irit. *Terra Infirma: Geography's Visual Culture*. London: Routledge, 2000.

Spitzer, Leo. "Persistent Memory: Central European Refugees in an Andean Land" in *Exile and Creativity, Signposts, Travellers, Outsiders, Backward Glances*, Ed. Susan Suleiman. Durham NC: Duke University Press, 1998. 373–396.

Van Alphen, Ernst. *Caught by History: Holocaust Effects in Contemporary Art, Literature and Theory*. Stanford: Stanford University Press, 1997.

Van der Kolk, B.A., & Van der Hart, O. (1991). "The intrusive past: The flexibility of memory and the engraving of trauma". *American Imago*, 48 (4), 425–454.

Wittgenstein, Ludwig. *Remarks on the Philosophy of Psychology*, vol. 1. Ed. G. E. Anscombe and G. H. Von Wright. Oxford: Blackwell, 1980.

Wolff, Janet, "On the Road Again: Metaphors of Travel in Cultural Criticism" in *Undoing Place? A Geographical Reader*. London: Arnold, 1997. 180–194.

Thamyris/Intersecting No. 17 (2007) 81-94

Diasporic Slavery Memorials and Dutch Moral Geographies

Joy Smith

There is so much more to remember and describe, for purposes of exorcism and salvatory rites of passage ... things must be made ... some fixing ceremony ... some memorial, something, some altar, somewhere ... where these things can be released, thought and felt ... but the consequences of slavery only artists can deal with.[1]

—Toni Morrison

In the above quote, African-American author Toni Morrison emphasizes the artist as mediator between past and present, a kind of interpreter, or alchemist, who melds conventional history with imagined personal memories, and collective memory. This involves the practices of excavation and reconstruction where the artist occupies the space between representations and the political, between the symbolic and the social. In the article "Monuments of the Black Atlantic" (2004), Dutch literary theorist Johanna Kardux credits Morrison's famous novel, *Beloved*, published in 1987, for having put the event of slavery on the map, reverberating throughout the black diaspora, igniting the current interest in slavery memorials. Kardux identifies this "paper monument" as firmly placing the cultural memory of slavery within the narrative of diasporic, communal identity and multicultural politics, influencing politicized aesthetic productions and slavery memorials on an international level. She makes the point that the slavery motif travelled, not only geographically, but also between aesthetic forms.

When dealing with representations of slavery and their influence on Afro-Dutch assertions of group identities, however, we need also consider the obvious influence of artists from the former Dutch colony of Surinam. In the same year as the publication of *Beloved*, Surinamese, Creole historian Cynthia McLeod's first novel, *Hoe duur was de suiker?* (*How Expensive was the Sugar?* 1987), was published in both Surinam and the Netherlands to a great deal of attention. The novel broke through a cultural silence surrounding Dutch colonialism and slavery. Fifteen years later, the commemoration of the newly erected Dutch national slavery monument occurred on July 1, 2002. This monument originally began as an internationally inspired, black diasporic project, that later retained the support of the national government. The monument was the culmination of ten years of political struggle. Years of heated debate were played out in a public context involving Afro-Dutch community activism, initiatives, and in the later stages, governmental, political backing and financial support. In this paper, I will discuss McLeod's novel, and the Dutch national slavery monument, as part of a migratory aesthetic surrounding the cultural memory of slavery. I will also position these written and architectural slavery memorials as forms of activism in present-day, multicultural Holland.

In *How Expensive Was the Sugar?* McLeod presents a highly inclusive version of historical Surinam to Dutch and Surinamese readers alike. The novel follows the lives of Elza and Sarith Fernandez, two stepsisters from a prominent, Jewish plantation family of Portuguese descent. The turbulent relationships the women experience with each other, their personal slaves, and a Dutch bank official of French-Huguenot descent, Rutger Le Chausseur, is played out against the backdrop of economic crisis, slave uprisings, and the war between the colonists and the escaped Maroons. Through these characters, we learn of the intricate relations between the European plantation owners, government and church officials, black slaves, and the free, urban, Creole community.

It is not an accident that so many groups are represented in this novel. The intersubjectivity between colonizer and colonized, and McLeod's emphasis on cultural hybridity and miscegenation, reiterate the Latin American tradition of asserting culturally inclusive myths as a way of creating a unified national identity (Somer 1990, Sansone 2003). Historically, literature has played a tremendous role in this kind of nation-building phenomena. This is certainly true for Surinamese literature, for Surinam is a country with one of the most diverse populations in the world (Dew 1978, 1994).

However, McLeod's book is a meditation on alterity. In focusing on alterity, a lack of symmetry in individual identities as well as group identities, she is not only bound to Surinamers and Surinam. Through various means she brings to the fore historical circumstances of continuous flows of people and cultures not only in Latin America with its multiplicity of colonizers, but also earlier, similar movements by groups throughout Europe. McLeod emphasizes temporal and spatial shifts throughout the novel, subverting the ethnic, racial lines between white colonists and slaves, Jews and gentiles. She does this through the use of various ethnic names, for example, the French name of Le Chausseur for the Dutch protagonist Rutger, and the Portuguese name of Fernandez for the Jewish protagonists. She demonstrates cross-continental connections between Surinam and Europe through descriptions of travel across the ocean by various characters because of familial bonds and economic ties between Europe and the colonized Americas. She does this also through references to slave auctions; descriptions of the slave population's African cultural practices, and the slave characters themselves invoke Africa and the ocean crossing of the middle passage.

Theorizing on group assertions and identity politics usually takes the nation-state as a given framework of debates, McLeod's novel while set in Dutch-colonial Surinam, can be viewed more broadly than the colonial period or the country of Surinam. It was published in 1987 during a period of decolonization and the height of mass-migration taking place between the late 1960s to the present. McLeod chose to deal with slavery, a not often discussed or well-known historical topic in the Netherlands, rather than the current issues of migration, that so many other postcolonial writers deal with during this period. She chose a culturally inclusive narrative, rather than one that deals with themes of exile currently in vogue for immigrant writers in the Netherlands. Important for this examination too, is that she wrote her novel in Dutch, allowing for a larger and Dutch audience, rather than Sranan, the "real national language" of Surinam, according to McLeod (4).

Given this time of tremendous migration and McLeod's attention to geographical movement and subversive identity play, *How Expensive was the Sugar?* can be situated within a contemporary, global context: between the registers of the painful historical past of slavery and colonization in Surinam, the present climate of neo-colonialism and mass migration of the former colonials to Europe, and the current tension-filled multicultural encounters in the Netherlands.

Many scholars testify to the overwhelming lack of knowledge by Dutch citizens of its colonial, slaveholding past, the little-known, dark side of this historically immigrant, and "tolerant" nation (Blakely 1993, Essed 1984, Oostindie 2001). According to a survey done in Dutch schools during the 1990s, only 50% discussed slavery in any depth, and two did not at all (Kardux 2004, 91). With this novel, McLeod places the past firmly within the present and brings public awareness to this not often acknowledged or discussed aspect of Dutch history (Oostindie 2001, Kardux 2004). This open and plural nation's denial and refusal to come to terms with its own past, and silencing of particular knowledges, presents another side to Holland's tolerant image and how it deals with its others.

McLeod's historical novel about colonialism and slavery gives voice to the disremembered and the unspeakable in Dutch society. As Mieke Bal writes in her edited volume *Acts of Memory*, "The memorial presence of the past takes many forms and serves many purposes, ranging from conscious recall to unreflected reemergence, from nostalgic longing for what is lost to *polemical use of the past to reshape the present*" (Bal vii, emphasis added). Cultural activism and criticism take many forms, and one is in the contestation of cultural memory. Her novel was perceived as piercing through a profound cultural amnesia in the Netherlands regarding colonialism. Some considered it as filling a void, or answering a call. Despite, or perhaps because of the non-recognition and long cultural silence about the dark side of Dutch history, *How*

Expensive was the Sugar? sold extremely well in the Netherlands and is still in print, readily available in bookstores to this day.

Dutch literary critic Ineke Phaf-Rheinberger (2001) interprets the success of the novel as a testament to the need for this kind of history. To my mind, the need to which Phaf-Rheinberger alludes is very much connected to the mass migration of postcolonial Surinamers to Holland, and their attendant need to create some kind of "narratives for a new belonging" in Europe (Bromley 2000). During the current neocolonial period, the movement of the former colonials to the metropoles is a common state of affairs. Third world countries that have won their independence are often still tied economically to Western, European nations. In the Dutch case, over half the population of Surinam has moved to Holland within the last thirty years.

With this mass migration, the Netherlands, a country renowned for and proud of its reputation as a progressive nation, has recently experienced tensions that call its "tolerant" image into question (Blakely 1993, Hoving 2004). In addition to the postcolonials, more recently, guest workers brought from southern Europe, particularly Morocco and Turkey, have stayed in the Netherlands and constituted families. While still a small part of the population, their Muslim religious and cultural beliefs are seen as problematic for cultural assimilation into Dutch society. The nation's current animosity toward its postcolonial and newer immigrants, while clinging to its reputation as a leader in progressive immigration policies, is a contradiction.

In the influential essay, "Moral Geographies and the Ethics of Post-Sovereignty" (1994), political science scholar Michael J. Shapiro, asserts that historical novels that rewrite popular and heroic myths about the nation's encounters with other cultures, is a powerful way to disrupt grand national, historic narratives. In the article, he describes the normalizing power of the state and its attempts to control identities as well as interpretations of space. A nation's "territorial map" is "maintained with a series of strategies of containment" (45). This is accomplished by narratives of national emergence, what Shapiro calls "the literary form of containment" that is concerned with "temporal as well as spatial rhetoric. (45)" Ultimately this creates illusions of a "continuous, homogeneous" state that relies heavily on the idea of a disrupted past (45).

This geopolitical map has been naturalized and "appears uncontentious." Yet it is a map that is lacking, selectively at any rate, historical depth. This constitutes for Shapiro a moral geography that he defines as "a set of silent ethical assertions that preorganize explicit ethico-political discourses" (41). Shapiro calls upon a remapping that has an ethical, temporal and spatial dimension. This can be achieved through an emphasis on historical genealogies that construct "frames of encounter" (57) rather than genealogies of forgetfulness. By so doing, dominant national and minority groups, and political identities, are contextualized, and marginalized groups, and their political movements, are then endowed with "historical assets." A concern for the past allows for marginalized groups to construct possible futures. This is particularly relevant for the situation of the postcolonial in Europe. McLeod's novel, set during the hundred years Maroon wars, subverts notions of complete Dutch colonial domination in Holland's encounter with Surinam, while also exposing a chapter in Dutch history that is disremembered.

With Shapiro's insights, it is possible to understand why McLeod would choose the field of cultural memory, more precisely the cultural trauma of slavery, not only in order to explore the historical encounter between Europe and Latin America, but to yield insights into the current, cross-cultural encounter between Surinamers in Holland. *How Expensive was the Sugar?* is an example of endowing this postcolonial community with "historical assets" lending weight to their right to be in Europe at the present time. The tremendous migratory movement of Surinamers to Holland not only effects understandings of their identity and aesthetics, but those of the new nation they call home. McLeod's novel invites readings of subjectivity that disrupt linear narratives of migration, call into question the meaning of "homeland," while also asserting a Surinamese, African-American identity within the new social order.

McLeod's rewriting of history can be viewed as having surpassed the national borders of Surinam, offering a critique on the current tension-filled multicultural situation in Holland and its lack of interest in its own history. To my mind, both the novel *How Expensive was the Sugar?* and the slavery monument are assertions of group identities. They are attempts at intervening on national, ideological narratives and forms of denial. The novel offers a public forum for the displaced or absent other in Dutch society, and like Morrison's *Beloved*, can be viewed as a catalyst for the Dutch national slavery monument. These cultural objects, written and architectural memorials, can function as catalysts for awareness and mourning of historic, traumatic events. They operate as the actual sites of remembrance themselves. Releasing these "things," as Toni Morrison would have it, and their potential to work through the historical past, in and for the present.

Exposing Slavery

If slavery is a leitmotif in the imagination of the diaspora that it created, it is because, as the Africans say, a wound may heal but a scar does not. Indeed, with regard to the deep wounds of slavery, even the prospect of healing is doubtful. The return to slavery and to images and tropes of its lingering trauma reiterates that what was done cannot be undone and that the memory of it must be kept alive so that both perpetrator and victim may live in the shadow of its knowledge. Only in this way, may we guard against its repetition. (Oguibe 100)

For people of the black diaspora, to "live in the shadow" of slavery has meant to live in complicit silence. In the decades since emancipation, slavery has been disremembered in Black Atlantic communities throughout the world (Eyerman 2001, Sansone 2003). It was for many conceived as a source of shame and causally linked to current social subjugation. For over a century, black diasporic communities took part in a collective forgetting. Recently, however, people of African descent have agitated for slavery memorials, days of commemoration, as well as representations and structures of remembrance, for some kind of recognition and acknowledgement of past and present harms. Despite the presence of identity movements since the 1960s whose ideas and identifications also surpassed national borders and circulated throughout the black diaspora, there has been an inability on the part of the larger society to make connections, see the current state of affairs contextualized within past injustices, and as enlightenment promises unfulfilled.

According to sociologist Ron Eyerman (2001), the centuries long event of slavery in the New World is a defining collective memory for African-Americans. He theorizes slavery as a cultural trauma around which black identities in the United States have been historically formed. For Eyerman, the unrealized promise of becoming full citizens after emancipation, a decades long process of disillusionment, contributed to making slavery the unifying theme and cultural memory through which American blacks have shaped their identities. Slavery was, and continues to be, a major topoi African-Americans utilize in cultural activism and negotiations with the dominant society. These processes take place in various social fields, not only within politics, social movements, and organizations like the NAACP (National Association for the Advancement of Colored People), but they also occur in aesthetic forms through struggles over representations and recognition.

While Eyerman limits his work to African-Americans in the United States, I find his emphasis on cultural memory with regard to identity relevant for African-Americans in a broader sense as well; people of African descent throughout the Americas. These processes of identifications and identity formation are not contained within a particular continent, but cross national boundaries and circulate.[2] Thus Eyerman's focus on the cultural memory of slavery can be extended and foregrounded in formulations of diasporic identities. These communities have been mainly envisioned in terms of space, where displacement and movement, the local and the global have been widely theorized. Human geographer Anne Marie Fortier (2001) offers a critique of that formulation and asserts the problems in assuming an originary point, or emphasizing a homeland, and pinpointing a "defining moment" of upheaval. It is a reductive move that binds diasporic identities within the linear time-space frame, the narratives of here and there, "continuity" and "progress," host society and homeland. It is precisely these categories that diasporic communities call into question.

Time and space is reconfigured and notions such as native, immigrant, third world and the West, are undermined. Former colonial and diasporic identities fall outside linear narratives of immigration and conceptions of the nation-state. In that sense, postcolonial identities could be considered "postnational." Fortier argues that a rethinking of categories is important for theorizing postcolonial identities. These old categories are particularly misleading for the population Stuart Hall calls the "twice diasporized" people of African descent whose ancestors were brought to the Caribbean, who then migrated, and now reside in Europe. According to Fortier, the emphasis shifts to memory and routes, rather than place, as the grounding for identities in diasporic cultures. The cultural memory of slavery has formed an enduring route, a landscape on which art is made and identities narrated, encompassing black diasporic communities throughout the world.

The Shape of Memory

Public art, erected as eternal monuments to past transgressions, occupy a different kind of site than written memorials, an "interior space," in which the "site of reading" becomes the "memorial space" (Young 7). Stone and concrete, architectural memorials, at times inspired from afar, but grounded and contested within the confines of individual nation-states, have become an important area within identity politics and the struggle for social visibility. The desire to invoke particular historical narratives, the nation's past crimes, often concealed, present opportunities for group assertions.

English and Judaic Studies scholar James Young's book on Germany and Holocaust memorials, *The Texture of Memory* (1993), managed to reinvigorate waning interest in monument scholarship. Young theorizes monuments as social texts to be read and views them as part of a dialogical process of contesting space by exploring the politics and rhetoric behind the monuments. In this same tradition, art historian Kirk Savage analyzes the fight for and contestations around African-American representations of slavery in the United States during the nineteenth century in his book *Standing Soldiers, Kneeling Slaves* (1999). He broadens Young's approach by employing Habermas' notion of the public sphere in his analysis. His book reinforces the notion that memory politics and identity politics often come together in the realm of art and representations.

More recently, Kardux's article, "Monuments of the Black Atlantic" (2004), incorporates a transnational theme when examining contestation and identity politics in her comparative work on slavery monuments in the U.S. and Holland. Kardux argues that the movement for the Dutch national slavery monument was inspired by a particular period during the '90s of grassroots activism in the United States for a slavery monument. The Middle Passage memorial was the obsession of one man, African-American fashion designer Wayne James, who with time, received a great deal of communal and financial support, as well as media attention for his activism. He managed to ignite the African-American community around a slavery monument that was to be constructed, commemorated, and immediately sunk into the sea. The "ephemeral" memorial was to mark the watery grave of millions of slaves who died on the way to the Americas in the middle passage. This successful, non-governmental initiative was part of an international agenda to inspire the building of slavery monuments throughout the world. Kardux also makes the point that the Middle Passage monument was, to a great extent, responsible for motivating Afro-Dutch communities in Holland to establish a slavery monument. The commemoration of the Dutch National slavery memorial in July 2002, after a ten year-long struggle, public unrest, negotiations, in-fighting, and public scrutiny, could appear to be a hard fought success. For the Afro-Dutch original proponents of the slavery memorial, the desire to erect a slavery monument was to finally invoke a disremembered and painful period. It was to preserve, in a benign form, a troubled past and leave a trace of former intolerance in a nation famous for its tolerance. A stone and metal monument representing Dutch historical involvement in slavery, and those of African descent who were enslaved, would act as a solid witness, weighty reminder, and concrete testament to social injustice.

The Dutch government, however, appeared to have another agenda. What began as a grassroots initiative by the Surinamese-Dutch community in order to raise national awareness about slavery, eventually came under the supervision of Roger van Boxtel, Dutch Minister of Urban Policy and Integration of Ethnic Minorities. When it then became a government-condoned project there was an attempt to raise public involvement not only from the Afro-Dutch population, but from the majority society as well. The result was that both the location of the monument, the decision to assign a theme for the artwork/design of the memorial, and the nine artists who would be invited to submit designs for the monument competition, all fell under the control of the Dutch government.

The monument came to rest outside the city centre of Amsterdam, and away from the prestigious memorials located in the heart of the city, where yearly, highly visible, public commemorations are held: The Dam square WWII monument, the Anne Frank house, and the Pink Triangle homosexual monument, that pays homage to the gay men and lesbians who died in concentration camps during WWII. Instead, the Dutch national slavery monument stands in a secluded area, surrounded by trees, in the southeast corner of Oosterpark, a name that describes its eastern location in the city of Amsterdam.

Near the monument stands a plaque with the inscription: "*Gedeeld Verleden Gezamenlijke Toekomst*." A translation of those words in English also appears underneath the Dutch words as "Shared Past Common Future." The Dutch word gedeeld, is a past tense form of the verb delen, "to share." The Van Dale dictionary lists five definitions for delen, but its first description may be translated as "to separate." Another variation of that definition also appears involving a monetary example with the translation, "to divide."[3] The inherent contradiction in the infinitive form of the verb delen, which includes " to share," and its opposite "to separate" or "divide," may guide us to the contradictory reality of the separate and unequal history of Holland's former enslaved colonials as compared to that of its temporal counter part, the Golden Age.

The Golden Age, that period proudly and often referred to, generated enormous wealth for the Netherlands and was in large part financed by colonialism and slavery. Yet it is seldom discussed in those terms. Newman, Clayton, and Hirsch (2002) suggest in *Time and the Literary* "... the present of reading is an encounter with other presents which reveals the contingency and impermanence of each, the coexistence of many mutually exclusive possible presents," and I would add pasts (6). In the Dutch case, the historical period of the "Golden Age" seems to have effectively blotted out the coexisting past of slavery and colonialism in Dutch society. The colonial past has been constructed as something that happened long ago and far away; simply no longer relevant. It occupies a separate, unequal, yet parallel space.

The contradictions in the definitions of the verb delen may also remind us of the status held by those who are marked as outsiders, named "allochtonen," meaning from another land, for generations despite being born on Dutch soil, as opposed to those who are considered natives, those who belong, called autochtonen. It alerts us to the ambiguities and ambivalences involved in exposing slavery to a nation invested in forgetting. The term "gedeeld," when translated as "shared" masks the power relations and uneven participation of colonialism and slavery between colonizer and colonized. The choice of the word "shared" glosses over the exploitative nature of the involvement of Holland with Surinam.

A year before the monument would be commemorated, the Dutch government held a competition for the design of the memorial. It mandated a theme for the monument. The artwork was to somehow depict the past, present, and the future.[4] Through a vote, Surinamese artist Erwin de Vries won the competition. He designed a large bronze monument that combines realist images with the abstract, and following the assignment, covers three sections. The past is represented by a group of slaves, bound together in what appears to be chains or ropes, facing forward to the next scene in the statue. The middle, present section, contains a human like figure walking beneath an arch, heading, like the bound slaves, toward the future section; a larger, abstract, female figure. She stands at the front of the monument looming, her back folded deeply, chest pointed outward toward the sun, with arms stretched wide.

Many artistic representations of slavery depict familiar historic images that have circulated around the world becoming designated markers: chains, kneeling slaves, and ships to name a few. Why then the need for a particular theme, the government's agenda around this three-part time construction for the Dutch slavery monument? For as Young claims, all memorials construct time (15). He asserts that, "like narrative, which automatically locates events in linear sequence, the memorial also brings events into some cognitive order" (7).

According to Kardux, the government insisted that the monument not only commemorate the historical slavery past, but that it represent the present and future multicultural society (97). This temporal stipulation shifts the emphasis from the past onto a utopic future. The visual representation of the monument becomes a teleological expression of this shift; three separate and distinct historical periods, past, present, and future, which come together, or rather, lead the viewer to a particular destination: the future. Even the size of the figures increase from life-sized slave figures in the back, building to the larger middle figure, and ending at the giant future/freedom figure to which one's visual attention is immediately drawn. Movement is an important theme in this memorial. The monument seems to race toward this imagined future of "happy multiculturalism."

Again, Young is useful here when he asks, "What meanings are generated when the temporal realm is converted to material form, when time collapses into space, a trope by which it is then measured and grasped? How do memorials emplot time and memory? How do they impose borders on time? A facade on memory?" (15). The Dutch national slavery monument's image, and its inscription, "Shared Past, Common Future" somehow allude to the present without expressly referring to it. The present remains somehow elusive in the monument's inscription and its images. Just as the middle figure lies somewhere between the realist and the abstract, the body facing forward, its head oddly and exaggeratedly tilted up and back, while walking forward, away from the present and towards the future, the on-looker is left with an unclear representation of the present and is directed toward an idealized and abstract future.

The present, unacknowledged, in that it is omitted in the words on the plaque, is a present where Dutch *authochtonen* resentments continue to rise, the kind of resentments that would spur slogans such as "Nederland voor Nederlanders." The viewer is directed, instead, to the figure of the future and all its promise. The abstract figure of the present, the representation of the present situation in Holland, is moving toward a longed-for future with all its claims to tolerance amidst multicultural strife. The figure is not kneeling or standing still, reflecting on the current social ills, but is facing forward, is in motion, moving away from the present, going toward a hopeful, imaginary future. The absence of the present on the plaque, and in the somewhat abstract form and forward moving posture of the figure in the monument, is a contradiction, much like the inherent opposition in the definitions of the infinitive verb "delen," (to share and to divide), that appears on the monument's plaque in the past tense form "gedeeld." There are inherent contradictions and ambivalences pervading the slavery monument's commemoration as national symbol *and* as an Afro-Dutch symbol of former and continued social subjugation.

There is a paradoxical challenge when a nation decides to commemorate, in monumental form, past wrongs and atrocities. Nations celebrate and represent their heroes, and reify memories that build the nation. Young refers to this process as a "self-aggrandizing locus for national memory." Victims, on the other hand, build monuments to their martyrdom, but "rarely," he stresses, "does a nation call upon itself to remember the victims of crimes it has perpetrated" (21). This "ambiguity of meaning" was assured perhaps, when the government became involved with the monument and "supported" it. The consequences for former colonials in Europe is an "our history," "their history" paradigm that creates a dilemma when nation-building impulses are paired with minority groups' desire for recognition of past atrocities. The Dutch national slavery monuments' slide from diasporic, transnational memorial, to national monument, was a situation inherently fraught with contradictions.

Moral Geographies: Nostalgia for the Nation

In order to be knowingly in each other's presence we must somehow share each other's past.
— "Remembering the Other" Johannes Fabian

I began this paper with a reading of Cynthia McLeod's novel, *How Expensive was the Sugar?* as a written memorial to slavery. I attempted to position McLeod's historical work, with Shapiro's theorizing on moral geographies, as a critique on present-day, Western European narratives of homogenous nation states. I also asserted a link between the novel and the Dutch national slavery monument as written and architectural memorials that act as forms of Afro-Dutch activism in the Netherlands. Tensions have been rising in Europe around multiculturalism, now that the ex-colonials are migrating to Europe. In the midst of this environment, McLeod's novel became the highest selling Surinamese novel ever. A little more than a decade later, the Dutch national slavery monument was commemorated.

I argued that the slippery slide from transnational, diasporic memorial to national monument created a shift where memory, the principle ground of identity formation for diasporic cultures, was replaced by place. Nostalgia for the tolerant image of the nation seemed to intrude on this diasporic process where national narratives of openness somehow prevailed, and with it, the disappearance of present multicultural strife. The slavery memorial that was to link various times and spaces, became, in a sense, cut off from the rest of the world, was usurped by the Dutch government as a nationalistic project celebrating an open and tolerant nation, oblivious to its present social problems, while emphasizing an imagined, hopeful future.

To many in the Afro-Dutch and majority Dutch population, the monument is seen as a meaningless and empty gesture. They believe it did very little to heighten general awareness and understanding of the colonial, slavery past for the majority Dutch population.[5] These dissonant and critical voices seem to echo the sentiments of scholars (Huyssen; Young) who have written about the invisibility of monuments, how monuments can often become a sort of wasteland for memories that are to be briefly acknowledged and then quickly forgotten rather than truly internalized into the society. The government's marginal placement of the monument in Oosterpark, and even within the park itself, seems to me to be a spatial metaphor for the current disconnection and exclusion of the Afro-Dutch population from full citizenship in Holland. The history of slavery, like the slavery monument itself, remains hidden from view from the vast majority of Dutch people.

For the Netherlands, a reconfiguration of time, space, and the other is needed. Surinam and the other former colonial countries' histories cannot continue to be held outside Dutch national history and cultural memory. Recent migration must be seen as part of a larger history of immigration, pluralism, and multiculturalism that historically allowed Holland to succeed. McLeod's novel, *How Expensive was the Sugar?* and the slavery monument are both written and architectural slavery memorials. They are traces of a *shared*, painful past, voiced within a present of cultural amnesia, positioned to affect a future that may realize a more stable Surinam, and a more successful multicultural Holland. These monuments can function as new ways of building community. As Young writes, "They become communities precisely by having shared (if only vicariously) the experiences of their neighbors. At some point, it may even be the activity of remembering together that becomes the shared memory once ritualized, remembering together becomes an event in itself that is to be shared and remembered" (7).

Endnotes

1. Nicola King recalls Morrison's appearance at the South Bank Show of 11 October 1987 where "Morrison suggests the inadequacy of 'historical discourse' in the claim she makes for art." *Memory, Narrative, and Identity* 2000: 153.

2. African-American studies has recently turned its focus toward a more international and transnational focus. See among other works *The Practice of Diaspora* by Brent Hayes 2003; *Blackening Europe* Ed. Heike Raphael-Hernandez 2004; *Black Imagination and the Middle Passage*, Eds. Maria Diedrich, Henry Louise Gates, Jr. and Carl Pederson 1999.

3. I am grateful to my ASCA colleague and friend Jolande Jansen for directing me to the infinitive form of the verb delen.

4. In an article written by Mark Duursma about Erwin de Vries and his design for the slavery monument, de Vries states that the past, present and future was to be included as a necessary part of the design in the contest assignment. "Ze vroegen in de opdracht om het verbeelden van verleden, heden, en toekomst, en daar heb ik me aan gehouden." July 12, 2001, NRC Handelsblad. Amsterdam. <http:/www.nrc.nl/cultuur expositie/994937502091>. Downloaded November 29, 2004. Kardux also mentions the past, present, and future design as a stipulation in the exhibition brochure for the competing designs and appears to be of two minds on the subject. On the one hand she quotes the brochure as saying that the artwork must "make visible the Dutch slavery past and its continuing impact on the present and the future in our multicultural society, and that it represent the struggle for freedom and emancipation of the slaves' descendants." Yet she also argues that there were divergent views for memorial designs and that different groups had "different narrative and ideological agendas" (2004: 96).

5. There is another aspect to the slavery memorial. A research institute was also founded, designed to be a "living monument." Space limitations prevent me from discussing it here.

Works Cited

Bal, Mieke. "Introduction" in *Acts of Memory*. Eds. Mieke Bal, Jonathan Crewe, and Leo Spitzer. Hanover: University Press of New England, 1998.

Blakely, Allison. *Blacks in the Dutch World*. Bloomington: Indiana University Press, 1993.

Bromley, Roger. Narratives for a New Belonging. Edinburgh: Edinburgh University Press, 2000.

Essed, Philomena. "Reflections on Everyday Racism" in *Race Critical Theories*. Eds. Philomena Essed and David Theo Goldberg. Oxford: Blackwell Publishers, 2002.

Essed, Philomena. *Alledags racisme*. Amsterdam: Feministische Uitgeverij Sara, 1984.

Eyerman, Ron. *Cultural Trauma: Slavery and the Formation of African American Identity*. Cambridge: Cambridge University Press, 2001.

Fabian, Johannes. "Remembering the Other." *Critical Inquiry* 26.1 (1999). 49–69

Fortier, Anne-Marie. "Diaspora" in David Sibley Ed. *Critical Concepts in Geography*. London: I.B. Tauris Publishers, 2001.

Goldberg, David. "Racial Rule" in *Relocating Postcolonialism*. Eds. David Goldberg and Ato Quayson. Oxford: Blackwell Publishers, 2002.

Hoving, Isabel. "Circumventing Openness: Creating New Sense of Dutchness." Paper presented at the *Goodbye Germany* Conference Berkeley, California, United States. October 28–30, 2004.

Huyssen, Andreas "Monumental Seduction" in *Acts of Memory*. Eds. Mieke Bal, Jonathan Crewe, and Leo Spitzer. Hanover: University Press of New England, 1999.

Kardux, Johanna C. "Monuments of the Black Atlantic" in *Blackening Europe: The African American Presence*. New York: Routledge, 2004. 87–105.

Kirby, Kathleen M. *Indifferent Boundaries*. New York: The Guilford Press, 1996.

McLeod, Cynthia. *Hoe duur was de suiker?* Amsterdam: Zilver Pockets/Maarten Muntinga bv 17th printing, 2003.

Newman, Karen. *Time and the Literary*. Eds. Karen Newman, Jay Clayton, and Marianne Hirsch. New York: Routledge, 2002.

Oguibe, Olu. "Slavery and the Diaspora Imagination" in Gert Oostindie (Ed.) *Facing Up to the Past: Perspectives n the Commemoration of Slavery from Africa, the Americas and Europe*. Jamaica: Ian Randle Publishers, 2001. 95–101.

Oostindie, Gert. (Ed.) "Stony Regrets and Pledges for the Future" in *Facing Up to the Past: Perspectives on the Commemoration of Slavery from Africa, the Americas and Europe*. Jamaica: Ian Randle Publishers, 2001. 9–18.

Phaf-Rheinberger, Ineke. *A History of Literature in the Caribbean Vol. 2* Amsterdam/Philadelphia: John Benjamin Publishing Company, 2001.

Prins, Baukje. *The Standpoint in Question*. Proefschrift Universiteit Utrecht, 1997.

Sansone, Livio. *Blackness Without Ethnicity.* New York: Palgrave Macmillan, 2003.

Shapiro, Michael J. "Moral Geographies and the Ethics of Post-Sovereignty." *Public Culture* 6 (1994). 479–502.

Young, James. E. *Texture of Memory: Holocaust Memorials and Meaning*. New Haven: Yale University Press, 1993.

Thamyris/Intersecting No. 17 (2007) 95-108

Travelling to the Colonial Past as Migratory Aesthetics: Aya Zikken's *Terug naar de atlasvlinder*

Sarah de Mul

The Dutch female author Aya Zikken (1919) spent a large part of her childhood in the Dutch Indies (colonial Indonesia). As were many Dutch colonial settlers, Zikken was forced to return to the homeland (the Netherlands) in the early 1940s during the struggle for Indonesian independence. The Netherlands, however, was almost completely unknown to Zikken. She tried to rework her East Indies childhood memories into numerous literary works. Suffering from feelings of rootlessness and homesickness for the Indies, Zikken also started travelling widely and has written a large body of such writing. Zikken's background as a Dutch child in colonial Indonesia and her forced migration to the Netherlands was predominantly the reason for her to write, to travel, and to write about travel.

In the interests of exploring the notion of migratory aesthetics, I will offer a critical reading of Zikken's narrative of "return travel" to Indonesia, entitled *Terug naar de atlasvlinder* (*Back to the Atlas Butterfly*) written in 1981.[1] The title of Aya Zikken's return travel narrative refers directly to Zikken's earlier written novel, entitled *De atlas vlinder (The Atlas Butterfly)* written in 1958.[2] *The Atlas Butterfly* is Zikken's most acclaimed work. It is a nostalgic recollection of a colonial childhood in a Dutch settlers' village in the highlands of South Sumatra. In *Back to the Atlas Butterfly*, the female travelling persona, named Aya Zikken, describes her return to this highland village where she was raised, here specified as Lahat, at South Sumatra. The intertextual relationship between the two aesthetic representations of Lahat in *The Atlas Butterfly* and *Back to the Atlas Butterfly* will be of crucial importance in the formulation of a migratory aesthetics.

I will argue that *Back to the Atlas Butterfly* is very fruitful for a discussion about the notion of migratory aesthetics for the following reasons. Firstly, Aya Zikken's return travel invites us to think about the notion of migratory aesthetics in a manner which is not restricted to stable identity categories, such as "the migrant." Secondly, the traveller's return takes shape by means of a specific form of intertextuality, which may well be considered as migratory aesthetics. In *Back to the Atlas Butterfly*, the narration of the physical return to Lahat is interspersed with imaginary evocations of Lahat, with intertextual references to *The Atlas Butterfly*. Realising that a physical return to the Lahat of her childhood is not possible in the late 1970s, the traveller negotiates between observations and acts of imaginary recall of Lahat in order to recapture her past. I will argue that Lahat, as the site of the traveller's childhood, exists in the negotiation of the slippage between the referential (but belated) and the memorial (but imaginary). The manner in which the traveller's return is constituted through migrating between two aesthetically crafted representations of Lahat – referential and imagined – will be discussed as migratory aesthetics. Hence, my reading of a traveller's return to Indonesia in *Back to the Atlas Butterfly* will yield insights into migratory aesthetics as a notion which does not only challenge conventional identity categories, such as "the Western traveller" and "the postcolonial migrant." In my formulation, migratory aesthetics also centralises the mobile dimension of intertextual relationships existing between different aesthetic representations of a singular space in the attempt to return to the colonial past.

The Trajectory of a Western Traveller Homesick for the Indies

In Aya Zikken's return travel narrative *Back to the Atlas Butterfly*, the travelling persona is constituted neither as a "Western traveller" nor as a "postcolonial migrant," but as possessing qualities of both. I consider return travel writing as a non-fictional first-person account about a journey back to the traveller's childhood site.[3] This understanding of "return travel writing" implies that, prior to the return, a departure from the childhood site to "elsewhere" has taken place. In return travel writing, the traveller departs from "elsewhere" and travels to what used to be her childhood "home."[4] This is in contrast with conventional Euro-imperial definitions of travel writing. Home is a crucial category within European travel, indicating a stable space where one departs from and returns to, and which is clearly demarcated from the space of "the foreign" and "the Other."

In *Back to the Atlas Butterfly*, the place where Zikken departs from is the Netherlands. However, this place is not considered as home, in the sense of a stable place. The I-person undertakes the return journey to Indonesia because she feels rootless and homesick in the Netherlands. Conditions of displacement from one's origins and feelings of homesickness have traditionally been connected to postcolonial or third world subjects who migrated to the West in a pathological way. In *Being/s in Transit*, Liselotte Glage argues, however, that " ... by implying that the West produced (self-) centred travellers and the former colonies, by contrast, produced fragmented, dislocated migrants ... in recent years, the figure of the migrant has acquired the status of a mythical beast, one that effectively blocks the view of our own history"(9). Given the travelling persona's homesickness and decentredness, *Back to the Atlas Butterfly* invites us to question the often-posited dichotomy between postcolonial migrants and Western travellers. Indeed, the assumption that Dutch ex-colonial subjects, such as Aya Zikken, might have migratory feelings too, requires thinking less constrictively about the figure of the migrant. In this manner, the travelogue draws the attention to the important idea that the notion of "migratory aesthetics" is unproductive if its meaning is reduced to such a thing as migrants' aesthetics, implying some form of aesthetics characterising migrant literatures.

Yet, it is important to note that the conflation of various migratory experiences and forms of aesthetics into a universalised category of "the migratory" is not desirable either. It is important to keep in mind Caren Kaplan's warning in *Questions of Travel*. The latter discovers a dangerous "mythologized narrativization of displacement" in recent theory that does not "question the cultural, political, and economic grounds of ... privileges, means and limitations" (13). We should bear in mind that Zikken's migratory situation is that of a very privileged Western person. Her migratory experience differs considerably from those individuals whose flights have been marked by extremities of loss, by persecution, and exile. In other words, the notion of migratory aesthetics could only yield insightful understandings if it is not predicated a priori upon normative identity categories such as "the migrant," and leaves room for the specificity of privileges, means and limitations that mark the subject in transit. Having examined the subjective dimension at stake in migratory aesthetics, I will now turn in a more detailed way to the aesthetic dimension of the notion.

The Return to Lahat in the Slippage between the Referential and the Memorial

The title of Zikken's return travel narrative refers to Zikken's earlier written novel *The Atlas Butterfly*, rather than to the referential destination of the journey, Lahat at South Sumatra. This indicates that the traveller in *Back to the Atlas Butterfly* does not only physically return to Lahat, but also re-visits the imagined version of this site in the novel, written some twenty years earlier. Both the physical and the imagined return, however, prove insufficient to retrieve the I-narrator's colonial childhood in Lahat around the 1920s. As will be argued, in *Back to the Atlas Butterfly*, the childhood site of Lahat is retrieved in the slippage between the physical Lahat, belatedly encountered during the return journey, and the imagined Lahat, encountered through intertextuality in the novel *The Atlas Butterfly*.

At stake in *Back to the Atlas Butterfly* is a complex interplay between representations of the childhood site at different time levels: firstly, the I-narrator's colonial childhood in Lahat around the 1920s; secondly, the colonial childhood of the Dutch girl Gembyr in the Dutch Indies described in *the Atlas Butterfly* written in 1958; and thirdly, an ageing woman's return to Lahat in the independent republic of Indonesia at the end of the 1970s. Through the use of observation, self-reflexivity, flash backs and memory, the I-narrator catalyses these different time levels.

The plot of *The Atlas Butterfly* revolves around the arrival of an extraordinary atlas butterfly in a Dutch colonial settlers' village at Sumatra. The butterfly announces "the arrival of a guest. To some it brings a miracle, to others a drastic change" (165). In fact, not one, but two guests, Miss Borneman and her daughter Oetari, arrive, and consequently the inhabitants' lives and the mutual relations among them change drastically. The protagonist is Gembyr, a dreamy thirteen-year-old Dutch girl, who lives a utopian imaginary world amidst the wonders of the tropical nature of the highlands, together with her Eurasian friend Ferdie. Gembyr is characterised as a Dutch colonial child that is going native (*verindischen*). She actively tries to imitate the physical behaviour of Indonesian women and the mythical story telling of her Indonesian nursemaid Jot. Unaware of the colonial context in which her childhood is staged, Gembyr feels a strong affiliation with Indonesian people. During the stay of the atlas butterfly, Gembyr's naïve world gradually collapses and she is confronted with the colonial world of adults, which she comes to know, in terms of class, ethnicity and gender, as a highly stratified microcosm. At the end of *The Atlas Butterfly*, Gembyr is obliged to say farewell to the surroundings of her childhood, the highland village in South Sumatra. Her father is promoted to a new job and the family moves to a city at Java Island.

Memory Through the Senses

In the opening pages of *Back to the Atlas Butterfly*, Zikken explains that her journey is in fact a pilgrimage to the figures and events staged in *The Atlas Butterfly*:

A pilgrimage to old Jot, who told me stories when I was a child. She sat with crossed legs on the tikar in front of my bed. The mosquito net was between us and we looked at each other through the white haze. Her voice was always soft. I know that I will never find her. I will not encounter her physically. Yet the journey is to Jot and Ibrahim and Moenah, the little monkey Kees, the cat Pepi, the dignified wooden house on poles and the garden of the seven marvels. … Not to do it better this time, but to experience the same again. Damn, it was such a nice part of my life. (7,9) [5]

The traveller's physical return is motivated by a nostalgic desire to retrieve her childhood, even though she is fully aware that a complete retrieval is not possible. In recollecting this childhood, the traveller refers to the characters and events staged in *The Atlas Butterfly*. In fact, she remembers herself as a child inhabiting the same setting as the fictional characters (Jot, Ibrahim, Moenah and so on) of *the Atlas Butterfly*. In this manner, *The Atlas Butterfly* seems to stand in a metonymical relation to the lived childhood of the travelling persona.

The returning traveller tries to recapture this childhood by way of a gradual immersion in the referential surroundings of late 1970s Sumatra:

I pretend that I am just travelling around a little without any reason. In my heart I know better. I do what I can to prepare myself, to become acclimatised a little, by taking the sounds of the language in my mouth and carefully taste them, by slowly remembering more, by slowly awaking. I have experienced this first day as a process of slowly awakening, while I did not even know that I had fallen asleep. (9) [6]

Her gradual approach to the final destination is laid out spatially. Aya Zikken does not take the shortest route to the village of Lahat. She starts her journey in North Sumatra and has planned to arrive at her destination very slowly and with detours. She departs from the region of the Batak in North Sumatra, and via the region of the Minangkabau and the Mentawai Islands she gradually arrives in Lahat in South Sumatra. Meanwhile, a process of familiarization is taking place. At first, the language of Bahasa Indonesia is totally foreign to her, but soon Zikken discovers that she intuitively grasps the language if she allows it to overwhelm her. At first, Zikken uses cutlery to eat rice, but later on she gets familiar again with the local habit of using fingertips. Considering her return as a "shock of recognition," Zikken compares herself in Sumatra with Alice in Wonderland.

In *Strange Encounters*, the black British feminist theorist Sara Ahmed argues that the notion of "home" primarily carries an affective and sensuous meaning. Home does not simply mean belonging or having one's origins somewhere, but rather that one *feels* at home. In terms of Sara Ahmed, home is "the lived experience of locality, its sounds and odours" (89). Moreover, it is not merely the subject who feels at home in a passive locality. The home actively intrudes the senses of that subject. "Locality determines what someone smells, hears, feels and remembers" (89). Departing from this affective dynamic relationship between the subject and locality, Ahmed thinks the notion of home through the metaphor of a second skin.

Ahmed's understanding of home is a fruitful lens to illuminate *The Atlas Butterfly's* imaginations of home as well as the attempt at homecoming in *Back to the Atlas Butterfly*. Gembyr's experience of her Sumatran surroundings in *The Atlas Butterfly* is precisely characterised by sensuousness, affectivity and harmony with the surrounding locality. For instance, Gembyr collects extraordinary natural elements, such as an albino chicken and a colourful piece of charcoal in a place she refers to as "the garden of the seven marvels"(89). The following fragment describes the seventh and largest marvel in the garden, Gembyr playing with green bottles filled with water, and a hammer:

She sat down with crossed legs on the ground in front of the row of bottles and lifted the hammer. All animals were silent. There was no more wind and noises from the kampongs did not reach the garden any longer. ... Gembyr [started] playing. It was a self-created song, a melody that is both sad and happy, like all songs she had ever heard in her country. The glass is singing, the water is singing and Gembyr hums deep in her throat a counter melody. It is a song of the earth where everything is living. If you listen carefully, you could hear the wind blowing over the Boekit Barisan and the rain dropping. You could hear the tjemara trees whispering and the polecat fleeing over the roofs. There are odours in the song, the smell of the kembang sepatoeheg and the koempoel-ampat flowers and the smell of the grey monkey and the cat Pepi who just gave birth, the smell of the klapper oil and fried sateh and freshly baked kwee semprong. The song includes more: the high nightly air is in there, and the singing of Ramonah's wife who had lost her third child, and the embroidered mules worn by Moenah during the slematan, all that is beautiful, or startling or impressive or very sad is in the song, which lasted very, very long (113).[7]

In this fragment, the water, the bottles, the wind, the animals and other surrounding sounds participate in an orchestra with Gembyr by being silent or by singing along with her ("All animals were silent. There was no more wind and noises from the kampongs did not reach the garden any longer ... The glass is singing, the water is singing and Gembyr hums ...). Moreover, this orchestra, consisting of child and environment, creates a "song of the earth where everything is living." The melody is a sensuous song that evokes synaesthetic experiences of sounds, images, odours and feelings of extreme happiness and sorrow. For instance, "the singing of Ramonah's wife who had lost her third child" melts the sound of singing with the visual image of a woman singing and with feelings of mourning. In this manner, the creation of the song itself, as well as "the melody of the earth where everything is living" suggests an affective dynamic relationship between Gembyr and her surroundings. Through the actualisation of the musical metaphor of "harmony" in this fragment, the impression is created that Gembyr's actions are "in tune" with the environment, as if a mutual understanding exists between them. Gembyr's environment seems to be, in terms of Ahmed, a second skin.

Turning to *Back to the Atlas Butterfly*, Ahmed's understanding of home could also yield fruitful insights into the traveller's journey of homecoming. Zikken tries to retrieve Gembyr's affective understanding of home, as it is imagined in *The Atlas Butterfly*. At the moment of return, the traveller is not really interested in political, social or economic aspects of late 1970s Sumatra. Her interest and perceptions are particularly directed towards Sumatra's natural resources. Moreover, by rendering her impressions of nature in late 1970s Sumatra, Zikken does not merely describe and observe from a distance. Rather, establishing an affective connection with these surroundings, the first-person narrator channels these natural surroundings through *all* the senses. Hence, the impressions of nature in late 1970s Sumatra are narrated in affective and sensuous terms. Note in the following fragment the strong emphasis, not only on "to see" but also on phrases such as "odour," "taste," "emotions" and "to feel":

No, the real things have not changed. Odours, tastes, emotions connected to my youth, to feel formerly familiar things, to touch bamboo, the sections of sugar cane, sharp waringin with its roots in the air [standing] at the end of a double drive running to a house-of-then. (7)[8]

More specifically, the fragment displays that Aya Zikken draws upon all the senses in order to filter her childhood surroundings from nature in late 1970s Sumatra. Singular affective experiences, such as the touching of bamboo, seem to function as *pars pro toto*, directing the traveller to Gembyr's home in the past. Gembyr's homeliness in *The Atlas Butterfly* is suggested because of the affective dynamics between the girl and the natural resources of Sumatra surrounding her. At the moment of return to the site, the traveller tries to recapture this imagined homeliness through the senses. In other words, departing from Ahmed's assumption that home is the lived experience of locality, its sounds and odours, then *Back to the Atlas Butterfly* suggests that homecoming, too, is an experience occurring through the senses. Zikken's experience of homecoming exists within a sensuous movement from the referential representation of late 1970s Sumatran nature to the imagined representation of the locality of Gembyr amidst nature and back again. The migratory connection established between these two representations of Indonesia occurs through the traveller's acts of memory through the senses. Through sensing her referential environment, the I-narrator simultaneously imagines and recollects her colonial childhood in the past. Having discussed memory through the senses as one way in which the traveller moves between referential and imaginary representations of Indonesia, I will now move on to analyse the traveller's performance of the past as another act of migration between an imagined past, and a referential present.

Performing the Memory of the "Indonesian" Past

In *The Atlas Butterfly* Gembyr is characterised as a Dutch colonial child that is going native (*verindischen*). She actively tries to imitate the physical behaviour of Indonesian women and the story telling of her Indonesian nanny, called Jot. Unaware of the colonial context in which her childhood is staged, Gembyr feels a strong affiliation with Indonesian people. (Notice for instance the phrase in the fragment of "the garden of the seven marvels:" "like all songs she had ever heard in *her* country" [my emphasis]). In this manner, *The Atlas Butterfly* creates the impression that Gembyr shares with Indonesian women this affective and sensuous connection to the Sumatra surroundings.

From this perspective, Zikken's nostalgic desire to retrieve her affective childhood experience of Sumatra has wider implications. This desire indicates also a yearning for a particularly Indonesian experience, which is untouched by colonial intervention. It is brought home to the reader that the traveller used to be at home at Sumatra in affective ways similar to local Indonesians. At the core of Zikken's homecoming is thus a fundamental paradox. The traveller herself is an imperial national subject who is nostalgic for a precolonial, Indonesian time. Simultaneously, her presence as a child in the East Indies in the context of Dutch colonialism is responsible for the alteration of this Indonesian way of life. The anthropologist Renato Rosaldo refers to this form of recollection as "imperialist nostalgia"(69–70).[9] In *Tourists with Typewriters*, the British travel writing scholars Patrick Holland and Graham Huggan have noted that this mode of memory comes in handy for some contemporary travel writers: "who can deploy it to yearn for the 'simpler' ways of life – often rural, premodern, preindustrial – that they persuade themselves they need. … In general terms, imperial nostalgia describes a pastoral mode of wistful reminiscence that seeks control over, but not responsibility for, a mythicised version of the past" (29). Imperialist nostalgia plays on what Johannes Fabian calls "denial of coevalness" in *Time and the Other* (31). With this term, Fabian points to the curious way in which certain European representations about non-European peoples and places transform geographical distinctions into temporal and ideological ones. As a result, the European centre appears to be the vital present, while constructions of non-European places as areas of barbaric archaisms often prove a ready made rationale for colonisation in the name of modernisation. Even though some post-imperial travel writings, such as *Back to the Atlas Butterfly*, precisely celebrate this "backward" and "premodern" life, they continue drawing on the same ideologically uneven temporal distinction.

On her detour to her final destination, Aya Zikken actively searches for Indonesian life within the premodern nature of late 1970s Sumatra. Earlier I have underscored how *The Atlas Butterfly* imagines Gembyr's home as a harmonious and sensuous experience of her environment. Considering Gembyr's affective understanding of home within nature, Zikken's journey through premodern nature in late 1970s Sumatra could be explained as an attempt to re-enact or *perform* the memory of this imagined childhood. Knowing that a full retrieval of Gembyr's experience is not possible, the traveller reiterates the imagined childhood situation within the belated décor of 1970s Sumatra.

Zikken's performance of childhood memory is suggested particularly in the account of the visit to the Mentawai-islands. In the traveller's descriptions, the islands are portrayed with tropes of wilderness, tribalism and tradition. Her account indicates that the traveller's individual observations and memorisations are never solely her own. After all, the stereotype of the premodern unspoilt island is embedded in a European literary tradition dating back to Daniel Defoe's enormously influential novel *The Life and Adventures of Robinson Crusoe*, written in 1719. In ways similar to the figure of Robinson Crusoe, Zikken arrives to the island by ship. Even though the traveller of *Back to the Atlas Butterfly* is not shipwrecked, her ship is caught by stormy weathers, and navigates for many hours in front of the coast before the crew is able to go ashore. Zikken describes the islands from a distance. In her view it resembles "the unknown tropical island out of the boys' books I used to read" (67).[10] Because of the high waves, the ship cannot approach the island closely and the crew changes over to a smaller motorboat with which they will go to the island. When Zikken faces the arduous task of jumping into the motorboat, she comments:

It is a familiar event. Everyone has probably seen it before in films. But then the dangerous scenes are definitely played by 'doubles' and the heroine is always helped by a strong handsome man who is waiting in the little boat to catch her. Here, the heroes did not have time, not even for a helping hand. ... They were yelling and cursing at me, when I stayed on the stairs of the boat, for minutes long and scared to death, aiming before I jumped. In the end, I managed, bruised and soaked to the skin. (67) [11]

This scene has a slapstick effect. Zikken creates the image of herself as an older woman who trudges and experiences difficulties with arriving to the island. In *Back to the Atlas Butterfly*, the conventional "romantic portrayal of Robinson Crusoe" is replaced by an ironical self-portrayal of a female ageing traveller who is hardly up to the adventure (Ross, "Introduction" 15). Zikken is portrayed as an ageing travelling woman who is at great pains to complete the adventure she started. Before wading through the water, the I-narrator comments: "I understood that I have become quite old since years ago I would have managed easily but now I just found it really uncomfortable" (67).[12]

However, the fact that her female ageing body forms an impediment also underscores the arduousness of the entire undertaking. The difficult arrival contrasts with Zikken's experience of the island. Finally arriving at the beach, Zikken is happy to finally feel solid ground beneath her feet and she stumbles, dehydrated, to the nearest hut to ask for a bit of water. Slowly recovering and with a painful body, Zikken suddenly realises that she has retrieved the harmonious and simple way of life within nature similar to what she remembers. In spite of her encounter with two Western aid workers, Zikken portrays the island as premodern: "on the island, yesterday was not yet that long ago." She realises:

I am in paradise. Immense sand beaches with palm trees, crystal clear water, there are a river mouths where I have to wade through, back and forth shooting little crabs over the sand, coral riffs and no human beings, no houses to be seen. Only the pounding of the waves at the shore, the twittering of birds and the screaming of apes in the distance of the trees in the interior. Klappers are lying on the beach, shells in various colours and shapes. (68)[13]

As this fragment displays, the traveller seems to have "found" an environment similar to her imagined childhood site. In ways similar to Gembyr's experience of locality, Zikken easily merges with the surrounding nature. She does not only record nature with visual images, but also with tactile and aural impressions. The I-narrator indulges in nature, which is portrayed with benignity and harmlessness towards her. Regarding the symbiotic relationship between subject and surroundings described in affective and sensuous terms, it can be argued that Aya Zikken's experience of the Mentawai-islands re-enacts Gembyr's home in the Sumatran highlands. In both instances, the surrounding nature seems to be as a second skin.

Moreover, there is no doubt that *The Atlas Butterfly's* imagining of Gembyr's home feeling implies an idealised and aestheticised portrayal of nature. The idealisation of nature is reinforced because it is told and focalised from the naïve perspective of a child. Although the Mentawai-islands are focalised and narrated from the perspective of an adult woman in *Back to the Atlas Butterfly*, a similar idealisation of nature is suggested. In this instance, the difficult context of arrival to the Mentawai-islands exacerbates, by way of contrast, the harmonious dynamics existing between the traveller and nature.

Indeed, even though stormy weather and an ageing female body initially obstructed the traveller's arrival at the site, these elements rhetorically serve to heighten the sense of home when the traveller does finally arrive at the Mentawai Islands.

Hence, the traveller's imagined childhood site is an idealisation characterised by its close connection to notions of premodernity and "Indonesian-ness." It could be considered, in terms of Renato Rosaldo, as a form of imperialist nostalgia. During the return journey, Aya Zikken tries to perform the memory of home, more specifically Gembyr's sensuous experience within unspoilt nature, as imagined in *the Atlas Butterfly*. She retrieves such an experience within the premodern décor of the Mentawai Islands. Hence, the traveller's homecoming to Sumatra is a performative acting out of the memorised childhood site against the referential background of the Mentawai-islands in the late 1970s. Therefore, not only the act of recalling the colonial childhood through sensing the referential environment, but also the act of performing the past in the belated décor of late 1970s Indonesia is a way in which the I-narrator interconnects observatory representations of present Indonesia with imaginary representations of her colonial childhood. Thus, the traveller's return to the colonial past takes shape by means of a migratory aesthetics, denoting an aesthetics of migration between a referential (but belated) and a memorised (but imaginary) representation of Indonesia. As will be elaborated in the following section, however, the traveller's acts of memory through the senses and her acts of performing the past ultimately do not suffice to bring a full return to the past to completion.

The Schism Between the Referential and the Memorial

At the moment of return to Sumatra, Zikken's "retrieval" of the imagined home cannot always be actualised however. Her performance of the past is obstructed by the bare materiality of both herself and her surroundings. In many ways, the traveller's ageing female body prevents her from establishing an affective connection with Sumatra's natural resources in ways imagined in *The Atlas Butterfly*. At one moment, a local woman gives Zikken a bunch of *bawang*, little onions wrapped in a pisang leave, a traditional present given to guests. Reposing in her hotel room, the traveller leaves the bunch of onions on the rim of the washing table- the *mandibak*- to keep them cool, a custom she learnt during her childhood. Meanwhile, she hears a group of Indonesian people bathing in the river nearby. Linking up one sensuous experience with another, Zikken remarks that the spicy odour of the bunch of onions "triggers her desire to be outside, with the others, in the river." Here again, the experience of the spicy odour triggers memory through the senses. This time, however, the traveller cannot act upon it. She continues: "But I know that this is one of the many things that I will never be able to do over here" (33).[14] It is indeed very hard to imagine that the Dutch ageing tourist would harmoniously merge with her Sumatran surroundings and bathe in the river together with the group of Indonesians. In this instance, the power layers of age, gender, class and ethnicity surrounding Zikken's body in independent Indonesia of the late 1970s impede the harmony with the surroundings she probably would have wished for. Hence, the re-enactment of the imperialist nostalgia for the simple Indonesian experience fails. This performance fails because the traveller's material body does not coincide with the imagined child self of the memory of home.

Not only the traveller's material body, but also the referential surroundings of late 1970s Sumatra impede the performance of the memorised past. This is nowhere more clear than at the end of *Back to the Atlas Butterfly*, when Aya Zikken eventually arrives at her final destination, Lahat. Here the schism between the referential and the memorised childhood home becomes very visible. What the returning traveller sees and remembers are in stark contrast. The locality of home is indeed a very contingent category, which evidently affects the experience of homecoming. Time has invaded Lahat. The passing of time has turned the décor of the imagined childhood home into ruins: "The passing of time has gnawed at beloved houses and even entire gardens have been eaten" (174).[15] Aya Zikken is forced to realise that it is virtually impossible to bridge the yawning gap between the memory and the observation of Lahat, between memorised and referential home. This is to say that the I-narrator realises that the physical return to her childhood cannot be completed, despite her acts of recollecting and performing the past. Eventually Zikken wonders why she actually undertook the physical journey at all. She does not know anymore what to do in the village. What is left to do for her is only to wander amidst the debris of the past. She screens the referential site of Lahat in terms of voids and absences and finds her imagined childhood home in decay. In the end, the stark materiality of Lahat in the late 1970s shatters the traveller's hope that she could ever come home to a fantasy.

Having read Aya Zikken's *Back to the Atlas Butterfly* through the lens of migratory aesthetics, I have touched upon a range of issues that are crucial for a fruitful adoption of the notion. First, it became clear that it is absolutely required to avoid rigid identity categories such as "the migrant" in putting migratory aesthetics to work. In my analysis of *Back to the Atlas Butterfly*, I have pointed to the dangers of clear-cut dichotomies between the Western traveller and the postcolonial migrant, particularly as neither of these terms do justice to the complex (psychological, historical, geographical) realities of an autobiographical I-narrator, such as Aya Zikken. Whereas the latter might be considered a Western traveller regarding her class and ethnic position, her affective affiliations are not wholeheartedly with a Western home, but are divided between Indonesia and the Netherlands. Loyalities to multiple locations and decentredness are conventionally connected to migrant subjectivities. As a Western traveller who is homesick for the Indies, the figure of Aya Zikken compels us to consider specificities of privileges, means and limitations, marking the subjective dimension of migratory aesthetics. Therefore, in the previous analysis, I have emphasised the need to avoid reducing the notion of migratory aesthetics to an identitarian notion of a migrants' aesthetics.

Moreover, I have argued for a notion of migratory aesthetics as aesthetics of migration between various aesthetic representations. In the case of *Back to the Atlas Butterfly*, such a migratory aesthetics has been adopted for the purpose of describing the I-narrator's return to her colonial childhood past. At stake in the return travel narrative is the making of interconnections between representations of Indonesia at different time levels. In my analysis, I have specifically paid attention to the ways in which the traveller's homecoming to her past exists in the negotiation of the slippage between present and past, between referential and imagined representations of Indonesia. In various ways, the I-narrator moves from her late 1970s Indonesian surroundings to the recollected colonial surroundings of her childhood and back again. As I have suggested, through acts of recall through the senses as well as through acts of performance, the I-narrator links up the present observed with the past imagined. The assumption that the return to the colonial past is constituted through migrating between these representations of Indonesia is ultimately supported by the fact that the schism between the referential and the imagined, between the present and the past, eventually cannot be bridged. Having arrived at Lahat, the place where her childhood took place, the traveller is ultimately confronted with the yawning gap existing between her observations of the present and her recollected imaginations of the colonial past. At that moment she realises that a complete return to her personal colonial past is not possible. Then also, however, it becomes clear that migratory aesthetics, the aesthetics of negotiating the slippage between past and present representations of Indonesia, has been the only mode in which the return to the past has been possible at all.

Endnotes

1. All further references will be put after the quotations between parentheses. All translations are mine.

2. Zikken, Aya. *De atlasvlinder*. Amsterdam: Atlas 2002 [first edition 1958].

3. Whereas I do not wish to uphold the dichotomy between fiction and non-fiction, I use the notion of "non-fiction" to underscore that return travel writing is associated with notions such as "referentiality," "mimesis" and "truth value" in the genre's "horizon of expectations" (Jauss, 1555).

4. In fact, Zikken's return travel writing repeats the trajectory of her initial trajectory covered as a six year old with her parents from the Netherlands to the Netherlands Indies. In this essay, the presence of Aya Zikken in de the Dutch Indies will be considered to imply this initial trajectory.

5. "Een bedevaart naar de oude Jot die mij als kind verhalen vertelde. Zij zat dan met gekruiste benen op haar tikar die voor mijn bed lag. Het klamboegaas was tussen ons in en we keken naar elkaar door een wit waas. Haar stem was altijd heel zacht. Ik weet wel dat ik haar nooit meer zal vinden. Ik zal haar niet lijfelijk ontmoeten. Toch is het een reis naar Jot en Ibrahim en Moenah, de aap Keesje, de poes Pepi, het waardige houten huis op palen in de tuin met de zeven wonderen. ... Niet om het dit keer beter te doen maar om hetzelfde nog eens te beleven. Het was zo'n verdomd fijn deel van mijn leven."

6. "Ik doe of ik zomaar wat rondreis. In mijn hart weet ik beter. ... Ik doe wat ik kan door eerst een beetje te acclimatiseren, door de klanken van de taal weer in mijn mond te nemen en voorzichtig te proeven, door me langzaamaan steeds meer te herinneren, langzaamaan wakker te worden. Want deze eerste dag heb ik beleefd als een proces van langzaam wakker worden terwijl ik niet eens wist dat ik was ingeslapen."

7. "Ze ging met gekruiste benen op de grond zitten voor de rij flessen en hief de hamer op. Alle dieren zwegen. Er was geen wind meer en geluiden uit de kampong bereikten de tuin niet langer ... Gembyr [begon] te spelen. Het was een zelfgemaakt lied, een melodie die droevig was en vrolijk tegelijk, zoals alle liederen die ze ooit in haar land had gehoord. Het glas zong, het water zong in de fles zong en Gembyr neuriede diep in haar keel een tegenmelodie. Het was een lied van de aarde waarop alles leefde. Als je goed luisterde hoorde je de wind over de Boekit Barisan waaien en de regen vallen. Je hoorde de tjemarabomen ruisen en de bunzing over het dak vluchten. Er waren ook geuren in dat lied, de geur van de kembang sepatoeheg en van de koempoel-amaptbloemen en de geur van de grijze aap en van de poes Pepi die jongen kreeg, de geur van de klapperolie en gebraden sateh en van pasgebakken kwee semprong. Er was meer in dat lied: de hoge nachtlucht was erin en het zingen van de vrouw van Ramonah die al haar derde kindje had verloren en de geborduurde slofjes die Moenah droeg als er een slematan was, al wat mooi was of opzienbarend of ontzagwekkend of erg verdrietig, was in dat lied, dat heel, heel lang duurde."

8. "Nee, de echte dingen zijn niet veranderd. Geur, smaak, emoties verbonden met je jeugd. Het betasten van vroeger gekende dingen, het aanraken van een bamboestengel, van geledingen van suikerriet, scherp alang-alanggras langs je blote benen, het zien van een brede waringin met luchtwortels aan het eind van een dubbele oprijlaan die loopt naar een huis-nog-van-toen."

9. "Imperialist nostalgia revolves around a paradox: A person kills somebody, and then mourns the victim. In more attenuated form, someone deliberately alters a form of life, and then regrets that things have not remained as they were prior to the intervention. At one more remove, people destroy their environment, and then they worship nature. In any of its versions, imperialist nostalgia uses a pose of "innocent yearning" both to capture people's imaginations and to conceal its complicity with often brutal domination."

10. "Het onbekende tropische eiland uit de jongensboeken die ik vroeger las."

11. "Het is een bekend gebeuren. Iedereen heeft het wel eens op de film gezien. Maar daar werd het gevaarlijke werk beslist altijd door een 'double' gedaan en de heldin werd geholpen door een sterke knappe man die in het bootje gereed stond om haar op te vangen. Hier hadden de helden geen tijd. Zelfs niet voor een helpende hand. ... Aan die vrouw die perse in hun boot wilde hadden ze geen boodschap. Ze schreeuwden me verwensingen toe, toen ik minutenlang doodsbenauwd op het trapje bleef staan mikken voor ik sprong. Nu ja, ik kwam erin. Met blauwe plekken en doorweekt was ik toch al."

12. "Ik begreep ook dat ik eigenlijk al aardig oud was want jaren geleden zou ik voor dit alles mijn hand niet hebben omgedraaid, maar nu vond ik het gewoon bar oncomfortabel."

13. "Ik [ben] in een paradijs. Onafzienbare zandstranden met palmen, glashelder water, af en toe de monding van een riviertje waar ik doorheen moet waden, wat snel heen en weer schietende krabbetjes over het zand, koraalriffen en geen mens te zien, geen huis te bekennen. Alleen het gebeuk van golven op de kust, het gekwetter van vogels en het roepen van apen, ver weg in de bomen in het binnenland. Klappers liggen op het strand, schelpen in allerlei kleur en vorm."

14. "De kruidige geur van de bawang maakt dat ik ernaar verlang om daarbuiten te zijn, bij de anderen, in de rivier. Maar ik weet dat een van de vele dingen is die ik hier nooit zal kunnen doen."

15. " ... de tand des tijds die maar raak knaagt aan geliefde huizen en zelfs hele tuinen zijn weggevreet."

Works Cited

Ahmed, Sara. *Strange Encounters. Embodied Others in Post-Coloniality*. London & New York: Routledge, 2000.

Defoe, Daniel. *Robinson Crusoe*. London: Penguin Books, 1965.

Fabian, Johannes. *Time and the Other. How Anthropology Makes its Object*. New York: Columbia University Press, 2002.

Glage, Liselotte. Ed. *Being/s in Transit. Travelling, Migration, Dislocation*. Amsterdam: Rodopi, 2000.

Holland, Patrick and Graham Huggan. *Tourists with Typewriters: Critical Reflections on Contemporary Travel Writing*. Ann Arbor: University of Michigan Press, 2000.

Jauss, Hans Robert. "Literary History as a Challenge to Literary Theory." In *Toward an Aesthetic of Reception* (1978). Trans. Timothy Bahti. U of Minnesota P 1982. Reproduced in *The Norton Anthology of Theory and Criticism*. Ed. Vincent B. Leitch. New York: W.W. Norton & Company Inc., 2001. 1550–1567.

Kaplan, Caren. *Questions of Travel: Postmodern Discourses of Displacement*. Durham: Duke UP, 1996.

Rosaldo, Renato. *Culture and Truth: The Remaking of Social Analysis*. London: Routledge, 1989.

Zikken, Aya. *De atlasvlinder*. Amsterdam: Atlas, 2002 [first edition 1958].

Zikken, Aya. *Terug naar de atlasvlinder. Een reis door Sumatra*. Den Haag: Leopold, 1981.

III. Displaced Aesthetics/ The Aesthetics of Displacement

Thamyris/Intersecting No. 17 (2007) 111-128

"Exilic Narrativity": The Invisibility of Home in Palestinian Exile

Ihab Saloul

To articulate the past historically does not mean to recognize it "the way it really was" ... It means to seize hold of a memory as it flashes up at a moment of danger.
—Walter Benjamin, "The Storyteller: Reflections on the Works of Nikolai Leskov"

As our storytellers weave their identities across multiple geo-political communities and borders, the memories of the past are recovered in their narratives. This configuration is formed out of past and present images from their everyday cultural practices and lives, and links the palimpsest of Palestinian cultural identity to that of diasporic history. Such narrative-memories, however, do not strive towards articulating the past as self-identical, "the way it really was." Rather, the past within those memories is constantly modified. These transformations occur primarily because such memories are regularly unleashed at "a moment of danger," a moment of being nullified. In this article, I aim at reading this "moment of danger" through the visual narratives of Palestinian exile.

Importantly, the histories of (de)colonization, liberation movements and diasporas around the world have long destabilized essentialist notions of homogenous identity. Nonetheless, observing the contemporary history of world politics, we still witness the stubborn persistence of different cultural-political expressions of the unity at the heart of identity. Take for example the problematic ways such notions appear in today's context of the so-called "War on Terror," especially its main political idiom of "us" verses "them." The concept of diaspora, however, not only complicates such essentialist notions of unified identity, but through its ability to forge new post-essential, post-geographical and post-cultural realignments, it also helps decipher the fault lines of ethnic, religious, class and gender homogeneity on which such notions are based. This critique of homogeneity primarily emerges from the migratory frame of reference that the concept of diaspora signifies, grounded as it is in geo-political (im)mobility beyond the nation-state lexicon and its multi-linguistics. Such a migratory frame of reference compels us to take into consideration both voluntary and involuntary intercultural processes of (im)mobility, particularly when accounting for the construction of cultural identities and the ways in which they are perceived, activated and articulated.

In his article, "By Birth Or By Choice?" (1999), Edward Said puts forward a similar migratory impulse that characterizes the everyday experience of the Palestinian people whose recent history of forced deterritorialization and exile since the 1948 catastrophe (*al-nakba*) made it possible for them to take on "the choice of being Palestinians" for the purposes of political struggle and resistance. This argument that Palestinian identity is a "becoming by choice" rather than a "being" does not contradict Rashid Khalidi's thesis that one can discern a distinct Palestinian identity that goes well back in history through the culture, civil society, and political rhetoric (Khalidi 177–209). Rather, the point, for Said, is that Palestinian identity "by choice" can be interpreted first and foremost as an active political – cultural commitment to be Palestinian. Such an active commitment is not only directed at the establishment of statehood, but to the more significant cause of ending injustice and liberating Palestinians into an identity that is capable of assuming its position, like all other identities and without exception, within contemporary history. This notion of identity as becoming by choice is what I refer to as "active identity."

Through analyzing the visual narratives of *al-nakba* in Palestinian cinematic representations, I attempt to study a Palestinian aesthetic domain that still remains under-illuminated. And as a work on visuality, this article writes and un-writes Palestinian identity in its negotiation of the rigorous boundaries between home and "not-home" or exile. The object of analysis is a Palestinian cinematic narrative, the film: *Al Makhdu'un* (*The Dupes*, Saleh, 1972). With the phrase "Palestinian cinematic narratives," I do not mean a cinema that is exclusively made by Palestinians. Rather, I am referring to a cinema that is to a large extent preoccupied with the question of Palestine. By taking on this film, I will probe its visual characteristics both in relation to Palestinians' loss of the homeland in the past, and to the Palestinian diaspora's struggle to establish narratives of home and identity in the present of exile. First, I examine this film as a mirror of self and other through which narratives of the lost homeland as well as its history of subordination are constructed against the backdrop of exile. Second, I elaborate on these narratives in the film in terms of their mode of storytelling and focalization with special attention to their aesthetic affects – the ways they activate narratives of Palestinian cultural identity in relation to the concepts of home and exile.

"Exilic Narrativity": Exile as a Deadly Other

In contemporary culture, the relationship between cinema and exile is perhaps more complex than ever before. While modern technology of both artistic expressions and warfare enables a multifaceted theatricalisation of destruction and loss, the "cinematic" remains an aesthetic medium that sets out to transform the experience of migrancy and displacement, by turning exile into a force of creativity, and by turning a linguistic and cultural no man's land into a fertile soil. This is possible primarily because cinematic narratives, through their various devices, are capable of substantiating that behind the historical and statistical data of war and displacement, there are human beings and personal stories. In other words, cinematic narratives are capable of pointing out that the exilic experience is no longer something that *just* happens to someone else, in some distant place, but that it is a constitutive, albeit brutal, cultural phenomenon of our reality.

Egyptian director Tawfiq Saleh's *Al Makhdu'un* (*The Dupes*) articulates the question of Palestine, not only through invoking the tragedy of the lost homeland (Palestine), but also by screening the discursive effects of such loss on Palestinian cultural identity within the reality of exile. The film unravels this question by means of the stories of the three main characters – Abu Qais, Assad and Marwan – who represent different generations of Palestinians attempting to escape the poverty of the refugee camps to find employment in Kuwait. As an adaptation of Ghassan Kanafani's masterful novella *Rijal Fi Al Shams* (1962, translated into English as *Men in the Sun*, 1978), the film stages the struggle which these three Palestinians undergo in their arduous attempt to escape their impoverished and hopeless lives and to build a future in exile. The characters' journey to search for a material security in exile is alluring but unreachable as they suffocate in an airless water tank at the Iraq-Kuwait border. Both the story, the journey it tells, and the characters' lives end up on the garbage heap.

Although the film (*Al Makhdu'un*) operates within the boundaries of different cinematic genres, it still uses storytelling as an aesthetic device that produces its narrative. The discussion of genres and the categorical distinction between them is a prominent discussion, not only in cinematic theory, but also in other domains; the most popular among them literary theory. My analysis of this film departs from a narratological, rather than generic point of view. Therefore, in my analysis of *Al Makhdu'un*, I will focus my discussion on the narratological relationship between the multiple ways of storytelling within the film and the stories that are told. Conceptualizing the multiplicity of modes of telling this film deploys is significant in that it allows us to understand Palestinian exile as a compelling experience signifying place disorder and fragmented living. In this experience, the exiled subject is caught between a much desired home and a denied accessibility to it. Such a conceptualization also helps us to theorize a particular narrativity through which the stories of exile can be read.

This is what I call an "exilic narrativity." By "exilic narrativity" I mean a narrative-building through fragmentation in terms of place, self and other. This exilic narrativity, I contend, represents a specific instance of migratory aesthetics and it is noticeable in the fragmented sequence of storytelling of most narratives of exile. Such a fragmentation can be seen, for example, in *Al Makhdu'un*'s narrativization of Palestinian exile through multiple fictional and documentary images and voices. As a result of this fragmentation, a "drifting" mode of storytelling takes shape. This mode of telling introduces "drifting storytelling" as a tool suitable for narrating a mobile event like that of Palestinian exile. Such a "drifting storytelling" can be seen in the film's constant shifting (in images and voices) between the past of the lost homeland and the present time of exile. Time and space, then, are both set adrift to mirror an experiential "truth" beyond the fiction – the documentary divide.

It is precisely through this analytical understanding of exile and its "drifting storytelling" within the interconnected realms of space, time, language, memory and the everyday experience that *Al Makhdu'un*'s narrative moves from the realm of representation into that of theorization of exile. This shift, from representing into theorizing, enables us to understand exilic narrativity within a mode of reading that systematically accounts for its drifting in terms of memory and its temporality against linear time. Through this mode of reading, the film can be seen not as a representative of a migrant experience (Palestinian exile), rather as a "migratory aesthetic" which theorizes such an exilic experience. This reading of the film as a "migratory aesthetic" is an "affect-based" one that opens up a specific discourse which takes into consideration the multiple forms of storytelling an estranging experience like that of exile effectuates in the present. At the heart of this reading lies the transition from colonial other to self as other, which becomes possible in exile.

Al Makhdu'un's intense drama is set in a highly charged and awkward space, shaped by the characters' death in the blistering desert. Thus, the film represents the tormented realm of a Palestinian diasporic consciousness that has been living amid the plight of exile for more than half a century. The epic theme, and the cataclysmic ambiance extremely condensed into this film of 107 minutes, makes it a distinctive Palestinian exilic narrative. Moreover, it is one told through multiple voices and perspectives. Such multiplicity of telling not only allows the three stories told within the film to transmit historical details and personal memories, but also to revive Palestinian cultural memory both by conveying the ordeal of loss and exile and by offering empathy to the exiled Palestinians. The stories of the film range from Abu Qais's memories of the homeland he left behind and of his one month old daughter (Hosna) who died due to emaciation after the family was forced out of its village, to the story of the teenage boy, Marwan, who sets off on a hazardous journey into the unknown in order to support his impoverished family. As such, the melodramatic aspects of the stories within the film give voice to the voiceless exiled Palestinians both individually and collectively. Individually, because these aspects construct a plausible space wherein each one of these exiled characters could exist (live and die) as individuals. And collectively, by means of the thematic nexus of the stories and their storytellers as particular narratives of Palestinian exile told by exiled Palestinian subjects.

At the beginning of *Al Makhdu'un*, the camera descends from the sky and the midday blazing sun down to an empty desert. This image is accompanied by sentimental

Arabic flute music as the names of the film crew roll on the screen. While on the lower part of the screen we see what looks like human skeletal remains of someone who obviously died in this desert, on the upper side of the screen, the camera zooms in on a figure that is coming from a distance. As the camera moves to receive him, the image of the skeletal remains slowly disappears and is replaced by the image of a seemingly exhausted man with a white scarf covering his head and carrying a small sack on his shoulder. Just before we are able to take a closer look at the man's face and make sense of him, the following lines pop up on the screen:

> *And my father once said:*
> *A man without a homeland*
> *Will have no grave in the earth*
> *And he forbade me to leave [travel].*

Like many stories, the story of *Al Makhdu'un* has a storyteller who announces it. This storyteller, one of the narrator's several possible manifestations, is materialized through these lines which announce the story of the film. The conjunction "And" with which the opening sentence of these lines begins is more than a paratactic sign, a common style in Arabic language. It is also a sign that carries with it a temporal signification related to the linguistic dynamic of the sentence itself; that is its relationship with the sentence that precedes it and that which follows. What precedes this sentence, however, is absent and invisible.

From a narratological point of view, the invisibility of what precedes the opening sentence is a significant element that reflects on the larger story, and even on the film itself. Such invisibility turns into a demarcation which situates the film as a narrative beginning at a specific temporal point that does not coincide with the beginning of the whole story. In other words, the beginning of the story is missing – it is drifting somewhere before the dangling "And," and at the same time, the present of the story we will see in the film immediately starts after reading the words "my father once said." It is the story of exiled men "without a homeland," who will have "no grave in the earth." In spite of their father's warning not to "leave" the homeland, they still take on the journey, and now we will see the story of how they perish in exile; a foretold destiny of doom precipitated by their ignoring of the father's vision.[1]

In one sense, by exposing its beginning through such a vision of exile as a deadly place, the film focalizes the homeland – the other side of the binary opposition – in a way that allows it to stand as a privileged place. Yet, in another sense, by doing so the film also complicates any straightforward relationship between place and time. The fact that the beginning of the film foregrounds the father's gloomy vision of exile allows the construction of exile as an empty place from a temporality of before that predicts an after. The construction of exile as a void gives it its material presence as a specific place, yet such a construction does not entirely compose the temporality of the narrative of this place. In the film, the temporal composition of exile (and its narrative) is not at all foregrounded through the father's vision. Instead, the film radically questions the meaning of this vision. That is, the film questions what is envisioned (exile) discursively both in terms of how successful the travelling of the characters is, and how endurable the environment of exile.

In order to answer these questions, the film itself is compelled to take on the journey. It has to accompany the characters in their journey, and even become a traveller precisely like them. This is the mirroring of self and other I mentioned before. The film's travelling can be seen in the sequence of images, following the opening statement, through which the camera begins to track sideways to bring into view an oasis wherein the exhausted figure travelling (Abu Qais) could rest. The moment Abu Qais enters this oasis, he takes the white scarf off his head, and throws himself into the shade of a tree with his face on the ground. The shade of the tree, however, does not relieve Abu Qais from his trip, rather it opens another gate through which he (as well as the film) continue travelling; this time backward into the past.

While Abu Qais is facing the ground, he hears the sound of his heart beat. Immediately after, Abu Qais begins to recollect a similar scene from the past in which he is lying down in the shade of the trees of his field in the homeland, and chatting to his friend. When Abu Qais asks his friend about the sound, his friend answers: "it is the sound of your heart. You can hear it when you lay your chest close to the ground." Abu Qais shrugs off his friend's answer, and challenges him with another question, by asking: "And the smell, then?" When his friend does not provide an answer, Abu Qais grabs some ground in his hand and begins to sniff it and says:

Every time I sniff the ground, I seem to smell the scent of my wife's hair after a cold bath. The same smell. The same freshness. The same moisture. This moisture comes from yesterday's rain. But yesterday it did not rain. It could not have rained. Have you forgotten where you are?

As this statement suggests, Abu Qais's identification with the homeland not only takes place through romanticizing it in his projection of it onto the figure of a woman, but also through a (human) materialization of this homeland. Such materialization primarily emerges through the articulation of the romanticized figure of the homeland by means of the senses (hearing, smell and touch). As a result, the homeland encompasses the substance of Abu Qais's life through which his identification with it is formed as an unspoken existential bond.

Moreover, it is precisely through these senses that Abu Qais is brought back from his recollections into the present. It is only when he smells the ground that Abu Qais realizes that the "moisture comes from yesterday's rain" and that "it could not have rained [yesterday]," and therefore he must be in the wrong place (exile). The image on the screen corresponds to Abu Qais's realization in that, immediately after these words, we see him back in the oasis; this time not in the shade of the tree, but in the blazing sun of exile. This event, Abu Qais's transfer from past into present and from the shade of the homeland's trees into the blazing sun of exile, becomes symbolic of his overall transition from being a Palestinian peasant "with" a homeland into a homeless exiled "without." Such symbolism not only characterizes the film as a Palestinian exilic narrative, but it also focalizes Abu Qais as an exilic subject who embodies a memory that travels between multiple places (homeland and exile) and multiple times (past and present). The voice that tells this is also split. At the end of the monologue Abu Qais changes from first-person to second-person discourse. He can no longer "be" a unified person when the realization of exile hits him.

By Way of Travel: Memory Contexts

Abu Qais's realization that he is in the wrong place, in exile rather than in the homeland, leads him through a long recollection from the past through which his journey of dispersion is revealed. In the oasis, having momentarily regained consciousness, and still holding the ground in his hands thinking that the moisture must be from rain, Abu Qais's eyes begin cruising around until they finally settle down on a river. Abu Qais suddenly recognizes this river as the *Shatt Al-Arab* waterway in Iraq. He learned this one day when he was sneaking from the window watching his son (Qais) in the class of Ustaz Salim, the teacher from Jaffa who taught in the village's school. The moment Abu Qais identifies the river as the *Shatt Al-Arab*, Ustaz Salim's voice takes over as we see him teaching the village's kids about the river and asking them to repeat after him: "When the two great rivers, Tigris and Euphrates, meet, they form one river called the *Shatt Al-Arab*, which extends from just above Basra ..."

The story of Ustaz Salim not only serves as a plausible explanation of Abu Qais's sudden recognition of the name of the river, but it also allows the viewer a glimpse of the lives of the Palestinians before *al-nakba* both as simple peasants and as a people who were apparently unaware of the tensions building up to the catastrophe. This becomes obvious in the following scene where the men of the village, including Abu Qais and Ustaz Salim, are sitting in the headman's reception-room, smoking the water-pipe and chatting. When one of the men asks Ustaz Salim if he is going to lead them in the prayers on Friday, Ustaz Salim immediately answers: "No, I am a teacher, not an *Imam* (a religious cleric). I cannot lead the prayers." When the headman asks him to clarify his answer, Ustaz Salim admits that he "does not know how to perform the prayers." The men of the village, puzzled and shocked by Ustaz Salim's answer, turn their eyes to the headman, who bursts out: "What do you know, then?" As Ustaz Salim is rising to leave the room, he says: "Many things. I am a good shot, for example. When they attack you, wake me. I, who knows how to shoot. I can be of some use to you then." Again, as in the opening lines, a voice from the past proleptically evokes the future.

In the following scene, the military attack on the village begins, and thus confirms this prolepsis. We see Ustaz Salim defending the village – together with another man of the village who later appears in the film as Abu Al Khaizaran; the driver who smuggles the three main characters in the film through the desert. As we see Ustaz Salim is shot and dies, as Abu Al Khaizaran is running to help him, Abu Qais's voice comes in to comment on his death. Without seeing his face, we hear Abu Qais saying:

God rest your soul, Ustaz Salim. And may he bestow upon you his mercy.

Undoubtedly, you must have been among God's favorites, when he made you give up the ghost, Ustaz Salim, before the Zionists occupy the land. God must have loved you – may his mercy be upon you. You stayed over there, Ustaz Salim. Is there any divine bounty more glorious?

As this statement suggests, for Abu Qais, the death of Ustaz Salim appears as a fortunate happening; even as a glorious "divine bounty." Ustaz Salim is fortunate because his death took place "before the Zionists" occupied the land, and so he was saved from living under the occupation and enduring what Abu Qais, like all other Palestinians who survived *al-nakba*, is experiencing in the present.

This statement is followed by a sequence of images, a mix of archival footage of *al-nakba* combined with a single fictive image, exposing what Abu Qais's family and the rest of Palestinians are going through in the aftermath of the catastrophe and what Ustaz Salim has been spared, thanks to his death "you stayed over there." While in the archival footage, we see images of the Palestinians' forced dispersion of their villages and towns, their tents, their settling in the refugee camps, their hunger, and their dependence on the United Nation's aid – without which they would starve – in the fictive image, we see Abu Qais's wife and son as members of that group of Palestinians.

The use of archival footage of *al-nakba* in the film not only gives a sense of pastness to Abu Qais's story, but it also situates the film rigorously beyond the divide between fiction and documentary. Moreover, it foregrounds the film's own discursivity as a "traveller." As a "traveller," the film, like its character (Abu Qais) who is recollecting his memories of the past, also has a memory. The film's memory is composed of past images – preserved in archives – and is recalled by the insertion of this old filmic material. Conveying its memory in and through archives, the film seems to emphasize a particular conception of memory; one whose functionality is foregrounded in terms of archives as witness. Within such a conception, memory functions in different ways; both as a resort and as a harvest (consequence) in the interminable phases of flux. Memory, in this sense, appears as no more stationary in the limited space of filmic archives than it is in the labyrinths of our brains.

This is consistent with psychological theories of memory. In his book, *Searching for Memory: The Brain, the Mind and the Past*, Daniel Schacter argues that within the human brain, memory can function at different levels and that multiple interactive processes are required in order to experience memory. To enshrine and recall this experience, in addition, is inextricably associated with the contexts, or what Schacter calls "cues for memory," in which memories are recalled and to the contexts in which those memories were previously formed. In other words, memory not only appears as a specific "imprint" of the past to which we constantly resort when needed, but it can also be seen as a consequence that is temporally constituted in the present and that is performed both in response and through the processing and incorporation of "cues of memory" (or its contexts). It is precisely through such a cognitive-functional conception of memory as archival witnessing that the psychoanalytic notions of the (un)trustworthiness and (un)reliability of memory open up the possibility to see memory as a useful and continuously accessible process of disruption, rather than as an already distorting faculty. This is possible because these notions of memory (untrustworthiness and unreliability) are ultimately cognitive-functional notions themselves that are primarily related to the subject's emotions and desires (Schacter 70–80).

Seen from this perspective, memory in the archival footage becomes a good reader that fills the temporal gap between past and present by marking the absences of the past's events. The film's use of archives, then, seems to suggest that the temporal nature of memory changes over time so that its experience shifts accordingly from the mnemonic to the contextual wherein memory is generated, reduced and conflated. Thus, rather than being a faculty which misappropriates (misrepresents) the past, memory represented in and through archives becomes a cultural – historical process that regularly interrupts (and at the same time is interrupted) in order to compose the temporality of the present exile. In this sense, the archival footage not only suspends the story told by the film (the deadly journey of exile), but it also interrupts the viewer's evanescent memory of the story within the film (Abu Qais's story). This interruption is facilitated by the archives of *al-nakba* which mystify as well as synthesize historical information so that the contexts within which the exilic subject's memory is formed, enshrined and recalled can be unveiled. Moreover, this interruption of the viewer's memory does not only occur on the level of the narrative and its focalizing subject, but it also takes place in the film on formal levels such as the movement of the camera, angles and framings. Such an interruption is evident in the shifting from Abu Qais's story to the archival footage.

Consequently, the viewer's activity of meaning production shifts from the fictional images of the film (Abu Qais's story) to the reality referenced as it happened outside but determining the narrative of the film (the archives of *al-nakba*). This shift between inside and outside the narrative introduces yet another splitting of causality. The events "truthfully" presented in the memory images of the archives are both disconnected from the fictional story of Abu Qais by generic incompatibility, and presented as the cause of the character's present state. Thus, the archives as witness, which interrupts the fictionality of the story told by the film becomes a bearer of its referentiality; a reference itself that validates such fictionality by exposing both its narratological and its historical contextual latency. This effect is emphasized by the fact that this "witness" (archival footage) itself is interrupted by being juxtaposed to the single fictive image of Abu Qais's family; an image that functions as a thematic and temporal reminder of the story within the film.

Through this reminder, Abu Qais's family not only becomes an allegorical figure standing for exiled Palestinians, but also the memory of this family is articulated in terms of a particular history that exists in the context of *al-nakba* and its archives. Travelling between past and present and between fictional and archival images, the film not only processes memory in terms of its contexts, but also transmits the narrative of Palestinian exile in terms of its origins (*al-nakba*). It is precisely though the film's travelling between its own historical memory (archives) and that personal one of its subject (Abu Qais) that the contexts of memory become signs that not only frame the subject's memory in relation to the lost place, but at the same time trigger his storytelling of exile as a split of subjectivity.

Exile: By Way of Telling

In the film, the idea that exile is a place wherein subjectivity is split does not appear only in terms of the characters material travelling into exile where we see them aimlessly wandering in the desert, but also in terms of the shifting from individual into collective voices. This can be seen in the film in the way in which the individual narrative of Abu Qais is opened up and probed to its limits so that the other characters' stories (Assad and Marwan) within the film can be introduced as a further explanation of the story of loss and exile told by the film.

In order to do so, the film is compelled to travel back from its own realm of memory (historical archives) into the memory of its speaking subject. Later in the film, we see Abu Qais wandering between the olive and the cactus trees of the homeland where he further elaborates on the death of Ustaz Salim:

God rest your soul, Ustaz Salim. You stayed over there. And thereby, you saved yourself all that misery, and have spared your white hair that shame. If you had lived, Ustaz Salim, and if you were drowned in poverty, as I am, would you have done what I did?

In this address to the dead man from the past, Abu Qais reiterates that Ustaz Salim's death was a fortunate happening, primarily because his death saved him the misery of becoming a refugee suffering the shame of losing the homeland. At the same time, Abu Qais questions whether the impoverished lives of Palestinian refugees, their poverty and their dispersion would have forced Ustaz Salim to act similarly to what Abu Qais is doing now, leaving the homeland. Through this question, Abu Qais questions his own decision. The moment he asks this question, we see him walking in the blazing sun of the desert where his mind drifts forward and backward once again as he begins narrating, in detail, the misery and the humiliation Palestinians experience since they lost their homeland.

In a relatively long scene, Abu Qais not only recalls how Saad – his neighbour in the refugee camp who returns from Kuwait with a fortune – convinced him to undertake the journey, but he also reads the Palestinian plight in terms of its larger politics, Arab politics in particular. While Saad is talking to the men and women of the camp about his successful adventures in Kuwait, he turns to Abu Qais and asks him "why don't you go there, Abu Qais?" Confronted by this question, Abu Qais does not give an answer and instead a series of other questions echo in his head:

Why don't you go there? What are you waiting for? Are you still unaware that you lost your trees, your house, your youth and your whole country? What did you expect? Talks ... Talks arguing nonsense. They have sold you and bought you again ... you have the Zionists before you and the traitors behind. You are in between [the hammer and the nail]. Haven't you got it yet that all this is useless? They want you to remain a beggar with a drooping head. They want to make sure that you never raise your voice. That you quarrel instead of striving together and claim your rights. It is a fact. Whoever survived the bullets of the Zionists, dies in humiliation. And whoever survives both is a victim of the traitors and plotters. Wouldn't it have been better you had died like Ustaz Salim ... Why don't you move on ... What are you waiting for? That fortune should fall on you from the roof? But do you have a roof yet? No roof, no house. They brought you and told you live here and you stayed. A year later, they said that room is too big for you. Let us have half of it. And you made a partition with blankets and jute. What are you waiting for? Your baby, who is going to raise him? Who is going to feed him? Why don't you go and find work to recover what you have lost?

Set in the form of the split subjectivity infiltrated by "you" and "they," this passage not only points out the miserable circumstances which the Palestinians experience in the aftermath of the loss of the homeland. It also criticizes the passivity of Arab regimes and Arab leaders toward the Palestinians. Such a criticism is clear through the portrayal of the Arab governments as "traitors" who betrayed the Palestinians, "they have sold you and bought you again." This criticism is supported visually again by means of archival images that proclaim the "truth" of the fiction. While Abu Qais is uttering these words, archival images of Arab leaders such as King Hussain of Jordan and King Faisal of Saudi Arabia are shown. We see images of them gathering and discussing the Palestinian plight in the Arab league and other organizations. These images are instantly juxtaposed to images of Palestinian suffering and exile. It is in this sense that Arab leaders' discussions become, like Saad's fictional exhortations, "Talks ... Talks arguing nonsense," something that does not relieve the Palestinians.[2]

Immediately after this scene, we see Abu Qais and his wife talking to Saad who tells them that "just beyond the Shatt lie all the things that are denied you." When Abu Qais asks his wife what she thinks, she answers: "Whatever you say," and nods in a supportive manner. It is only then that we see Abu Qais looking up at the blazing sun as he leaves the oasis. Later on, we see him negotiating the cost of the trip with the smuggler who warns him that the journey is not easy, and he asks for fifteen dinars as a price. When Abu Qais proposes to pay him ten dinars instead, the smuggler turns to Abu Qais and says, "we don't force you to do it [the journey]." At this point, and in the same scene of the smuggler, the film interrupts the story of Abu Qais as we see the smuggler asking for a similar charge (fifteen dinars) from someone else, the young man Assad, who also, like Abu Qais, wants to be smuggled into Kuwait.

As he is bargaining with the smuggler, Assad finally agrees to give him the fifteen dinars he is charging, on the condition that the smuggler will only get the money after the end of the journey. The smuggler refuses, and tells Assad what he said to Abu Qais before, namely that he did not force him to take the trip and that if Assad does not accept his conditions, he should leave him alone, "Get out, and don't stop before you are on the main road." The moment Assad hears these words "the main road," his mind drifts back into the past as we see him wandering on the road and lost in the desert.

This way, his reasons for taking this journey are exposed. We see Assad, like Abu Qais, as a Palestinian who is victimized and whose situation forces him to leave his home. Moreover, we see him as a young man whose life cannot become any worse than it already is. He is involved with the resistance movement and therefore persecuted by the authorities. In order to solve his problems, Assad decides to escape the land and to make a new start in Kuwait. Unlike Abu Qais who clings to the mirage of exile, yet hesitates before taking on the journey and doubts that the reality of exile will live up to its expectations, Assad is completely convinced that leaving the homeland is the best solution for his problems.

When Assad turns to his uncle to borrow the money he needs for the trip, his uncle warns him in the beginning that he should not be too optimistic about his trip to Kuwait because many people have gone before him and "came back empty-handed." Soon after, however, Assad's uncle changes his mind and decides to give him the money:

[uncle says:] All the same, I will give you the fifteen dinars. But remember, these are my last. [Assad says:] Why give it to me since you are sure I'll never be able to refund it? [uncle:] Do you know why? [Assad:] Why? [uncle:] You don't know why? Because I want you to start even in hell. So that you can marry my daughter.

The moment Assad hears his uncles' motivation for lending him the money, he realizes that his uncle wants to buy him for his daughter "just as one buys a bag of manure for one's field." When Assad – agitated by his uncle's proposition – complains to his friend about his uncle and asks him whether he should marry his cousin "just because her father read *al-fatiha* – the first Sura of the Quran, customarily recited at the conclusion of an agreement – when we were born the same day," his friend answers:

No doubt he believes it's destiny… Why should you sell yourself? Why do you grab those fifteen dinars in such a way? Stay here, Assad. It's your place. Don't run away … Do you think of running away at every difficult step? … Stay with us. Why should you sell yourself?

Despite his friend's appeal to him to stay in the homeland and face the problems rather than run away from them, Assad is determined to take on the journey – even if it meant that he has to "sell" himself – as we see him taking the money from his uncle.

After this scene Assad cuts a deal with Abul-Abed, another Palestinian from the camp, who takes the money from him in advance, swears by his honour not to betray him, and later on smuggles him across the Jordan-Iraq border and abandons him on the way in the desert.

At this point, the film returns to the present where it left off, as we are brought back to the scene where Assad was bargaining with the smuggler in Iraq. This return is not a ploy to continue with Assad, but to introduce the story of the teenager, Marwan, who also bargains with the same smuggler and even threatens him – in case the smuggler does not accept the five dinars he is offering – that he will report him to the police. The smuggler, then, becomes angry and slaps Marwan on the face and kicks him out of the shop. As Marwan runs away crying, he meets Abu Al Khaizaran, who appeared earlier in the film fighting with Ustaz Salim. Abu Al Khaizaran tells him that he is also a Palestinian and that he agrees to smuggle him to Kuwait for five dinars on the condition that Marwan should not tell anyone that he charged him five dinars only, and also to help him find other people who want to go to Kuwait. When Marwan tells Abu Al Khaizaran that he knows someone who is staying with him at the hotel (Assad), Abu Al Khaizaran says that he also knows someone who used to be his neighbour in the village where he lived in Palestine (Abu Qais).

Only at this point do the different story lines come together. Soon after, the four of them meet and discuss the details of the trip. Abu Al Khaizaran tells them that he has to go to Kuwait since he works there, and that he drives a truck in which he can smuggle them in. He also tells them that the truck belongs to a rich Kuwaiti man and that is why it does not get checked at the border. All they have to do is to hide inside the empty water-tank "for six or seven minutes" on the Iraqi border and a similar amount of time on the Kuwaiti one. When Abu Qais shows his doubts about the safety of the journey, "This is a dangerous business. Maybe we die," Abu Al Khaizaran smiles to him and asks him not to worry since "I am the one who drives ... the leader." When the men are finally convinced, cut the deal with Abu Al Khaizaran and agree to depart the next day, Abu Al Kaizaran turns to Marwan and asks him if he knows anyone in Kuwait. When Marwan says that his brother works there, Abu Qais asks why Marwan, then, has to go and work in Kuwait instead of going to school? It is only then that the film travels into the past once again as Marwan tells his story. In the following scenes, we see how Marwan's brother stops sending money to his family after he gets married and how he sends letters to Marwan telling him that it is his turn to leave school and take responsibility, "dive in the pan." We also see how Marwan's father, struggling to feed his wife and five children, divorces his wife for no reason and runs off to marry Shafiqa, the rich handicapped women who lost her leg during *al-nakba* – and leaves his kids, forcing Marwan to take on the responsibility of supporting the family.

These stories within the film, ranging from Abu Qais to Assad to Marwan, not only reflect a wide scope of suffering through which Palestinians experience exile, but at the same time these stories portray the multiplicity of the narratives of the loss of the homeland during *al-nakba*. Such multiplicity is emblematized in the three stories both through the subjects' ages and order of appearance from old to young as a way for composing the larger story told by the film. Each of the three stories is exposed through analepses that are connected ultimately, albeit differently, to the same event, the loss of the homeland. All this takes place while the three characters are encircled within the present of exile. As a result, this exilic present becomes an integral part of the storytelling itself. In this sense, exile, like memory, cannot be understood and analyzed without its contexts: that is, both the contexts in which exile is experienced in the present and the contexts from which it previously originated. It is precisely through such entanglement between exile and the multiple and fragmented stories within the film that the story it has told becomes an instantiation of exilic narrativity.

Death By Heat: Exilic Time

Immediately after the exposition of the characters' stories is completed, we return to their actual journey in the desert, the closing part of *Al Makhdu'un*. The journey towards Kuwait is riveting and emotional. This journey is presented through different short scenes all of which lack synchrony except for the first one (the beginning of the journey). The first scene of the journey – where we see Marwan and Abu Qais sitting on the roof of the truck and Assad sitting next to Abu Al Khaizaran chatting – primarily serves to expose yet another story within the film, that of Abu Al Khaizaran.

In this scene, Abu Al Khaizaran is talking to Assad and mockingly comparing the one hundred and fifty kilometre journey to "the path which God promised his creatures they must cross before being directed either to paradise or to hell." Assad replies that they entrusted him (Abu Al Khaizaran) with leadership and it is up to him to take them to heaven or hell. When Assad asks Abu Al Khaizaran whether he has ever been married, Abu Al Khaizaran quickly answers with a question: "why do you ask?" and immediately begins telling his story. Through Abu Al Khaizran's story, not only are we reminded of Ustaz Salim's death in the story of Abu Qais where Abu Al Khaizran was present, but also we see a "latent" continuation of that story from the perspective of Abu Al Khaizaran. Shortly after the death of Usatz Salim, Abu Al Khaizran is injured while defending his homeland and stripped of his manhood. When one of the doctors, while he is on the operating table screaming that he "does not want to," tells him that losing one's manhood is better than dying, Abu Al Khaizaran screams "No. It's better to be dead." It is through Abu Al Khaizaran's preference of death over life "without manhood" that his view resembles that of Abu Qais who also sees the death of Ustaz Salim as a fortunate happening which prevented him from living on "without homeland." This scene connects both characters' perspectives on loss through which the first's preference of death over life "without manhood" becomes a synecdoche for the latter's preference of death over life "without homeland."[3]

Also, through this scene Abu Al Khaizaran is focalized, like Abu Qais, as a victimized Palestinian who deserves sympathy. However, the viewer's sympathy with Abu Al Khaizran – unlike that with Abu Qais, Assad and Marwan – remains only partial. This is so because in the following scenes of the journey, not only do we see him as a man who sacrificed his manhood for the homeland, but through his actions we see him also as a man who lost the "morals of manhood." Throughout the journey, he keeps describing himself as someone whose goal in life is to collect money: "All I want is money, and when I have money I want more and more." Moreover, in general he acts like a man without morals. In one of the scenes, while the men are resting after they crossed the Iraqi border, and after Abu Qais, Assad and Marwan barely survived their trip in the extremely hot and airless water tank, Abu Al Khaizaran grabs the water-skin attached to the truck and starts pouring it into his mouth and then with the rest of the contents starts washing his head and his whole body without offering any to the dying men. It is because of such actions that the viewer withdraws sympathy from Abu Al Khaizaran's character. Such lack of sympathy with this figure, I contend, functions to complete the story told by the film through which his character (and story) becomes an allegory of those Palestinians who rather than staying in the homeland, prefer to leave in search of material security in exile. Such allegorization is facilitated by the temporal structure of the scenes that compose the context (the journey in the desert) within which Abu Al Khaizaran's story is revealed.

As I suggested above, the remaining scenes of the journey lack synchrony. To paraphrase Mieke Bal, when a scene lacks synchrony, ellipsis often becomes prominent (Bal 105–07). This is what happens in *Al Makhdu'un*, time is compressed. Unlike the first part of the film, where all the characters are given enough space to return to their past in the homeland, in the final part (the journey) ellipsis occurs in the characters' present signifying that there is no time to go back to the past. During the journey, instead of the characters going into the past by means of memory acts, the past itself erupts in the present as we hear the voices in the characters' minds and see images of their past pop up on the screen. This scarcity of time not only interrupts the progression of Abu Al Khazaran's story – we only see how he lost his manhood, but what we don't know is how he travelled into exile like the other three characters – but also the journey itself is presented in an accelerated manner as if the film itself seems to be running towards its ending.

Such a scarcity of time becomes most visible in the film's ending. Abu Qais, Assad and Marwan, tired and barely able to stand, go into the lorry's tank for the second (and final) time doubting that they would come out of it alive as Marwan declares: "We all lost it." At this point, Abu Al Khaizaran tells them to set their watches and that this time it would not take him more than "seven minutes." While Abu Al Khaizaran is rushing into the empty border checkpoint, he is suddenly held up by the officials on the border. As he repeatedly shouts "I am in a hurry," the officials keep ridiculing him by asking him about his secret mistress in Iraq (the dancer girl Kawkab).

In the officials' room, while Abu Al Khaizaran consults his watch indicating that he has already lost four minutes, the camera keeps shifting between the inside of the room where he is being delayed and the outside where the truck with the men is standing. We hear the three men inside the tank knocking, yet the sound of their knocking never reaches anyone, no more than it has for the past fifty-eight years since *al-nakba*. Finally, as Abu Al Khaizaran finishes his papers, after he promises to introduce the officials to his imaginary mistress, he consults his watch again to ascertain that he is indeed late and that it took him more than seven minutes (fifteen minutes). Driving out of sight from the border, with the men inside the tank already stopped knocking, Abu Al Khaizaran stops the truck after awhile, and goes to check on the men. When he opens the burning hot tank, he finds the three of them dead.

The scarcity of time in this scene is manifested through the use of watches. These watches give access to exilic time, by indicating that time in exile is both moving rapidly (from four to fifteen minutes) and at the same time the suffering is endless. They also suggest that there is time in exile, yet it is never enough. Through their death, such vision of exilic time becomes exemplary of the characters' short lives in exile. For Abu Qais, Assad and Marwan, life can possibly begin in exile, but it is a life that is not to be lived and not to be continued. This is simply so because it is a life that is planted in an airless environment under the blazing sun. This sun brands the three of them with pain as it acts as a "decoy" implanted in time: one that can make a day of their lives seem like a year, yet also one which shortens the time they have to live.

In *Al Makhdu'un*, after Abu Al Khaizaran finds out that Abu Qais, Assad and Marwan died, he continues the journey alone in total silence. Without uttering a word, he stops on the way to Kuwait, carries the three bodies off the truck and abandons them on the garbage heap. On the screen, while we see Abu Al Khaizaran walking back to his truck and driving away, the camera slowly brings into view the three bodies laying next to each other. This image is accompanied by the same sentimental music with which the film began. More importantly, the moment the camera brings into view the three bodies on the garbage heap, it begins scanning them and moving forward until it reaches Abu Qais's hand which is in the shape of someone who is holding his fingers on the trigger; symbolizing resistance. It is only then that the same lines with which the film started pop up on the screen once again:

> *And my father once said:*
> *A man without a homeland*
> *Will have no grave in the earth*
> *And he forbade me to leave [travel].*

Ending the film with these lines brings back the father's vision of exile. Between the first and the second quotation of the lines, the film has travelled in order to discover their meaning. Moreover, through the images of the characters' dead bodies as well as Abu Qais's fingers as if on the trigger, the film seems to suggest that it has understood what the father's vision "have no grave in the earth" means and therefore it subliminally evokes in the image of the trigger, the choice of staying in the homeland to work in the resistance instead of "existing" in the desert of exile.

Yet, in another sense, the repetition of the beginning in the ending, particularly through the use of the same sentimental music and the father's vision, can also be read in narratological terms as a device that characterizes "drifting storytelling" in the film. The death of Abu Qais, Assad, and Marwan signifies that the stories embedded within the film also lost their storytellers. This loss, however, is compensated by the fact that the film itself turns into a "travelling storyteller." This compensatory shift is achieved primarily through the silence of Abu Al Khaizaran as well as the camera's movement forward, which replaces the movement of the ones who died. In this sense, circularity and movement stand for endless repetition and retrovision. In other words, as much as the closing images in the film represent the ending of the story it has told, these images could possibly also be just the beginning of another story of the lost homeland.

The story of this lost homeland is constructed by multiple storytelling. Perhaps to be a Palestinian in exile, then, is the condition of constantly travelling to the outside with that which is inside oneself. The place of the lost homeland is exchanged with the stories of its loss and the aptness of "drifting storytelling." These exilic stories, represented within and told by *Al Makhdu'un*, exist, like their storytellers, on an exilic juncture between the factual and the fictional, between the archives and the acted scenes, and between documentary and fictional cinema. It is through this dialectical "in-between" viewing position that the three exiled men in the film together with the viewer are perpetually left with the visibility of the lost home and at the same time, most significantly, with the invisibility of exile as a new home.

The invisibility of exile as a new home is a focus of most contemporary Palestinian narratives of *al-nakba*. The details of the relationship between exile and the Palestinian subject vary from narrative to narrative, but how these details alternate and effect Palestinian cultural identity in the present remains a critical question in those narratives. In my analysis of *Al-Makhdu'un*, I have discussed how reading exilic narrativity, as an instance of migratory aesthetics, is constantly grounded in a "drifting" mode of visual storytelling between multiple fictional and documentary images and voices. In this drifting the voice of the exilic subject is given a vision appropriate to his/her journeys in the desert of exile.

Endnotes

1. M.H. Abrams defines paratactic style as: " ... one in which the members within a sentence, or else a sequence of complete sentences, are put one after the other without any expression of their connection or relations except (at most) the noncommittal connective, 'and'" (Abrams 304–05). On the storyteller as a specific version of the narrator, see (Bal 16–77).

2. In fact, the film was banned twice in Egypt and in other Arab countries for its criticism of Arab regimes articulated in this scene. See a description of the film on <www.arabfilm.com>.

3. Some critics read this story – Abu Alkhaizaran's loss of manhood – in terms of the Palestinian loss of the homeland as a "national defeat that is experienced as castration" (Amireh 753).

Works Cited

Abrams, M.H. *A Glossary of Literary Terms*, 6th Ed. Fort Worth, Texas: Harcourt Brace College Publishers, 1992.

Amireh, Amal. "Between Complicity and Subversion: Body Politics in Palestinian National Narrative". *The South Atlantic Quarterly* 102:4, Fall 2003, 747–772.

Bal, Mieke. *Narratology: Introduction to the Theory of Narrative*, 2nd Ed. Toronto: University of Toronto Press, 2002.

Benjamin, Walter. "The Story-Teller: Reflections on the Works of Nikolai Leskov". *Illuminations*. Ed. Hannah Ahrendt, trans. Harry Zohn. New York: Schocken Books, 1968.

Frassanito, William. A. *Gettysburg: A Journey in Time*. New York: Charles Scribner's Sons, 1975.

Khalidi, Rashid. *Palestinian Identity: The Construction of Modern National Consciousness*. New York: Colombia University Press, 1997.

Kanafani, Ghassan. *Men in the Sun*. Trans. H. Kilpatrick. London and New York: Three Continents Press, 1978.

———. *Rijal Fi Al Shams*. Cairo: American University in Cairo Press, 1962 & 1991.

Said, Edward. "By Birth Or By Choice?", *Al-Ahram Weekly Online*, Issue No. 453. 1999. URL: <http://weekly.ahram.org.eg/1999/453/op2.htm>.

Schacter, Daniel. *Searching for Memory: The Brain, the Mind and the Past*. New York: Basic Books, 1996.

Film

Al Makhdu'un (*The Dupes*). Dir. Tawfik Saleh. VHS. Arab Film Distribution, 1972.

Thamyris/Intersecting No. 17 (2007) 129-144

Unsettled Settlers: Postcolonialism, Travelling Theory and the New Migrant Aesthetics

Graham Huggan

In this essay, I want to explore the apparent discrepancy between historical experiences of migration and aesthetics theories of "migrancy" that have emerged from contemporary cultural studies. I shall posit a link between the metaphorisation of migration and the – often utopian – spatial poetics/politics of postcolonial theory. I shall examine this link by looking at two recent works by cultural theorists that attempt, in different ways, to bridge the gap between postmodern "travelling theory" and postcolonial cultural politics. These works – Paul Carter's *Living in a New Country* (1992) and Iain Chambers' *Migrancy, Culture, Identity* (1994) – can be seen as examples of a new "migrant aesthetic" which uses poststructuralist theories of displacement to account conceptually for migrating people, goods and ideas within the so called New World Order. I shall assess both the benefits and the limitations of such an approach; finally, I shall consider the extent to which the current cultural studies debates surrounding migration shed light on Australia's contested status as a postcolonial settler society.

I want to begin, though, with four no doubt unfairly decontextualised quotations on the subject of migration: the first from a political scientist (Aristide R Zolberg); the second from a sociologist (Hans-Joachim Hoffmann-Nowotny); the third from an economist (Robert E B Lucas); and the fourth from a cultural theorist (Iain Chambers). Here are the quotations, which I shall juxtapose without further comment:

If we conceive of a world which consists, on the one hand, of individuals seeking to maximise their welfare by exercising a variety of choices ... and, on the other, of mutually exclusive societies, acting as organized states to maximise collective goals by controlling the exit or entry of individuals ... the deviant character of individual migration is thus seen to be related to a fundamental tension between the interests of individuals and the interests of societies. (Zolberg 7)

Migration results from structural and anomic tensions ... and is a process by which such tensions are transformed and transferred ... [Two cases may be cited. In the first, an] individual may have a more or less balanced status configuration within a societal system, but may experience anomic tension because he or she is a member of a power deficient system ... In such a case, the member may give up system membership status and migrate to another system with a lower power deficit or a power surplus ... [In the second, an] individual experiences an anomic tension which can be traced back not to the external position of the system but to the internal status quo. If the individual unit perceives the chance of achieving a reduction of the anomic tension internally as low, the individual can try to achieve an improvement of status configuration by emigrating. (Hoffmann-Nowotny 70)

It is ... perhaps natural to consider weighing the pros and cons [of migration] within a cost-benefit framework ... [T]his type of study would divide the population into various categories: children, semi-skilled men, professional women, and so on. The emigration or immigration of each is then viewed as a project to be subjected to cost-benefit criteria ... I shall assume the objective is one of efficiency, though in principle it is quite possible to introduce distributional weights recognising perhaps a greater concern for the incidence of costs and benefits on lower income groups. (Lucas 104)

In the oblique gaze of the migrant that cuts across the territory of the Western metropolis there exists the hint of a metaphor. In the extensive and multiple worlds of the modem city we, too, become nomads, migrating across a system that is too vast to be our own, but in which we are fully involved – translating and transforming what we find and absorb into local instances of sense ... It is, above all, here, that we are inducted into a hybrid state and composite culture in which the simple dualism of First and Third Worlds collapses and there emerges what Homi Bhabha calls a 'differential communality', and what Felix Guattari refers to as the 'process of heterogenesis'. The boundaries of the liberal consensus and its centred sense of language, being, position and politics, are breached and scattered as all our histories come to be rewritten in the contentious languages of what has tended to become the privileged topos of the modern world: the contemporary metropolis. (Chambers 14)

The day-to-day struggles of many contemporary migrants within today's so-called new world order encounter a further level of conflict here in the competing jargons of academic prose. This essay is in part about the difficulty of reconciling the often convoluted language of academic abstraction with the equally complex lived experience, in both past and present, of individual migrants and migrant groups. I shall argue (as many academics do) for a dialectical understanding of migration as both adaptable conceptual tool and ongoing sociohistorical process; I shall also argue – with some reservations – for an inter- and/or multidisciplinary methodology with which to analyse migration as an intricate nexus of social, political, economic and historical forces. This line of thinking tallies with several recent studies on migration, from the literary/geographical collaboration *Writing across Worlds: Literature and Migration* (King, Connell and White, 1995) to the multidisciplinary Swedish-based project *International Migration, Immobility and Development* (Hammar et al, 1997) to Robin Cohen's magisterial multi-authored *Cambridge Survey of World Migration* (1995). What is common to these projects, and several others like them, is the recognition that migration cannot just be seen in terms of the "transference of human capital," but must also be gauged in terms of cultural impact and the shifting winds of global change (Sowell 391; see also Castles and Miller). As Stephen Castles and Mark J. Miller suggest in their somewhat misleadingly titled study *The Age of Migration: International Population Movements in the Modern World* (1993), "immigration changes demographic and social structures, affects political institutions and helps to reshape cultures" (96). Never more so than today; for while international migration is hardly "an invention of the late twentieth century ... [i]t has grown in volume and significance since 1945 and most particularly since the mid-1980s" (3), with every chance of further, possibly spectacular, growth in the new millennium. This growth is not merely demographic, but indicates a mounting realisation that migration is "one of the most important factors in [effecting and analysing] global change" (4). "The hallmark of the age of migration," for Castles and Miller, "is the global character of its migration: the way it affects more and more countries, and its linkages with complex processes affecting the entire world" (260).

It is not the place of this essay to examine these complex global processes, but rather to reflect on the various discourses through which ideas about migration are produced, disseminated and consumed. One such discourse pertains to contemporary critical/cultural theory, which (particularly since the work of Edward Said and James Clifford in the 1980s and early 1990s) has had a great deal to say about migrants and migration.[1] What is noticeable in much of this work, which might be loosely bracketed under the fashionable heading of "travelling theory," is the metaphorisation of migration as a composite figure for a series of metaphysical, as well as physical displacements. The metaphor of migration serves a variety of different purposes: to illustrate the increasing fragmentation of subjecthood and subjectivity under (post)modernity; to reflect on the semantic instability underlying all constructions of (personal/cultural/national) identity; to insist on the homology between experiences of dislocation and the destabilisation of essentialist ideologies and fixed paradigms and patterns of thought. Migration has become a useful code-word for the different kinds of conceptual slippage that are characteristic of postmodern/poststructuralist approaches toward linguistic and cultural systems; in addition, migration functions as a catalysing metaphor for the exploration of cultural change and the apprehension of new, mobile cultural subjects in the nominally postnational era.[2]

The dangers attendant on the metaphorisation of migrant experience are not lost on many of these theorists: James Clifford, for example, in *Routes: Translation and Travel in the Late Twentieth Century* (1997), warns against "talk[ing] of travel and displacement in unmarked ways, thus normalising male experience" (258; see also Wolff, "On the Road Again"); while Caren Kaplan in her book *Questions of Travel: Postmodern Discourses of Displacement* (1996) makes the valid if obvious point that travel metaphors, including those of migration, risk levelling out discrepant historical experiences, blurring the boundaries between voluntary and involuntary forms of movement, and at worst acting as an alibi for the privileges of a worldly cosmopolitan elite.

As Kaplan suggests, migration and other patterns of human movement in the modem era tend to carry an imperial legacy that is often mystified in the voguish academic categories of nomadism, migrancy and displacement. One might expect these mystifications to be of interest to postcolonial critics, who have arguably made it their business to bring imperialism back to the centre of self-involved postmodern debates surrounding language, identity and representation in the present late-capitalist conjuncture. Yet even a cursory glance at some of the latest postcolonial theory reveals a similar propensity to use spatial metaphors loosely – even, in some cases, interchangeably. A particular culprit here is Homi Bhabha, whose celebrated notion of a "third space of enunciation" – a space he sees as being occupied by, among others, migrants in the Western metropoles – involves a vertiginous conflation of different metaphors of displacement.[3] Revealingly, in an interview with Paul Thompson for the collection of essays *Migration and Identity* (1994), Bhabha speaks of the emergence of a "new complex, culturally problematic kind of cosmopolitanism ... of migration, which has a very specific postcolonial and Third World history" (196). Yet it is precisely the elision of a certain kind of cosmopolitan privilege that arguably limits – and also locates – Bhabha's project.[4] Postcolonial theorists like Bhabha have justifiably been criticised for their tendency to mystify the same – uneven – relations of power their work claims to uncover. The same might also be said of some of the writers whose works they discuss; as Elleke Boehmer argues in her introductory study *Colonial & Postcolonial Literature* (1995) (the subtitle of which, appropriately enough, is *Migrant Metaphors*), postcoloniality refers to the emergence of a set of conditions for the globalisation of "migrant writing," which she defines somewhat ungenerously as "a literature written by elites, and defined and canonised by elites" (239–40). This type of literature, for Boehmer, runs the risk of "evacuating commitment" in the pursuit of celebrating rootlessness and cosmopolitan joie-de-vivre (240). To define a literature of migrant floating as the culmination of the postcolonial, Boehmer concludes sardonically, "does represent something of a diminution in a long tradition of self-consciously political writing" (240).

Boehmer's comments are self-confessedly generalised; but they indicate the anxiety hovering around the edges of postcolonial discourse that "the postcolonial" may be less a marker, as is usually claimed, of opposition than a kind of brand-name for the palatable "otherness" purveyed and consumed by metropolitan elites.[5] In the 1990s according to Boehmer, "the generic postcolonial writer is more likely to be a cultural traveller, or an 'extra-territorial', than a national" (233). To trade in migrant metaphors can thus become a profitable business, with rewards handed out to writers who, self-conscious border-crossers, know how to manipulate the transcultural codes of a postcolonial "migrant aesthetic." (The best example here is, unsurprisingly, Salman Rushdie, who has always taken care to position himself – both pre- and post fatwa – as a cosmopolitan migrant writer belonging to what he calls "a world community of displaced writers" (15) that includes such figures as Milan Kundera, Maxine Hong Kingston and Günter Grass).[6] And yet, I want to suggest, it is not just creative writers who have subscribed, consciously or not, to the preset "geopolitical aesthetic" rules of literary cosmopolitanism (Brennan). A variety of literary critics and cultural theorists have also jumped on the bandwagon, fostering a fraught alliance between the allegedly transgressive manoeuvres of postmodern travelling theory and the putatively oppositional politics of postcolonial cultural practice. The figure – the rhetorical figure – of the migrant plays a key role here, allowing both for claims of resistance to dominant (state) formations and for self-liberating linguistic play in the "borderline engagement with cultural difference" (Kunow).

A good example of this alliance is in Iain Chambers' acclaimed study – part travelogue, part cultural commentary, part philosophical meditation – of the impact of cultural diversity on today's increasingly transnational world. *Migrancy, Culture, Identity* (1994), says Meaghan Morris in a dutifully admiring blurb on the back cover, has enhanced Chambers' reputation as "of contemporary cultural studies." The book's interconnected essays "tell stories of different worlds that already define our own; moving lightly through border-zones of culture dense with new ideas, they stop to chat with strangers on the way; and they share with us the wise joy in dialogue as a way of working towards a common horizon." This generous tribute, as blurbs often do, tells us more about Morris' engaging brand of breezy populism than it does about Chambers' project, in which the lyrical ambitions of the author are frequently stymied by turgid prose. (I should probably confess to a certain irritation at the relentless modishness of Chambers' writing, its aura of street-smart intellectualism and sophisticated worldly savoir-faire. Possibly, this signals my – no doubt snobbish – dis-ease with hypertheorised approaches to popular culture, which risk fetishising the cultural phenomena they claim to be explaining, and which arguably supplant one form of elitism – the Arnoldian connoisseurship of high culture – with another, the postmodernist unravelling of the complexities of everyday life.)

That said, what exactly is the nature of Chambers' project? Ostensibly, it is an analysis of forms of global movement under modernity – mass migration, the worldwide transportation of consumer goods, the transnational circuitries of capital, and so on – which create a volatile mix that belies (white) European pretensions to cultural superiority and stability. As Chambers puts it:

When the 'Third World' is no longer maintained at a distance 'out there' but begins to appear 'in here', when the encounter between diverse cultures, histories, religions and languages no longer occurs along the peripheries ... but emerges at the centre of our daily lives, in the cities of the so-called 'advanced', or 'First', world, then we can perhaps begin to talk of a significant interruption in the preceding sense of our own lives, cultures, languages and futures. (2)

"Migrancy" – a cultural studies neologism I have been unable to trace in any dictionary – describes this condition of "interruption" and historical disturbance; involving a psychic, as well as physical shift in which "neither the points of departure nor those of arrival are immutable or certain, [it] calls for a dwelling in language, in histories, in identities, that are constantly subject to mutation" (Chambers 5). Migrancy registers as much a semantic as a historical disruption, one in which:

the nomadic experience of language ... is no longer the expression of a unique tradition or history; [in which] thought [itself] wanders ... migrates, requires translation; [and in which] reason runs the risk of opening out on to the world, of finding itself in a passage without a reassuring foundation or finality. (Chambers 4)

Migrancy, finally, describes a project of conversion through which diverse histories of displacement, often highly painful to those affected, are to be assimilated to an aesthetic of pleasurable intercultural contact.

There are several obvious problems associated with this utopian venture. For one, as Chambers himself recognises, there is the danger of blurring boundaries between, on the one hand, those coercive forms of dislocation that are

induced by war, economic deprivation, political repression, poverty [and] racist slavery ... and [on the other hand] that diffuse sense of mobility that characterises metropolitan life, [and that is] charted in the privileged channels of movement represented by the media, information technology, advertising, tourism and a generalised consumerism. (28)

For another, there is the risk of overemphasising the city as the locus classicus of migration, the place where different, and often contradictory, realities mix and mingle. Migrancy, as Chambers admits, is very much a metropolitan aesthetic, based on the mutability and restless creativity of urban praxis, but also on the potential exclusivism of a view in which "the model of the city becomes ... the model of the contemporary world" (27).[7] And for a third, there is the tendency to collapse the understanding of cultural difference into the consumption of (multi)ethnic products whose otherness is easily assumed. Consider the transition in the following passage between political intent and personal pleasure:

In the migrant landscapes of contemporary metropolitan cultures, de-territorialised and de-colonised, re-situating, re-citing and re-presenting common signs in the circuits between speech, image and oblivion, a constant struggling into sense and history is pieced together. It is a history that is continually being decomposed and recomposed in the interlacing between what we have inherited and where we are. In the shifting interstices of this world, whether moving to the acoustic patterns of our bodily beat or the techno-surrealist design of computerised simulations, there exists the opening that redeems and reconstitutes our being ... It is perhaps something that we can hear when Youssou N'Dour, from Dakar, sings in Wolof, a Senegalese dialect, in a tent pitched in the suburbs of Naples. [Chambers lives in Naples, where he teaches at the Istituto Universitario Orientale.] *Only six months earlier I had heard his haunting voice in a New York club, this time in the context of the Japanese techno-pop/New Age sound of Ryuichi Sakamoto and No Wave New York guitarist Arto Lindsay. It is surely in these terms, well before intellectual and institutional acknowledgement, that we come most immediately and effectively to recognise the differentiated territories in which the imaginary is being disseminated and the eurocentric voice simultaneously dispersed.* (Chambers 14–15)

Chambers is unembarrassed by this transparent assertion of "conspicuous cosmopolitanism" (Roberts), through which the "de-colonised landscapes of contemporary metropolitan cultures" provide a stage for the straining affect of a would-be postcolonial sensibility. My diction is no doubt too harsh here, but suffice to say I am unconvinced by Chambers' attempt to wed a putatively radical postcolonial cultural politics to an ambivalently indexed postmodern response to cultural consumerism on a global scale. As I have already suggested, the tensions contained within Chambers' version of a migrant aesthetic are already present within postcolonialism as a contemporary currency of intellectual exchange. (Elsewhere, I have analysed these tensions in terms of the competing "regimes of value" (Appadurai 1986) that surround the global production and consumption of culturally "othered" artefacts and ideas (Huggan). Theories of migrancy might similarly be seen in terms of the apparent contradiction between explicitly anti-colonial imperatives to open up new cultural horizons and implicitly neo-colonial designs to keep cultural difference in its place. I want to turn at this stage to another recent attempt to bridge the differences between migration as historical process and migrancy as aesthetic creed. This is the work of the Australian cultural critic and theorist Paul Carter, who is best known for his excursions into the field of spatial history (*The Road to Botany Bay*, 1987; *The Lie of the Land*, 1996), but who is also – as I shall demonstrate – an accomplished, if maverick, aesthetician and philosopher of language. I shall concentrate here on Carter's second book, *Living in a New Country: History, Travelling and Language* (1992), partly because it serves as a useful counterpoint to Chambers' study, and partly because it provides me with a segue into the last part of my essay, an assessment of Australia's current status as a mixed migrant society and, more controversially perhaps, as a rapidly changing postcolonial settler culture.

Carter's book, as its title announces, is about living in a new country, one which is marked by a certain fluidity – a provisionality – of interpersonal exchange (5–6). Whereas Chambers, based in Europe, must make the case for rejuvenation, Carter in Australia already assumes it, not so much in the country as it is, but in the ways in which it is seen (5). This perception of novelty is implicitly associated with a migrant society in which "language has ... yet to detach itself from the contingencies of speaking and hearing;" in which communication involves the continual renegotiation of "dialogical contracts;" and in which a "migrant psychology," recognising the arbitrariness of social/linguistic conventions, both registers and inhabits the gap that inevitably separates names and things (6–7). This migrant sensibility, as Carter notes, has not prevented the vilification of "foreign elements" in Australia as elsewhere, in the so-called old world as well as the new. In a global climate in which mass migration co-exists with, and sometimes fuels, recrudescent nationalism:

it becomes more than ever urgent to develop a framework of thinking that makes the migrant central, not ancillary, to historical processes. We need to disarm the genealogical rhetoric of blood, property and frontiers and to substitute for it a lateral account of social relations, one that stresses the contingency of all definitions of self and other, and the necessity always to tread lightly ... to make migratory haphazardness the material out of which [our social fabric] weaves its identity. (Chambers 7–8)

One recognises here, if in a more lucid form, the emphasis on intercultural dialogue and the celebratory insistence on the performative basis of identity formation that are characteristic of Chambers' work. One recognises also the common desire to aestheticise migrancy, to posit it as an alternative to the poetics of settled spaces and as a rejoinder to the linear discourses associated, somewhat loosely, with Enlightenment thought. In Carter's last, astonishing chapter this migrant aesthetic is explored further through a reformulation of the modernist techniques of free association and arbitrary juxtaposition. These techniques are brought together in the rhetorical device of collage. For the modernists, Carter explains, "collage was a disruptive device, a mechanism for undermining bourgeois notions of representation and tradition;" but in a postcolonial society (which Carter equates in Australia with a migrant society) collage is not anomalous, but

the normal mode of constructing meaning. Everyday speech does not flower out of any deeply held and mutually shared unconscious grammar but is patched together from heterogeneous lexical, syntactic and grammatical sources that are generally produced imitatively, without any sense of context (186–7).

Carter cites the example of Australia's "major suburban streets, with their eclectic mix of commercial signs, advertising hoardings and historically parodic architectural styles" (187). Most of his other examples, though, are less visual than auditory or phonic; for the primary effect of what Carter calls "post-colonial collage" is to "relocate and sound the spaces in between" different utterances, and to reveal "[w]ithin the ritualised performances of language ... a deeper poetics, a suppressed association mediated through sound, cadence, rhythm, pitch and stress" (187, 198).

It is in the spaces opened up by migrant (mis)communication that Carter locates a poetics of movement, of productively interrupted speech. Like Chambers, Carter views migration as a metaphysical as well as physical itinerary:

An authentically migrant perspective would, perhaps, be based on an intuition that the opposition between here and there is itself a cultural construction, a consequence of thinking in terms of fixed entities and defining them oppositionally. It might begin by regarding movement, not as an awkward interval between fixed points of departure, but as a mode of being in the world. The question would be, then, not how to arrive, but how to move, how to identify convergent and divergent movements; and the challenge would be how to notate such events, how to give them a historical and social value. (101)

This challenge might come as welcome news to historians of migration; but like Chambers, Carter makes little effort to distinguish between different migrant experiences, preferring instead to assimilate these to an overarching migrant aesthetic or, in his ambitious claim, to "a migrant theory of meaning." Empirical evidence is abandoned in favour of metaphysical speculation; the ingenuity of Carter's theories – which are, of course, in part a celebration of migrant ingenuity – is arguably diminished by his idealist reliance on a generic "migrant situation." Migrancy, or Carter's version of it, thus risks becoming a totalising theory even as it accentuates improvisation and the gaps in established systems of meaning and thought.

To be fair to Carter, his is not only a brilliantly poetical defence of "the migrant condition," but also a thoughtful alternative to what he calls the "prosaic" type of narrative history in which "the master historian, carefully contextualising, ingeniously iron[s] out differences in the interests of his grand narrative" (191). Migrancy emerges in this latter context, less as a theorisation of migrant histories than as an attempt to understand the grounds of historical thinking in figurative, that is to say aesthetic, terms. These terms are closely allied to the principles of travelling theory: the need to understand culture, not as a stable entity but as an intersection of different trajectories (Clifford); the need to understand identity as being formed and reformed on the move; and, not least, the need to understand theory as a horizon of figuration, as a shifting composite of metaphors that travel, as ideas themselves travel, in time and space (Said). Travelling theory, in cultural terms, allows for perspectives on global movement that stress the provisionality of all forms of intercultural connection. This raises the complex question of how to fashion group solidarities, and of how to locate agency, in a global cultural economy punctuated by incommensurable "differences" and "disjunctures" (Appaduarai 1994). It could be argued against Carter that his aestheticised theory of migrant meaning traps migrants themselves in a semantic loop, propelling them into situations where their adaptive genius, their capacity to improvise and create new meanings, merely reconfirms their disempowerment at the hands of the cultural orthodoxy – and of state authority. If "migrancy" registers the speculative attempt to apprehend movement "as a mode of being in the world," it is surely not an answer to those who seek to control, meaning mostly to restrict, migrants' actual movements. The suspicion emerges that "migrancy" might be a form of anti-essentialist essentialism which disguises the uneven relations of power between different migrant groups, including the power of course to decide who is or is not a migrant. This begs the question of the particular "migrant situation" in Australia, and of changing definitions and perceptions of migration and of the mixed migrant society. "We are mostly all migrants," says Carter in his introduction to *Living in a New Country*, and even "if we have tried to stay at home, the conditions of life have changed so utterly in this century that we find ourselves strangers in our own houses" (7). Yet as I have suggested, this universalisation of "the migrant experience" in travelling theory overlooks often conspicuously hierarchical attitudes toward different migrant groups. In Australia, these attitudes not only indicate a history of selective immigration policy, but also the continuing inequalities of access – to education, economic opportunity, political power and so on – for different migrant communities within a supposedly multicultural society.[8] The two pieces on twentieth-century Australia in Robin Cohen's *Cambridge Survey on World Migration* restrict themselves to immigration patterns for southern Europeans and Asians.[9] This picture is potentially misleading; for while immigration to Australia in the last few decades has certainly derived from southern Europe and, increasingly, Asia, with Asians accounting for some 40 per cent of intakes in the early 1990s, post-second world war efforts to bring in migrants to Australia focused on Britain, operating on a ratio of roughly ten British migrants for every "foreigner" accepted (Castles and Miller). The tendency to overlook migrants of British (or, more problematically, "Anglo-Celtic") origin replicates the common view that, while technically the vast majority of Australians are migrants, some – to adapt Lolo Houbein via George Orwell – are more migrant than others.[10] A similar forgetfulness has affected some studies of so-called migrant writing in Australia, in which it is assumed that migrant writers are, by definition, non-Anglo-Celtic (Gunew and Longley). The view of migrant writing as predominantly transgressive or counter-hegemonic merely reinforces ethnic compartmentalisation, both by manufacturing a series of representative migrant voices and by homogenising the target group – Anglo-Celtic Australians – against which they are presumed to speak. Thus, one of the ironies in the otherwise valuable work of anthologiser/critics like Sneja Gunew is that, while they rightly dismiss the view of migrant writing as sociological evidence, sociology itself might provide rather different, possibly corrective views of their working categories. Certainly, the view of migrant writing as operating against normative Anglo-Celtic practices tends to be founded on a largely essentialised – perhaps even jaundiced – view of Anglo-Celtic culture.[11]

A similar argument might be brought to bear against the view of Australian literature/culture as postcolonial. As Bob Hodge and Vijay Mishra, among others, have suggested, the term "postcolonial" has been applied in a variety of tenuously comparable contexts, tending paradoxically to obscure the very asymmetries of power its proponents wish to examine. In Australia, these relations of power pertain to a history of internal colonialism, of continuing white discrimination against, especially, Aboriginal people that makes a mockery of the claim that Australia, and its literature, have emerged in opposition to European cultural norms. While the "postcoloniality" of Australian literature and culture can certainly be contested, Hodge and Mishra's argument – like Gunew's – risks merely substituting one set of essentialisms for another. Thus, Aborigines are to be celebrated, as Gunew endorses non-Anglo-Celtic migrants, as Australia's authentically colonised subjects or as their "true" dissenting voice (Lawson). [12] In fact, postcolonial critics and theorists, including many of those whom Hodge and Mishra finger, are only too well aware of the contradictions embedded in Australia's relationship to its colonial past – and its neo-colonial present. Alan Lawson, for instance, in an essay on postcolonial theory and "the settler subject," points to the ambivalence already inscribed within the terms "settler" and "settler culture." The term "settler," says Lawson, is a "tendentious discursive phenomenon [which] foregrounds the slippage from invader to peaceful settler as a strategy within the project of imperialism" (24). "Settler cultures," similarly, are internally conflicted, "liminal sites at the point of negotiation between the contending authorities of Empire and Native" (Carter, *Living* 114). The task of postcolonial theory and criticism is to analyse these internal conflicts and contradictions, in such a way as to demonstrate the inadequacy of the binary constructions (Europe and its others, the coloniser and the colonised, the west and the rest, and so on) that dominate a certain, foundationalist type of anti-colonial critique.

These arguments and counter-arguments, by now, probably have a familiar ring to them. I have rehearsed them briefly here to make a general point about the hazards of literary/cultural labelling, and to illustrate that terms like migrant, settler and postcolonial are necessarily political in their descriptive and affective force. It is axiomatic that terms like these are anchored to power structures, and that the effectiveness of each to convey a certain, perhaps subliminal, meaning must depend on those who control the channels of communication at any given point. The value of travelling theory is to destabilise these meanings, disrupting, for example, the ideological opposition between the "temporary" migrant and the permanent settler by showing the semantic slippage that exists within, as well as between, each of these terms. Another benefit of travelling theory is to suggest that migrancy is a condition of possibility; that it harbours the potential to transform a historical record of exclusion and discrimination into a utopian aesthetic which suggests that "it is the figurative possibility in language itself that makes the future possible."[13] The danger always exists that this transformative project may be self-serving, and that the multiple histories it seeks to convert may be misrecognised, even overlooked. Travelling theory – cultural theory in general – certainly needs the support of history, less as an empirical check on its idealist excesses than as a guide to accompany it on its divagatory journeys, down its tangled tracks. Theories of migration and migrancy are a test-case for this companionship: a reminder that theories of displacement are always historically inflected; but equally, that the scattered histories of displaced and relocated peoples are also records of the metaphors they have used to justify their movements – and chart their quests.

In this essay, I have tried to state a case for the usefulness of cultural theory in approaching the historical experiences of migration, to Australia and elsewhere. While cultural theory's prevarications might seem merely irritating to some historians, its value might lie precisely in its capacity to act as a gadfly to received perceptions of the historical record. If, as I have suggested, the metaphorisation of migration sometimes helps to obscure the specificities of historical experience, it also draws attention to what we might call the metaphoricity of human life itself. Cultural theory – even of the most extreme relativist variety – has nothing to gain from refuting the factual, or from collapsing historically verifiable events into a play of indeterminate fictions. At its worst, of course, it seems to fall afoul of a kind of sophistry, a perverse determination to complicate issues beyond the reach of historical truths. At its best, though, it provides a set of workable, if often complex, methodologies for an interrogation of the unevenness that cuts across all – necessarily metaphor-laden – forms of human representation. It is perhaps utopian if nonetheless salutary to think that history can be remade from below, or that the neglected experiences of migrants might rewrite the narrative of the nation. Yet in present-day Australia, these are more than just saving illusions – as migrants themselves often know, and as historians, cultural theorists and scholar-writers of many different stripes will no doubt continue to make it their business to find out.

Endnotes

1. See for example, the seminal essays Edward Said, "Travelling Theory" in *The World, the Text, and the Critic*, Harvard University Press, Cambridge, 1983, pp 226–47 and James Clifford, "Travelling cultures" in Lawrence Grossberg, Cary Nelson and Paula Treichler (Eds), *Cultural Studies*, New York, Routledge, 1992, 96–116.

2. See, for example, Arjun Appadurai, *Modernity at Large: Cultural Dimensions of Globalisation*, University of Minnesota Press, Minneapolis, 1996 and Dean MacCannell, *Empty Meeting Grounds: The Tourist Papers*, Routledge, New York, 1992.

3. For a brilliant critique of Bhabha's obfuscatory terminology, see Neil Larsen, "DetermiNation: postcolonialism, poststructuralism, and the problem of ideology" in Fawzia Afzal-Khan and Kalpana Seshadri-Crooks (Eds), *The Preoccupation of Postcolonial Theory*. Durham: Duke University Press, 2000.

4. Bhabha shares this privilege with other members of a highly mobile postcolonial intelligentsia – for a further discussion of the compromised status of the cosmopolitan postcolonial intellectual, see Aijaz Ahmad in *Theory: Classes, Nations, Literatures*, Verso, London, 1992 and, particularly, Timothy Brennan, *At Home in the World: Cosmopolitanism Now*, Harvard University Press, Cambridge, MA, 1997.

5. See here Graham Huggan, *The Postcolonial Exotic: Marketing the Margins*, Routledge, London, 2001 and, especially, Brennan's critique of the marketing of Third World literature.

6. For a thoroughgoing critique of Rushdie's self-positioning as a "migrant writer," see Krishnaswamy. Krishnaswamy is also critical in more general terms of "mythologies of migrancy" which "ironically reinvent ..., in the very process of destabilising subjectivity, a postmodernist avatar of the free-floating bourgeois subject" (Revathi Krishnaswamy, "Mythologies of migrancy: Postcolonialism, postmodernism and the politics of (dis)location", *Ariel*, vol 26, no 1, 1995, p 143). For a similar argument, see also Kaplan, p 140, for whom theories of "postmodern migrancy" may have the effect of "obfuscating and even erasing the representation of social relations in historically grounded and politically meaningful ways."

7. This metropolitan bias is often noticeable in cultural studies, which generally has little to say about those who have no access to urban culture. This is also the case with certain kinds of postcolonial criticism, which assume the metropolis to be the privileged site for (intellectual) resistance. For an example of this kind of criticism, see Edward W. Said, "Third World Intellectuals and Metropolitan Culture", Raritan, Winter 1990.

8. See Jerzy Zubrzycki, "Migration in Australasia and the South Pacific" in *Kritz*, op. cit., pp.158–880.

9. See Gillian Bottomley, "Southern European migration to Australia: Diasporic Networks and Cultural Transformations" in Cohen, pp 386–91 and Jock Collins, "Asian Migration to Australia" in Cohen, op. cit., pp 376–79.

10. Houbein's comments, in the early 1980s, were directed at so-called "ethnic" writers, the term of choice having since switched from "ethnic" or "migrant" to "multicultural" (see Sneja Gunew, *Framing Marginality: Multicultural Literary Studies*, Melbourne University Press, Melbourne, 1994). Whichever of these terms is used, Houbein's ironic self-description (she is Dutch Australian) still seems relevant: "Technically, everyone is ethnic; in practice, some of us are more ethnic than others", (Lolo Houbein, 'The role of "ethnic" writers in Australian literature' in J Daalder and M Fryar, *Aspects of Australian Culture*, Abel Tasman Press, Adelaide, 1982, p 98).

11. Gunew's more recent work recognises the problem of setting up straw categories; but the "Anglo-Celtic" label sticks, and is used elsewhere less discerningly.

12. For a similar argument in Canada, see Linda Hutcheon, "Circling the Downspout of Empire" in Ian Adam and Helen Tiffin (Eds), *Past the Last Post: Theorising Post-colonialism and Postmodernism*, University of Calgary Press, Calgary, 1990, p 172: "[W]hen Canadian culture is called post-colonial today the reference is very rarely to the Native culture, which might be the more accurate historical use of the term ... Perhaps, given [Native and metis writers'] articulations of the damage to Indian culture and people done by the colonizers (French and British) and the process of colonization, theirs should be considered the resisting, post-colonial voice of Canada."

13. See also George Lakoff and Mark Johnson, *Metaphors We Live By*, University of Chicago Press, Chicago, 1980.

Works Cited

Ahmad, Aijaz. *In Theory: Classes, Nations, Literatures*. London: Verso, 1992.

Appadurai, Arjun, Ed. *The Social Life of Things: Commodities in Perspective*. Cambridge: Cambridge University Press, 1986.

———. "Disjuncture and Difference in the Global Cultural Economy." *Colonial Discourse and Post-Colonial Theory: A Reader*. Ed. Patrick Williams and Laura Chrisman. New York: Columbia University Press, 1994. 324–39.

———. Modernity at Large: Cultural Dimensions of Globalisation. Minneapolis: University of Minnesota Press, 1996.

Bhabha, Homi K. "Between identities: interview with Paul Thompson." *Migration and Identity*. Ed. Rina Benmayor and Andor Skotnes. Oxford: Oxford University Press, 1994.

Boehmer, Elleke. *Colonial and Postcolonial Literature*. Oxford: Oxford University Press, 1995.

Bottomley, Gillian. "Southern European migration to Australia: Diasporic networks and cultural transformations." Cohen. 386–91.

Brennan, Timothy. *At Home in the World: Cosmopolitanism Now*. Cambridge, MA: Harvard University Press, 1997.

Carter, Paul. *The Road to Botany Bay: An Essay in Spatial History*. London: Faber and Faber, 1987.

———. *Living in a New Country: History, Travelling and Language*. London: Faber and Faber, 1992.

———. *The Lie of the Land*. London: Faber and Faber, 1996.

Castles, Stephen, and Mark J Miller. *The Age of Migration: International Population Movements in the Modern World*. New York: The Guilford Press, 1993.

Chambers, Iain. *Migrancy, Culture, Identity*. London: Routledge, 1994.

Clifford, James. "Travelling cultures." *Cultural Studies*. Ed. Lawrence Grossberg, Cary Nelson and Paula Treichler. Routledge: New York, 1992. 96–116.

———. *Routes: Travel and Translation in the Late Twentieth Century*. Cambridge, MA: Harvard University Press, 1997.

Cohen, Robin, Ed. *The Cambridge Survey of World Migration*. Cambridge: Cambridge University Press, 1995.

Collins, Jock. "Asian migration to Australia." Cohen. 376–9.

Daalder, J, and M Fryar. *Aspects of Australian Culture*. Adelaide: Abel Tasman Press, 1982.

Gunew, Sneja, and Kateryna O Longley. *Striking Chords: Multicultural Literary Interpretations*. Sydney: Allen and Unwin, 1992.

Gunew, Sneja. *Framing Marginality: Multicultural Literary Studies*. Melbourne: Melbourne University Press, 1994.

Hammar, Tomas, Grete Brochmann, Kristof Tamas and Thomas Faist, Eds. *International Migration, Immobility and Development: Multidisciplinary Perspectives*. Oxford: Berg, 1997.

Hodge, Bob, and Vijay Mishra. *The Dark Side of the Dream: Australian Literature and the Postcolonial Mind*. Sydney: Allen and Unwin, 1991.

Hoffmann-Nowotny, Hans-Joachim. "A sociological approach toward a general theory of migration." Kritz et al.

Huggan, Graham. *The Postcolonial Exotic: Marketing the Margins*. London: Routledge, 2001.

Hutcheon, Linda. "Circling the downspout of empire." *Past the Last Post: Theorising Post-colonialism and Post-modernism*. Ed. Ian Adam and Helen Tiffin. Calgary: University of Calgary Press, 1990.

Kaplan, Caren. *Questions of Travel: Postmodern Discourses of Displacement*. Durham, NC: Duke University Press, 1996.

King, Russell, John Connell and Paul White, Eds. *Writing across Worlds: Literature and Migration*. London: Routledge, 1995.

Krishnaswamy, Revathi. "Mythologies of migrancy: Postcolonialism, postmodernism and the politics of (dis)location" Ariel 26.1 (1995).

Kunow, Rudiger. "Salman Rushdie and the art of the contact zone." *Multicultural Perspectives On Salman Rushdie's Fiction*. Ed. Liselotte Glage. Forthcoming.

Lakoff, George and Mark Johnson. *Metaphors We Live By*. Chicago: University of Chicago Press, 1980.

Larsen, Neil. "DetermiNation: postcolonialism, poststructuralism, and the problem of ideology." *The Preoccupation of Postcolonial Theory*. Ed. Fawzia Afzal-Khan and Kalpana Seshadri-Crooks. Durham, NC: Duke University Press, 2000.

Lawson, Alan. "Postcolonial theory and the 'settler' subject." *Essays on Canadian Writing* 56 (1995).

Lucas, Robert E B. "International migration: Economic causes, consequences and evaluation." Kritz et al.

MacCannell, Dean. *Empty Meeting Grounds: The Tourist Papers*. New York: Routledge, 1992.

Roberts, Martin. Private conversation, 1997; with thanks.

Rushdie, Salman. *Imaginary Homelands: Essays and Criticism 1981–1991*. London: Granta Books, 1991.

Said, Edward. "Travelling Theory." *The World, the Text, and the Critic*. Cambridge: Harvard University Press, 1983. 226–47.

Said, Edward. "Third World intellectuals and metropolitan culture." *Raritan* (Winter 1990).

Sowell, Thomas. *Migrations and Cultures: A World View*. New York: Basic Books, 1996.

Wolff, Janet. "On the road again: Metaphors of travel in cultural criticism." *Cultural Studies* 7.2, (1993): 224–39.

Zolberg, Aristide R. "International migration in political perspective." Global Trends in *Migration: Theory and Research in International Population Movements*. Ed. Mary M Kritz, Charles B Keely and Silvano M Tomasi. New York: Center for Migration Studies of New York, 1981.

Zubrzycki, Jerzy. "Migration in Australasia and the South Pacific." *Kritz*.158–880.

Thamyris/Intersecting No. 17 (2007) 145-160

Storytellers, Novelists, and Postcolonial Melancholia: Displaced Aesthetics in Chinua Achebe's *Things Fall Apart*

Sam Durrant

I

Migration threatens the destruction of aesthetics, if aesthetics is understood in the Kantian sense as the appreciation of the beautiful. If no aesthetic judgement can be made outside a tradition of appreciation, the migration of peoples inevitably introduces alternative traditions, disrupting the framework of interpretation and rendering universal judgement impossible: migration, then, might be said to produce incommensurable aesthetics or even an aesthetics of the incommensurable.

Conversely, perhaps, one might argue that aesthetics has always been as migratory as culture itself. Has there ever been art without at least the idea of visitation, of the stranger, without the thought of her arrival, without her potential to disrupt the parochialism of tradition? No art, perhaps, without the disruption of tradition. This would be a specifically modernist understanding of tradition as a series of ruptures with that which has gone before, an unceasing attempt to make it new, a series of collisions at the limits of a culture's understanding: art would then become the record of cultural collision, a kind of discontinuous cultural memory that does not simply absorb difference into the sameness of tradition but rather bears the mark of a series of blows to self-identity. Migratory aesthetics, then, would thus describe the constitutive migration of culture across its own borders. But then what need for the qualifier "migratory," if aesthetics is always already in movement between cultures and traditions? If there is indeed a migratory aesthetics, then wouldn't one also have to posit the existence of an aesthetics that stays at home, a sedentary or indigenous aesthetics that predates the arrival of modernity and attempts to resist the various forms of modernity's migration?

II

I will try to answer some of these questions through an exploration of Chinua Achebe's *Things Fall Apart*, a novel that is usually read as a recuperation of an indigenous aesthetics but which is in fact in constant migration between modernity and tradition, and between pre-colonial, colonial and postcolonial temporalities. My wider suggestion will be that postcolonial literature, as a record of cultural collision, as a record of the multiple histories of migration (colonisation, so called reverse colonisation, forced transportation, economic migration, asylum) that characterize (post)modernity,[1] is continuous with the discontinuous aesthetics of modernism, its understanding of tradition as rupture and of art as the attempt to register the shock of the new.

Such a reading of the postcolonial is implicit within Homi Bhabha's attempts "to rename the postmodern from the position of the postcolonial" (Bhabha 175). In his (in)famous essay "DissemiNation," Bhabha draws on a Benjaminian understanding of time in order to track the return of the history that happened overseas. For Bhabha, the homogenous empty time of historicism, which produces a continuist, patriotic narrative of Englishness, is disrupted by "the time of the now" which, in flashing up moments from the past (Britain's history overseas), disturbs the national narrative and creates a space for a more hybrid version of national identity (according to the popular reading of Bhabha), or, more accurately, disturbs any claim to (national) identity.

Bhabha's essay is problematic in many respects, not the least of which is the way in which the figure of Gibreel, from Salman Rushdie's *The Satanic Verses*, becomes the figure for the return of the repressed history that happened overseas, or what Bhabha dubs "the principle of avenging repetition" (169). Bhabha cites the following passage from *The Satanic Verses*:

> *These powerless English – Did they not think that their history would return to haunt them? – 'The native is an oppressed person whose permanent dream is to become the persecutor' (Fanon) ... He would make this land anew. He was the Archangel Gibreel. –* And I'm back! (Rushdie 353 qtd in Bhabha 319)

Bhabha's all too cursory reading fails to recognise that Gibreel's fantasy of revenge is just that – a fantasy. Although his desire to "tropicalise" London may explain the prolonged heat wave that the population of England experiences, the nation remains resolutely unhybridised; racism, in Thatcher's Britain as in today's, remains the order of the day. Rushdie presciently indicates that this racism is at its most systemic in the police force and the immigration authorities, whose officers force Gibreel's double, Changez Chamchawala, to eat his own shit (159–60). Crucially, Gibreel ends up the victim of his own hallucinations, succumbing to schizophrenia and committing suicide. Despite the novel's comic framework, Rushdie's citation of Fanon is deadly serious and reminds us that the native's dream of revenge leads either to self-destructive psychosis or what, since the 11th September 2001, has become known as "blowback."

In other words, Bhabha's romanticisation of the effects of immigration is a dangerous misreading of both Rushdie's novel and of history itself. Migrancy cannot magically transform the traumatic experience of the migrant into a cure for metropolitan chauvinism. Immigration has in fact served to focalise intolerance even while the presence of immigrant sub-cultures is made to sustain the illusions of multiculturalism. Bhabha's reading also ignores the hostile reception of *The Satanic Verses* in certain quarters of the Islamic world and the resulting Fatwah. Rushdie's novel, for all its attempts to negotiate a relation between the West and the East, modernity and tradition, the secular and the sacred, now perhaps marks the moment where a global schism was seen to open up and two world views became understood as ever more violently incommensurable.[2]

In the decade and a half since Bhabha's essay, the field of "trauma studies" has emerged, largely without reference to Bhabha's reading of the belated temporality of the postcolonial. Although the field is primarily centred on the kinds of memory-work produced by survivors of the Holocaust, there are signs now that the field is beginning to encompass other histories and memories.[3] One of the problems involved in "postcolonializing" trauma studies is clearly the origins of psychoanalysis as what Ranjana Khanna has termed a "colonial discipline" (Khanna x). But rather than seeing this historical implication/complicity as a problem, as an indication of the inappropriateness of deploying psychoanalytic models for "non-Western" subjects, one might instead see psychoanalysis as a form or modernism, as a response to, and critique of, modernity. As such, like the work of contemporaries such Benjamin, we might see the work of Freud not only as a theory of trauma but also a traumatised – or better, an inconsolable – theory: works such as Freud's *Beyond the Pleasure Principle* might be read alongside essays such as Benjamin's "The Storyteller" as parallel attempts to "work through" modernity and as themselves registrations of the blow to (Western) consciousness that came to be associated with the events of World War One.

In the famous passage from "The Storyteller", modernity seems to arrive without warning:

> *A generation that went to school on a horse drawn street-car now stood under the open sky in a countryside in which nothing remained unchanged but the clouds, and beneath those clouds, in a field of force of destructive torrents and explosions, was the tiny fragile human body.* (84)

If postcolonial writing is continuous with modernist writing it is precisely because modernity arrives even more suddenly, and at least as destructively, when it is violently imposed from without by a colonial power.

The disjunctive nature of postcolonial temporality was signalled long before the advent of either "postcolonial theory" (as currently conceived) or trauma studies. In "Interior of the Novel: Amerindian/ African/ European Relations," an essay published in 1970, the Guyanese novelist and philosopher Wilson Harris argued that the postcolonial novel has to break free from the conventions of realism in order to represent the negation of individual agency and humanity at the heart of the colonial enterprise. In order to bear witness to this negation, the postcolonial novel has to abandon its moorings within individual consciousness:

> *Where [Georg] Lukács speaks of a 'middle-of-the-road' hero within his besieged marxist premises I must speak of a middle-of-the-landscape sculpture or waterfall or river or escarpment of jungle or rockface down which a phenomenal erosion happened, quite suddenly, precipitately, of conquered peoples. The Igbo [or Ibo] of Nigeria are a terrifying example of the engulfment which can suddenly overtake a people within a trauma of helplessness – external conquest, internal collapse. There is reason to believe that the earliest forms of tragic art were born out of a necessity to compensate such losses within the human psyche.* (16)

In place of Lukács' representative individual, Harris offers a non-human "character," a waterfall or river that bears witness to colonisation as the erosion of the human subject. Although this erosion obviously took place over a period of time, Harris stresses the precipitate nature of the event; for Harris, the "trauma" of colonisation is not so much a historical occurrence as a collapsing of history. The logic of this "phenomenal erosion" of time is indicated by the sequence "trauma of helplessness – external conquest, internal collapse." Colonisation is experienced as a breach of the Ibo's own world-historical view, as a dislocation of their ability to witness what is happening to them. Not only does colonisation seem to take place outside the tribe's own history, but it also places the tribe outside of itself, jettisoned into an alien modernity. The encounter with the white man is, in Cathy Caruth's formulation, an "unclaimed experience," an experience that was too overwhelming to experience at the time of its occurrence.

Caruth's work, with its origins in Freud's description of individual trauma, does not really yield a model of collective trauma.[4] Harris's description of trauma is useful precisely because it recognises the inadequacy of the category of the individual for dealing with collective catastrophes such as colonisation. One hesitates to understand such catastrophes as productive of collective trauma because it is precisely the sense of a collectivity that is destroyed by colonisation. I prefer the term "cultural trauma" here because the colonisation of the Ibo involved a precipitate loss of culture, the loss of precisely those rituals and beliefs that would enable a people to memorialise their history.

This brings us to the last part of Harris' claim: "There is reason to believe that the earliest forms of tragic art were born out of a necessity to compensate such losses within the human psyche." Tragedy is above all about community; although it often retells the story of the dissolution of community, the retelling is in itself a communal experience, a reclamation of a sense of being-in-common. Harris' analysis of the colonisation of Iboland is no doubt derived from his reading of Chinua Achebe's *Things Fall Apart*, the canonical novel of decolonisation published in 1958, two years before Nigerian independence. I want to spend the remainder of my essay revisiting Achebe's novel in order to investigate my claim that there is a certain continuity between modernism and postcolonial literature as responses to the "profound perplexity" (Benjamin 87) of modernity. In so doing, I want on the one hand to suggest that Bhabha is right to draw on Benjamin's diagnosis of modernity in order to explore the traumatic temporality of the postcolonial, but on the other to question Bhabha's claim that a suppressed history of colonial oppression can return as a celebratory, even redemptive, form of migratory aesthetics. By focusing on a novel that deals not with a postcolonial migration to Europe but with the prior European colonisation of Africa, I want to suggest that migratory aesthetics is already in play from the first moment of cultural contact, a moment that heralds the destruction of "indigenous aesthetics"[5] but also brings forth a postcolonial aesthetics that belatedly attempts to compensate for this destruction. This new aesthetics is migratory in the sense that it is without a homeland, inconsolably caught between the culture of the coloniser whose triumph it protests and the culture of the colonised whose disappearance it laments. Far from recuperating an indigenous tradition, *Things Fall Apart* marks the impossibility of a traditional aesthetics and the violent insertion – or, one might say, migration – of the Ibo into modernity.

III

Things Fall Apart is traditionally read as a kind of anthropology or what one might call ethno-realism, as the recovery of an authentic pre-colonial cultural tradition and as such antithetical to modernist aesthetics. But I want to suggest that Achebe's attempt to recall the colonisation of Iboland, the irrevocable disruption of custom and tradition that occurred in the late-nineteenth and early-twentieth century, is itself deeply modernist; that far from recovering a lost tradition, the novel is elegiac, melancholic, inconsolable. Achebe's titular citation of Yeats' poem "The Second Coming" ("Things fall apart; the centre cannot hold;/Mere anarchy is loosed upon the world") testifies to the violent process of acculturation to which Achebe himself has been subjected as a colonial subject. The title is sometimes understood as an ironic mode of "writing back" to the Western canon, and at other times as a sympathetic nod to Ireland's own experience of colonisation. But leaving aside the difficult question of (Achebe's understanding of) Yeats' relation to British and Irish culture, it seems to me undeniable that the title establishes a continuity between modernist poem and postcolonial novel as attempts to respond to apocalypse, or more specifically or symptomologically, as attempts to respond to the apocalyptic arrival of modernity.

In 1905, a certain Dr. Stuart rode into a village called Abame on a bicycle. The villagers, who had never seen a bicycle, killed the stranger. The British, in accordance with the nascent Collective Punishment Ordinance (1912), which legalised disproportionately violent responses to native insurrection, wiped out the entire village. In the novel, the inhabitants of another village hear of this massacre and struggle to understand the event, and to accommodate it within their worldview:

'They have paid for their foolishness,' said Obierika. 'But I am greatly afraid.' We have heard stories about white men who made the powerful guns and the strong drinks and took slaves away across the seas, but no one thought these stories were true.

'There is no story that is not true,' said Uchendu. 'The world has no end and what is good among one people is an abomination with others. We have albinos amongst us. Do you not think that they have come to us by mistake, that they have strayed from their ways to a land where everyone is like them?' (99)

While the characters can imagine difference/strangeness and grapple with what is often diagnosed as the "postmodern" problem of cultural relativism, what they are unable to think directly is the possibility of their own annihilation, the annihilation of their own stories, world view and value system. While Yeats attempts to conceive of cultural catastrophe through the Judaeo-Christian concept of the Second Coming, Achebe's characters attempt to understand their own annihilation as always already foretold by their oracle, and as the punishment for their own misdeeds. Both writers write history as apocalypse in an attempt to present the sublime advent of the new, the violence of the formless "rough beast" which, in its migration towards Bethlehem, confounds aesthetic judgement and produces a crisis of representation.

It is a critical truism that Achebe draws extensively on African oral traditions in his novel, incorporating proverbs, folk tales and other oral devices into his narrative. Read alongside Walter Benjamin's essay on storytelling, however, one begins to realise that Achebe's novel is caught between Benjamin's description of the pre-modern (pre-colonial) storyteller and the modern (postcolonial) novelist. Achebe, as the son of an Anglican minister, is historically and ideologically removed from the pre-colonial village life which he attempts to narrate. Writing on the eve of Nigerian independence, he is irrevocably part of modernity and his novel bears witness to the "profound perplexity" of that moment in which Nigerians must seek some sort of bridge between their postcolonial future and their precolonial past, a bridge over the gap in their history produced by the "missed experience" of their own colonisation.

The act of narration itself functions as this temporal bridge, as an act not of historical recovery but of the recovery of the means to remember. Achebe projects himself into the midst of the tribe[6]: veiling his status as the "isolated modern novelist … uncounselled [and unable to] counsel others," Achebe performs an act of temporal ventriloquism, adopting the voice of the pre-colonial, pre-modern storyteller able to draw on the wisdom of the tribe in order to tell the story both of how things were before the arrival of the British and of how the tribe – the intricate network of cultural practices and beliefs that constituted Ibo civilization – fell apart. The critical question becomes to what extent this projection of novelist as storyteller allows Achebe to function as a belated witness, and how far this belated witnessing allows his "people" to reclaim, to experience, as if for the first time, the history that they were not able to experience at the time of its occurrence.

This is how Achebe describes his role as a postcolonial African writer:

The worst thing that can happen to a people is the loss of their dignity and self-respect. The writer's duty is to help them regain it by showing them in human terms what happened to them, what they have lost. There is a saying in Igbo that a man who can't tell where the rain began to beat him cannot know where he dried his body. The writer can tell the people where the rain began to beat them. (159)

Like Harris, Achebe emphasises that the traumatic kernel of colonisation, that which severs the colonised from their history, is the ideological negation of their humanity, the calling into question of their very capacity for experience. Like Harris, Achebe draws attention to a collapsing of time and space, a radical disorientation that unhinges the Ibo subject from its own experience. In the quotation from Harris, the experiential subject is replaced by the landscape itself, the waterfall, river or escarpment that testifies to a "phenomenal erosion." In the passage from Achebe, the experiential subject is replaced by an African body, a body that registers only the brute sensation of being beaten by the rain. This sensation does not truly become a claimable experience until the writer belatedly reveals, "in human terms," what has happened to them.

On another occasion, Achebe goes even further in order to emphasise the inhuman dimensions of colonialism, the way it calls into question the category of experience itself.

Experience is necessary for growth and survival. But experience is not simply what happened. A lot may happen to a stone without making it any the wiser. Experience is what we are able to do with what happens to us. ... I believe that if we are to survive as a nation then we need to grasp the meaning of our tragedy. (*Morning Yet* xiii)

Here the rain-beaten body is replaced by an insensate stone, as if even the material affect of colonisation were not registerable. In all three passages it is art that seems to offer a way out of this failure of experience. Each passage effects a transition from the passive objectivity of the colonised body to the agency of the postcolonial artist, he who is retrospectively able to raise sensation or even a lack of sensation to the level of a meaningful experience.

In interview, Achebe underlines this fundamental *activity* of the artist: "The storyteller *creates* the memory that the survivors must have – otherwise their surviving would have no meaning" (Gikandi 10). But what would it mean to create a memory of a traumatic event? If trauma is defined as a radical loss of memory, then how is Achebe's novel able to remain true to the negation of experience at the heart of colonialism? What is Achebe doing when he translates the inhuman into human terms, trauma into a meaningful experience?

For postmodernist thinkers such as Jean-François Lyotard, sceptical of the artist's claim to redeem history, Achebe would be guilty of chronologising the achronology of trauma. The decision to narrate or historicise is always taken, Lyotard argues, against the formlessness of trauma, "in order to lend it form, a place in space, a moment in temporal succession" (17). Lyotard, writing primarily about the representation of the Holocaust, sees realist representations of traumatic events as *an*aesthetics, modes of anaesthetising ourselves against the affect of history, ultimately ways of denying that the rupture ever occurred.

Although Wilson Harris' own novels retain a humanist faith in the redemptive power of art, they eschew the conventions of realism in an attempt to represent the fundamental achronology of trauma. For Harris, the historical viewpoint of the colonised subject is not fully recoverable. His narratives are thus metafictional, unable to escape the consciousness of the author himself, as he shuttles between past and present in an attempt to bear witness to the lost tribes and absent presences of colonial history. Achebe's novels, by contrast, hide their status as authorial conjecture, and attempt to conceal their shuttling between past and present. Firmly located in the past, *Things Fall Apart* naturalises the act of narration, rather than drawing attention to its deliberate "creation" of a memory that the tribe – by Achebe's own account – never possessed.

But my point is not to condemn Achebe's novel for being insufficiently metafictional or self-reflexive. Rather, I want to analyse the consequences of Achebe's decision to recover, or rather to create, an experiential African subject. In Achebe's references to his own role as an African writer, there seems to me to be a wholly legitimate reclamation of African agency, a movement from the passivity of the stone or rain-beaten body, through the neutrality of survival, a state that lies midway between passivity and activity, to the activity of writing itself. Nevertheless, it is one thing to reclaim the *post*colonial agency of the African writer; quite another to reclaim – retrospectively – the agency of those who underwent the traumatic experience of colonisation. While his critical comments draw attention to his own agency as a writer and thence to the agency of his contemporary African readers and the active role they need to play in decolonising the African mind, his novel seeks to foreground the agency of its major protagonist, Okonkwo.

In order to recentre African history around an African subject, Achebe structures his narrative around a hero whose own actions, according to the conventions of tragic realism, drive the narrative. This ultimately leads to the suggestion that Okonkwo is himself responsible for the dissolution of the tribe. Rather than see this as a perverse rewriting of history, I want to suggest that this is the only way in which Achebe can translate the catastrophe of colonialism into human terms. In order to reclaim a history of estrangement as one's own, it would seem ultimately necessary to claim some sort of responsibility for that history. History that merely happens to us, arriving without warning from another time and place, is not understandable as history. It is instead only experienceable as the absence of history, rupture, discontinuity. If Achebe is going to "create a memory" of this anti-historical event, he needs to reverse the sequence. What Harris describes as "a trauma of helplessness: external conquest, internal collapse" needs to be translated into a historical narrative in which internal collapse *precedes* or even *invites* external conquest, in which the tribe, far from being helpless, plays a real part in its own downfall. The dissolution of the tribe needs to be presented as the logical culmination of *internal* contradictions, and the coming of the white man as an event that merely precipitates a process of falling apart that was already inevitable, a catastrophe that, like the conquest of the Incas, had already been foretold by the tribe's own oracles. To claim that the tribe's falling apart had already been foretold is in itself a way of gaining a measure of control over the catastrophe.

If tragic art does indeed attempt to compensate a community for their losses, it does so by lending catastrophe form, by placing the catastrophic event within a narrative of cause and effect. However, unlike other forms of narrative, tragedy usually offers a very limited degree of explanation: it asserts the inevitability of a given sequence of events and establishes the relationship between these events but remains silent as to the ultimate cause of these events. As Abiola Irele, in an essay on *Things Fall Apart*, puts it, tragedy is "the working out in men's lives of a rigorous fatality that transcends the individual's ability to comprehend or arrest its preordained events." If tragedy contains catastrophe within a narrative of "men's lives," it also opens up within that narrative an unknowable space "beyond men's comprehension." In Lyotard's terms, it lends catastrophe human form while simultaneously respecting its arbitrary, inhuman nature, its formlessness.

This suspicion of the ultimate arbitrariness of catastrophe is always in tension with the question of human agency and responsibility. The tragic event is presented on the one hand as the direct result of an individual's actions, as the consequence, invariably, of transgressing a cultural taboo, and on the other hand as an event that was pre-ordained and inevitable. On the one hand, the downfall of the hero is the result of his/her *hubris*. On the other, the action is foretold by an oracle and the hero's attempts to escape his/her destiny in fact merely hastens it, most famously, perhaps, in Sophocles' *Oedipus Rex*.

In *Things Fall Apart*, the question of free will and destiny is translated into the terms of Ibo theology, according to which a man's destiny is controlled by his personal god or *chi*. Early in the novel it seems as if the force of Okonkwo's personality and desire will persuade his *chi* to grant him success. After he is exiled from the tribe, the narrator comments: "Clearly his personal god or *chi* was not made for great things. A man could not rise beyond the destiny of his *chi*. The saying of the elders was not true – that if a man said yea his *chi* also affirmed. Here was a man whose *chi* said nay despite his own affirmation." (92). The passage is partly presented as a glimpse into Okonkwo's thought processes, as evidence of his lapse into despair, a major sin in both Ibo and Christian cultures. In an essay on "Chi in Igbo Cosmology,"

Achebe writes against such a nihilism, and reemphasises the Ibo belief in personal responsibility:

The Igbo believe that a man receives his gifts or talents, his character – indeed his portion in life generally – before he comes into the world. It seems there is an element of choice available to him at that point; that his chi presides over the bargaining. [When] a man's misfortune is somehow beyond comprehension, [it] can only be attributable to an agreement he himself must have entered into, at the beginning, alone with chi, for there is a fundamental justice in the universe and nothing so terrible can happen to a person for which he is not somehow responsible. (*Morning* 97, my emphasis)

Colonisation ruptures the Igbo world view precisely because it disturbs this sense of "fundamental justice." Achebe's novel, in attempting to recover this world view, must present the dissolution of the tribe as an event for which the tribe itself – or at least one of its members – is "somehow responsible." The narrative is thus structured around Okonkwo's violation of a series of taboos. If a community is to be held responsible for its own destruction, then it can only be because it has violated its most sacred beliefs. In turning his hero into the agent of his own tribe's destruction, Achebe finds a way of translating a history of powerlessness into a history of self-destruction, a way of keeping a history of alienation in the family, of *re-indigenising a displaced aesthetics*.

The novel thus begins with a celebration of Okonkwo's physical strength, a natural virtue that has led him to a position of preeminence within the community:

Okonkwo was well known throughout the nine villages and even beyond. His fame rested on solid personal achievements. As a young man of eighteen he had brought honour to his village by throwing Amalinze the Cat. (3)

The narrative then launches straight into an account of this famous victory. The opening thus operates as a direct (over)statement of African agency: here is an individual who, despite his weak and effeminate father, seems to have taken his destiny into his own capable hands. But the opening also operates as a tacit warning: Okonkwo's strength is also a liability. Known also for his short temper, Okonkwo is equally capable of bringing dishonour to his village. If his early actions bring him recognition and a place at the heart of the community, his later actions will cause him to be exiled and estranged. As the tribe collapses, Okonkwo's violence turns first upon his own next-of-kin and finally upon himself. The super-active body on which all eyes are focused in the initial wrestling match has been transformed by the final chapter into a corpse hanging from a tree, a taboo object from which the tribe must avert their gaze lest they recognise in it confirmation of their own alienation and the end of the warrior-values that at least in part defined their community.

Although Obierika claims that it was the British "who drove [Okonkwo] to kill himself," Okonkwo's suicide is in fact the culmination of a series of transgressions or "abominations" that Okonkwo himself has committed. The first of these is his violation of the Week of Peace, during which he beats one of his wives and thereby commits a crime against the goddess of the earth Ani. A priest tells Okonkwo that "the evil that you have done can ruin the whole clan. The earth goddess whom you have insulted may refuse to give us her increase, and we shall all perish" (22). It is significant that Okonkwo sins against the goddess of fertility: his phallic strength is here presented as radically unregenerative, as a force that may ultimately cause the tribe to wither and die. He is eventually fined for his violation, but clearly remains a liability to the tribe: a few weeks later he nearly shoots a second wife in another fit of temper.

The transgression that eventually secures the fate of both Okonkwo and the tribe is a repeated act of infanticide. Okonkwo is driven to murder a succession of sons, almost as if he were consciously severing the tribe from its future, actively seeking his own disinheritance. Okonkwo's violent nature is itself a reaction to the weakness and perceived effeminacy of his father, who would rather play the flute than labour to accumulate wealth and power. Okonkwo's whole life is devoted to disavowing this memory of his father. However, Okonkwo's disavowal of his father ends up forcing his own son in turn to disavow *him*: alienated by his father's violent ways, Nwoye turns to what he sees as the gentler religion of the Christian missionaries. Hearing of his son's defection, Okonkwo is only prevented from strangling him by the intervention of another tribesman. Nwoye then leaves his father forever.

Okonkwo's relation to his son parallels his relation to Ikemefuna, a boy from a neighbouring village who is given to the Umuofia in order to avert a war between the two clans. Ikemefuna comes to live in Okonkwo's compound and builds up a rapport with both Okonkwo, who comes to treat him like a son, and Nwoye, who regards him as his brother. A few years later, the Oracle decrees that Ikemefuna must be taken outside the village and sacrificed. Okonkwo is warned not to bear a hand in his death, precisely because "[Ikemefuna] calls [him] his father" (40). However, Okonkwo accompanies the men outside the village and when Ikemefuna runs towards him seeking his paternal protection, he draws his own machete and deals the final blow himself. As his friend Obierika puts it, this "is the kind of action for which the [Earth] goddess wipes out whole families" (46).

However, no action is taken by the tribe until Okonkwo kills another son, this time entirely inadvertently. During the funeral of one of the village elders, Okonkwo's gun explodes and kills the dead man's son. As with his previous transgressions, Okonkwo's crime is an offence not simply because of its violent nature, but because it is a violence that is turned inward, against his own kin: "it was a crime against the earth goddess to kill a clansman, a man who committed it must flee the land" (87). Okonkwo is exiled to his mother's clan in an attempt to right the imbalance caused by his renunciation of his effeminate father.

The seven years of Okonkwo's exile also function as an image of the tribe's own exile, for it is during Okonkwo's absence that the Christians consolidate their power-base. It is almost as if the narrative finds itself unable to narrate this period of history directly, as if it finds it necessary to banish its hero from the scene of the tribe's impotent decline. In Cathy Caruth's terms, it finds itself unable to reclaim the experience of colonisation: the insider perspective is temporarily lost and the narrator is forced to narrate the tribe's history from the perspective of a neighbouring clan.

One might say that the narrative is forced to *become migratory in order to record the destruction of its own home.* When Okonkwo eventually returns, after his seven years in exile, it as if his tribe has experienced, as Harris suggests, a phenomenal erosion of time: history, it seems, has taken the tribe unawares. Thus when Okonkwo finally takes matters into his own hands, "it is already too late" (124) and his actions merely serve to precipitate the tribe's dispersal.

Earlier in the novel, we hear of the massacre at Mbaino (which historically occurred at Abame): I have already discussed the characters' attempts to come to terms with this story of the stranger. As well as acknowledging that there is "no story that is not true," they also attempt to assimilate the event into their own understanding of historical causality: "Their clan is now completely empty. Even the sacred fish in their mysterious lake have fled and the lake has turned the colour of blood. A great evil has come upon the land as the Oracle has warned" (98). Although it is the British who act as the agents of the god's destruction, ambushing the village market day, it is again the tribe that is ultimately held responsible for its own destruction, for their foolishness in "kill[ing] a man who says nothing" (98). In the novel's end-game, Umuofia calls a meeting to decide whether to wage a war against the new government, another messenger arrives, Okonkwo's machete descends for the last time, and the tribe break into "tumult rather than action" (145). Realising that the tribe will now never go to war, Okonkwo commits the ultimate sacrilege of taking his own life.

Achebe thus transforms the history of an external conquest into a history of self-destruction, a catastrophe that the Ibo brought upon themselves by their own actions. A history that reveals the extreme vulnerability or helplessness of one's ancestors is transformed – at least partially – into a morality tale about the self-destructive nature of power. But the image of Okonkwo's corpse remains, because it carries with it the force of a certain incommensurability: Okonkwo feels that his warrior values are no longer commensurable with the reduced capacity of his tribe to act in defence of those values. Ironically, his own act of suicide transgresses that same code and his body becomes a taboo object that can only be buried by strangers. The self-destructive ending to the tragedy preempts the possibility of closure, and Okonkwo's dangling corpse becomes an image of the unconsolable.

Earlier on in the novel, meditating on how he has begotten an effeminate son, Okonkwo, popularly known as the "Roaring Flame," stares into a fire and comes to understand "that living fire begets impotent ash" (109). However, just before Okonkwo arrives at this rare moment of understanding, Achebe presents the reader with an extraordinary vision of what it means to be disinherited, a passage that recalls Macbeth's vision of his own usurpation and de-generation:

Why, he cried in his heart, should he, Okonkwo, of all people, be cursed with such a son? ... Now that he had time to think of it, his son's crime stood out in its stark enormity. To abandon the gods of one's fathers and go about with a lot of effeminate men ... was the very depth of abomination. Suppose when he died all his male children decided to follow in Nwoye's steps and abandon their ancestors? Okonkwo felt a cold shudder run through him at the terrible prospect, like the prospect of annihilation. He saw himself and his father crowding round the ancestral shrine waiting in vain for worship and sacrifice and finding nothing but ashes of bygone days, and his children the while praying to the white man's god. If such a thing were to happen, he, Okonkwo, would wipe them off the face of the earth. (108)

Within the terms of the narrative, the passage is partly ironic: for it is Okonkwo himself who has committed a succession of abominations or crimes against the earth. It is his own self-destructive nature, and not that of his son, that has left him contemplating "the ashes of bygone days." But the passage also resonates because it seems to speak across the gulf that divides Okonkwo and his ancestors from the modern Nigerian novelist. The passage almost amounts to an act of *prosopopeia*, an evocation of the speech of the dead. And the substance of this speech is both a lament and an accusation, an accusation that is in part directed against Achebe himself, the son of a Christian minister. Since Achebe is himself one of those whom Okonkwo accuses in advance of having abandoned their ancestors, is the novel tacitly conceding its failure to bridge the gap between them, even while it provides a belated expression of grief for those who "have not found the mouth to tell of their suffering" (125)?

What Achebe offers us, finally, is thus not the recovery of the culture of his homeland, but rather a novel that is itself in flight/fright, a migratory aesthetics that is perpetually on the move from a history that, for all its use of indigenous proverbs and folklore, it is finally unable to reinhabit. Just as Obierika is unable to countenance the sight of Okonkwo's dead body and must ask the white man's men to cut it down and perform the burial rites, the narrative itself seems to turn away from the site of its own ending, conceding the task of narration to the District Commissioner, from whose perspective the last paragraph of the novel is written:

The story of this man who had killed a messenger and hanged himself would make interesting reading. One could almost write a whole chapter on him. Perhaps not a whole chapter but a reasonable paragraph at any rate. There was so much else to include, and one must be firm in cutting out details. He had already chosen the title of the book, after much thought: The Pacification of the Primitive Tribes of the Lower Niger. (148)

Is the irony here aimed at the District Commissioner or at Achebe himself? Does the postcolonial novel supercede the colonial record? It certainly succeeds in displacing the colonial account, but it replaces it with an aesthetic that is in transit between pre- and postcolonial world views. For this alternative aesthetic is itself so implicated in modernity, so ruptured, that it can never constitute a return to the world of Okonkwo. Rather, its power derives from its capacity to bear witness to the discontinuities of (post)colonial history. Achebe's art cannot restore the precolonial tradition and must leave Okonkwo and his ancestors to light their own ancestral shrine, but, as Harris suggests, his tragedy may well function to compensate the living for their losses and provide them with a way of dealing with the perplexity of living the multiple migrations of modernity.

Endnotes

1. My syntax intentionally sidesteps the question of the relation between modernity and postmodernity here. Suffice to say that I simply see the latter as an intensification of the former, rather than a different socio-economic condition.

2. The events of 11th September 2001 are often cited as confirmation of Samuel Huntingdon's controversial thesis concerning a purported " clash of civilizations."

3. See, for instance Bennett and Kennedy (Eds) and Durrant.

4. Caruth's chapter on "Moses and Monotheism," which concludes that "history is precisely the way we are implicated in one another's traumas" (24), is nevertheless highly suggestive of the inter-subjective or even inter-racial nature of trauma.

5. One might argue that Achebe's presentation of Ibo life reveals a culture that is itself on the move, capable of adaptation to changed circumstances. Nevertheless, colonisation is overwhelmingly presented as catching the tribe unawares, pre-empting any internal dynamic of change.

6. I am aware of the colonial origins of the term "tribe," but use it not as the negative of supposedly more sophisticated forms of modern social relations, but to denote the melancholic desire for a pre-colonial community that is at the heart of Achebe's novel.

Works Cited

Achebe, Chinua. 1959. *Things Fall Apart*. New York: Ballantine, 1991.

———. *Morning Yet on Creation Day: Essays*. London: Heinemann, 1975.

Benjamin, Walter. "The Storyteller." *Illuminations*. Trans. Harry Zohn. London: Cape, 83–108.

Bennett, Jill and Roseanne Kennedy. *World Memory: Personal Trajectories in Global Time*. Basingstoke: Palgrave Macmillan, 2003.

Bhabha, Homi. *The Location of Culture*. London: Routledge, 1994.

Caruth, Cathy. *Unclaimed Experience: Trauma, Narrative and History*. Baltimore and London: Johns Hopkins UP, 1996.

Durrant, Sam. *Postcolonial Narrative and the Work of Mourning: J.M. Coetzee, Wilson Harris and Toni Morrison*, Albany: State University of New York Press, 2004.

Freud, Sigmund. *Beyond the Pleasure Principle.* 1920. In *On Metapsychology* 269–339.

Gikandi, Simon. *Reading Chinua Achebe: Language and Ideology in Fiction*. London:

James Currey, 1991.

Harris, Wilson. "Interior of the Novel: Amerindian/ African/ European Relations" (1970). In *Explorations: A Selection of Talks and Articles*. Ed. Hena Maes-Jelinek. Mundelstrup, Denmark: Dangaroo Press, 1981. 10–19.

Huntington, Samuel. *The Clash of Civilizations and the Remaking of World Order.* New York: Simon And Schuster, 1996.

Irele, Abiola. *The African Experience in Literature and Ideology*. Bloomington, Indiana University Press, 1990.

Khanna, Ranjana. *Dark Continents: Psychoanalysis and Postcolonialism*. Durham and London: Duke UP, 2003.

Lyotard, Jean-François. *Heidegger and "the jews."* Minneapolis: University of Minnesota Press, 1990.

Rushdie, Salman. *The Satanic Verses*. 1988. Dover, Delaware: The Consortium, 1992.

Thamyris/Intersecting No. 17 (2007) 161-176

Transgression of Everydayness in Heddy Honigmann's P®IVÉ: A Dutch Case Study in Stanley Cavell's Film Ethics

Wim Staat

In the Fall of 2004 it became part of Dutch average everydayness to see politicians, religious leaders, talk show regulars etc. discuss Islamic fundamentalism on television. Populists claim that the murder, November 2nd 2004, of one of Holland's national jesters, Theo van Gogh, proves that they were right when they warned about the influence of political Islam in the Netherlands; Dutch government officials claim that they were right when they led the way into a national debate on values and norms in Dutch society. For a while, it was not uncommon to find everyday discussions addressing the limits of free speech in Dutch public life. Paradoxically, the everydayness of our conversation was thematically determined by discussions of highest democratic values, free speech, in relation to cultural identity and migrant integration. These themes have not subsided in everyday discussions on European unification in relation to the so-called gap between the citizens of Europe and their democratically elected representatives. Even if disappointed by the outcome of referenda, politicians have claimed to be satisfied by the fact that the highest values in democracies have found their way into common debates. In film and media studies, therefore, it appears to be a good idea that if we study the film medium's relation to morality, we should focus on the way in which widely acknowledged values, like the freedom of speech, are given a specific audiovisual form, possibly reflecting the *Zeitgeist* of a specific community. Film scholars interested in ethics, it would seem, could simply ride the waves of popular demand and supply descriptions of mediated moralities.

In contrast, it has become difficult to claim that in everyday life we usually do not talk about highest values but rather embody values in and through the norm of our everyday conversations. In other words, these are no opportune times for those who claim that morality is not so much thematically expressed by participants in everyday discussions about free speech and fundamentalism, but is rather reflexively embodied by everyday habits, including habits of conversation. It is probably even harder to claim that the changes in the morality of Dutch culture do not revolve around values like free speech, majority rule and minority protection, and the separation between Church and State, which are, to be sure, democratic values expressed by constitutional norms, honourably and rightfully reiterated in public debate. It seems an act of self-marginalization, nowadays, to claim that the changes in Dutch morality might actually entail uncertainty about which values and norms are really at stake.

Consequently, Stanley Cavell's recent book on the moral relevance of film seems only marginally relevant as it tries to answer questions like "What is the public's business? How do we come to our knowledge of what bears on the common good of our lives?" through a discussion of films ostensibly lacking "front-page moral dilemmas."[1] There seems little currency in Cavell's way of dealing with morality, now that the time seems right for a (re-)introduction of film ethics thematically through dilemmas of free speech, of migrant integration vis-à-vis the preservation of cultural identity, or even of the rule of law in a European context. Nevertheless, like Cavell, I would want to resist the temptation of contributing to a discussion of morality and politics in terms of front-page dilemmas and indeed follow Cavell's lead. Therefore, I will first further specify Cavell's philosophical questions towards a film-theoretical evaluation of the way in which the everydayness of the common good relates to the film medium. My first question, then, is: how can film provide us with insights into the common good of the everyday? This entails an inquiry into the moral lessons inherent in Cavell's own canon of Hollywood comedies and melodramas of the '30s and '40s. Combining Cavell's descriptions of the everyday with what theorists of cultural identity claim to be the relevance of other (film) cultures for the understanding of their own, I should at least also ask: how do we come to understand the common good in the everyday through films that are more contemporary than Cavell's examples? If we acknowledge that film is part of our everyday experience, always also inhibiting us, not letting us see beyond the limitations of the everyday, we need to find out how contemporary film can get us past the confines of everydayness. My case study, in conclusion, explores the way in which Heddy Honigmann's documentary film P®IVÉ (2000) actually shows the workings of confines and possible migratory transgressions in and through the everydayness of Dutch religious fundamentalism.

Cavell on Everydayness in Film

In *Cities of Words* (2004), Cavell explores the common good as the public's business precisely through films because he believes they offer insight into the "ways in which ordinary human beings confront and question each other's conduct and character every day."[2] Cavell refers to Wittgenstein's late work and to J.L. Austin, and he sides with "their redemption of what they call the ordinary from its rejection in much of philosophy."[3] *Cities of Words* is a peculiar book, directly related to a university lecture course on ethics in which Cavell loosely combined the classical philosophers on morality and ethics with close readings of popular Hollywood films, mostly from the 1930s and '40s. Cavell's selection of films does not come as a surprise for anyone familiar with his film preferences already described in *The World Viewed, Contesting Tears* and *Pursuits of Happiness*.[4] In *Cities of Words* Cavell suggests a parallel in his reading of favourite films and favourite philosophers. Texts on canonical moral philosophers are wed to texts on Cavell's own canon of Hollywood films. Yet, there is no synthesis towards what could be an ethical film theory or a theory of film ethics. Typically, Cavell's philosophy develops towards a plea for the recognition of "moral perfectionism" as a truly American contribution to philosophical ethics.[5] However, as Stanley Bates points out, "moral perfectionism as Cavell understands it is not itself a *theory*."[6] There is some difficulty already, then, in any attempt to describe Cavell's moral philosophy as ethical theory, if not in the attempt to distil a theory of film ethics out of Cavell's writings on cinema. Nevertheless, Cavell's work on cinema, which is often presented as new descriptions of familiar Hollywood genres, offers a possibility to more positively characterize his moral philosophy otherwise than repeating what it is not. In *Cities of Words*, Cavell's ethical film theory should not be considered as a theory but probably more like a genre in which each genre member is a particular instantiation in and through which we can learn about the genre as a whole. Cavellian film scholar William Rothman points out the inherently reflexive relation between a genre and its members:

> *Each member* studies *[generic] conditions, interprets them, revises the way in which they have been interpreted, and thereby earns membership in the genre by bearing the* responsibility *of its inheritance.*[7]

The coupling of texts in *Cities of Words*, then, should not be mistaken for a hierarchical ordering in which a theoretical text is subsequently illustrated by a film interpretation. Each text of every couple is a different yet equal member of the genre of "pedagogical letters on a register of the moral life" (Cavell's subtitle).

Given the problems inherent in the attempt to characterize Cavell's moral philosophy as a theory, it should come as no surprise that Cavell in his books on cinema does not appear to want to position himself vis-à-vis film theorists. Still, with his emphasis on the redemption of the ordinary and his interest in reflexive instantiations of genre within film theory Cavell comes close to Siegfried Kracauer's (1889–1966) notion of the "redemption of physical reality" in so far as the latter claims the medium's appropriateness for the exploration and extension of habits in everyday interaction:

> *Films tend to explore this texture of everyday life, whose composition varies according to place, people, and time. So they help us not only to appreciate our given material environment but to extend it in all directions. They virtually make the world our home.*[8]

Everydayness, according to Kracauer, is not a contingent feature of some films; the everyday is featured in all films. Everydayness belongs to the nature of the film medium. This is not to say, however, that Cavell would endorse Kracauer's intimations of everyday life's redemption in and through film. For Cavell an appreciation of everyday life through film in some sense should provide us with the possibility of transgressing the very limitations that average everydayness imposes on us.[9] The insight into everydayness that films provide should be described as an insight into the changes of values and norms that have always dynamically determined the everyday as a process. For this purpose, Cavell relates Plato's "Allegory of the Cave" in *The Republic* to Howard Hawks' 1940 comedy *His Girl Friday*.

For Cavell, Plato's cave is "the cave of the everyday."[10] Hence, the trajectory that leads us out of the cave and into the light is a journey that frees us from the confines of the everyday and lets us transgress average everydayness. In this sense, there's nothing redeeming about the everyday. But that is not all: in spite of this critical presentation of the everyday, Cavell does not dismiss it. He extends the metaphor of the journey and claims that in our travels towards a concluding state of being human, "the measure of direction, or progress, is not assured by a beacon from afar, or what seems to be meant by ... a moral compass" that keeps us on the path, straight. Instead, what guides us is the motion we are in. When we are walking out of the cave, Cavell holds, it is quite possible that there is nothing other than the everydayness of the act of walking that actually gets us out of the cave. In this case, the journey "is no longer expressed in the image of a path, but rather ... in the idea of walking as such."[11] Differently put, the light that guides us is provided by the everyday habit that constitutes our very act of walking. Hence, the everyday features twice in Cavell's extended metaphor. We are moving out of the darkness of everydayness, and yet, we are guided by everyday activities themselves. We should recall that for Cavell the redemption of the everyday has emanated from Wittgenstein's *Philosophical Investigations*, not from Plato's *Republic*. Yet, there is no necessary contradiction, Cavell appears to emphasize, between Plato's disparaging description of the cave of everydayness and Wittgenstein's redemption of everydayness by way of the everydayness of ordinary language itself. In Cavell's metaphor, everyday activity itself is the embodiment of the good, as there is no moral compass outside everydayness. We should not expect any insights into the common good, therefore, from moral principles outside the everyday embodiment of the good.[12] Films, then, should not be expected to establish moral principles with which we can judge the moral rights and wrongs inherent in front-page dilemmas. They can, however, be considered as explorations of everydayness, and, more significantly, as explorations of the embodiment of the common good in the everyday.

How does this work for a black comedy like *His Girl Friday*? Provocatively, vis-à-vis Plato's exile of the poets from the city-state, Cavell claims moral relevance, not for classical tragedy, but for Hollywood comedy. As could be expected after his description of the moral relevance of the everyday, "there is no obvious way to get to the green world" out of what Cavell calls the everydayness of "the black world" of *His Girl Friday*.[13] Still, the common good is already there, right in the cave-like darkness of a Hollywood comedy:

A black world ... creates its own virtues. The virtues required for the limited good you can do in a black world (all the world we know there is) are, as divined by this film, for example, deviousness, charm, wit in the face of danger, a knowledge of what is of human interest, the appeal to others through sentiments you may not be in a position to authenticate, hardness in the face of desperation you cannot alleviate, a dangerous addiction to freedom, and an immunity to flattery and other bribes. (Are these virtues? Vices?).[14]

This list of virtues or vices (should we call them "inclinations," or "dispositions" perhaps?) characterizes both the protagonists in this film; it is what they share and what makes them belong together. Every virtue or vice in this list corresponds to what the protagonists do in particular scenes of the film. The list characterizes the film's characters, and in this sense "character" is an appropriate translation of Greek *ethos*, also referred to as "custom." The characters in this film form a community identified by its customs, by the day-to-day expression of wit, charm, and deviousness embodied by the characters' habitual reactions to the world and to each other. In *His Girl Friday* this sense of belonging is even made public: Hildy (Rosalind Russell) and Walter (Cary Grant) will get (re-)married. Note that according to Cavell it is the film, in an act of "divination," that lets us know what Hildy and Walter's virtues are; it makes one wonder how Hildy and Walter have come to know what it is that they share, for there is no moral compass outside their black world. For Cavell the answer is clear: it is only after the films' characters have separated that they are able to appreciate what it is that they were missing, i.e., their community based on character (*ethos*). This answer actually grounds Cavell's grouping together of a range of Hollywood comedies from the 1930s and 40s: these are the comedies of re-marriage, and here *His Girl Friday* is paradigmatic.[15] Hildy and Walter know, here and now, that they belong together because the temporary distance between them, a reflexive distance established within their own world, has served as the precondition for their divine insight.

Note, moreover, that Hildy and Walter's belonging together is recognized by them even before they know whether wit, charm etc. are virtues or vices. For a couple in the comedy of remarriage, Cavell explains, "what they do together is less important to them than the fact that it is together that they do it."[16] This recognition constitutes what Cavell identifies as a character friendship between Walter and Hildy, a precondition for their (re-)marriage.[17] As the relationship between Hildy and Walter is presented by Cavell as paradigmatic for the exploration of the common good in everyday life, we begin to understand that the limitations of the everyday and the resources the everyday may offer, saving it from atrophy, are both part of a description of a non-transcendental form of reflexivity.[18] The comedy of remarriage shows us, its viewers, that a careful exploration of the everyday might actually be a form of scholarship. In Cavell's terms:

[T]he origin and goal of the study that constitutes the highest activity of friendship is precisely the study that takes friendship … as its object. It is to achieve a new perception of your life, new speculation about it, but one whose condition is the friendship itself. Only in the state of friendship is it possible to "study" it, to perceive it … Of course there is something of a paradox here: the condition of friendship, the study that makes it possible, is not possible until the friendship has already been achieved.[19]

In this paragraph Cavell describes the paradox of not just one particular state of human being; indeed, the "highest" state of friendship, for Cavell a state of perfection, is paradigmatic for human relations in general. Within the community of friends, we study our own friendship. But to identify ourselves as a community, the community has to have been already there. It is the paradox of identity based on notions of culture as a shared way of life. Clearly, then, friendship is not confined to re-marrying couples, and what Cavell writes about the reflexive constitution of identity is not confined to Cavell's film canon either.

Everydayness and Cultural Identity

The mediating role of the comedy of remarriage is not an illustration of a philosophical problem by-way-of film. In actuality, the film medium appears to be closer to the everydayness of communal reflexivity than the language of philosophy can ever be. This is why it is film and not philosophy that will reveal, divine, to us the character of customs in everyday life. The film medium for us is what separation is for Hildy and Walter, a precondition to recognize the community we are in. And again, this precondition that allows our reflexive identification of ourselves, does not reside anywhere else than within the community of which average everyday media usage is a part. There is no guarantee that a film would make us reflexively reach beyond its average everydayness, and yet the transgression of the everyday is immanent to the film medium. In a vocabulary more familiar to critical film theory: this is why films can be considered not only as expressions of a) hegemonic power relations and b) petty bourgeois aestheticism, but also as expressions of c) social and political engagement, as "First," "Second" and "Third Cinema" respectively – although it would be a mistake to understand the taken-for-grantedness of hegemonic cinema as the equivalent of its confines, and the counter strategy of the politics of Third Cinema as an equivalent of the transgression inherent in the film medium. As Paul Willemen points out, a film almost never belongs to one category exclusively; moreover, a change of context can make a clear cut Third Cinema Film belong to the auteurism of Second Cinema.[20]

For Willemen, when writing "The Third Cinema Question," the Latin-American connotations of Third Cinema were less important than the Englishness of his own scholarly community in which left cultural theory had developed into a post-populist and post-deconstructionist intellectual crisis. To be sure, Willemen's article does refer to the political manifesto's of the late 1960s, of which "Hacia un Tercer Cine" (Towards a Third Cinema) by Latin-American filmmakers Fernando Solanas and Octavio Getino has become best known. However, rather than articulating an interest in 1960s filmmaking, Willemen's piece more concerns the 1980s revival in film studies of interest in the Third Cinema movement. This revival allowed Willemen's present scholarly community "to re-pose the question of the relations between the cultural and the political."[21] In terms of our discussion of Cavell's filmic everydayness, i.e., transgression as the precondition of reflexivity determining the identity of a community, here the community of British film scholars, was evoked by a reverential reference to Third Cinema's political commitment. More often than not, Third Cinema has functioned in discourses of "own," Western national-cultural identity, and according to Willemen it has done so in three different, albeit related ways. Willemen is critical about these three ways, but he is adamant in securing the stakes of this identity construction: "it is the precondition for a critical-cultural practice in Britain."[22] Willemen, then, does not so much want to avoid the reference to Third Cinema; instead, he wants to secure one of the three ways in which this reference might serve its purpose in the construction of a particular day-to-day practice, i.e., in the construction of an own communal identity.

This third way for Willemen is inspired by Mikhail Bakhtin. Willemen even gives it a Bakhtinian name: "creative understanding."[23] In his chapter on the national in film, Willemen develops "creative understanding" as the alternative to the two other ways of relating to the otherness of Third Cinema. The first he disqualifies because of its "projective appropriation."[24] It uses Third Cinema and other cinematic cultural practices to prove the universal applicability of the West's own norms. It is thoroughly assimilationist. The second reference to other cultures is criticized for its exoticism. Willemen calls it "ventriloquist identification."[25] It is the total immersion in oppressed cultures in order to speak in their voice. Despite its good intentions, however, this is a masquerade, Willemen explains, because it is just "the monopolist-imperialist's guilty conscience" speaking here.[26] Non-assimilationist, non-ventriloquist, creative understanding, then, is presented as "an approach which concentrates on the need to understand the dynamics of a particular cultural practice within its own social formation."[27] It is as creative as the Münchhausenesque transgression of the everyday from within the everyday, which we encountered in the comedies of remarriage. According to Willemen, Third Cinema should not be understood as an exotic film culture, it rather belongs to the everyday practice of one's own community, in Willemen's case: left cultural theory in the UK. Note that Willemen explicitly denounces using the term "dialogue" here, because "dialogue" in Bakhtin characterizes all communication and does not differentiate between the transgression of and confinement to cultural practices. Proponents of intercultural dialogue, then, should be tempted to abandon their "inflated reference to The Dialogic" and introduce "the crucial concept of alterity, of otherness."[28] But then again, this otherness should not be foreign to one's own community; the other is not a trespasser, so to speak. Nevertheless, otherness should let a community transgress its own cultural practices, and in this sense the intrusion of otherness into communal habits is a precondition for a community to understand its own identity. Habit change, induced by alterity, is a precondition for our insight, or should we say hindsight, into our own habits.[29] In Cavellian terms: alterity is not a moral compass outside everydayness; yet, it is alterity that redeems the everyday.[30]

In *An Accented Cinema: Exilic Filmmaking and Diasporic Filmmaking*, Hamid Naficy has identified Third Cinema as a "progenitor of the accented style."[31] Naficy, like Willemen, presents his readers with a re-appreciation of Third Cinema, because Naficy, again not unlike Willemen, believes that Third Cinema is not the exotic other of Western identity, but should be welcomed, just like Accented Cinema, for its transnationality, remarkably offering transgressive insights into the (im-)mobility of the national. Naficy indicates what contemporary films and filmmakers to look for, other than the Third Cinema of the late-1960s and the Hollywood comedies of the 1940s, when we want to consider contemporary film as the medium through which we explore our own cultural identity. Here in Holland, at the beginning of the 21st Century, our understanding of the common good, the everyday embodiment of values and norms should be helped by accented filmmakers, because their films supposedly offer us the best insight into what actually is closest to us, our habitual, everyday cultural identity. Exilic filmmakers, Naficy explains, are paradigmatic: "Because in exile the familiar becomes unfamiliar and the natural denaturalized, one is forced to face ... the essential constructedness of one's own structures of belonging."[32] Looking for a Dutch case in point, this would mean that even in a filmic collection of front-page moral issues, specifically, a series of documentaries about the *Ten Commandments*, the exilic filmmakers would let us see most clearly what would be the common good hidden behind those front pages.[33]

Towards Transgression in P®IVÉ

Let us look more closely at just one of the *Ten Commandment* documentaries, and try to understand what this film reveals about the habitual everyday. Heddy Honigmann's P®IVÉ (2000) is a film about the eighth commandment: *Thou shalt not steal*. What is it then that we are looking for in this film made by a child of the diaspora who is a migrant herself, clearly belonging to the group of what Naficy considers to be exilic and diasporic filmmakers? As we are interested in a creative understanding, in this case, of Dutch cultural identity, we should probably not focus on how Naficy describes filmmakers like Heddy Honigmann, i.e., as finding themselves "in an enviable position of being able to remake themselves."[34] This would side track us and venture us on a way towards the attribution of *auteur*-ship to Honigmann, unless of course Honigmann's "performed identity" would tell us more about the reflexivity required for the constitution of cultural identities in general, including that of the Dutch. The latter is a real possibility for the film medium because the distance that is "the engine of all exilic identities"[35] can also be understood as the precondition of the transgression of everydayness. What we are looking for, then, is not Honigmann the *second cinema auteur*; instead, we should ask whether the characteristic forms of accented films, i.e., Naficy's description of the aesthetics of exilic films, can be found as marks of transgression in P®IVÉ as well. As we have learned from Cavell, we should not expect these transgressions to shed any immediate light on front-page moral issues. These transgressions provide an insight into the actual workings of habits in the everyday. Obviously, then, we could work our way down Naficy's list of aesthetic features of identity construction in accented films (diegetic staging; the doppelganger motif; self-reflexivity; and self-inscription), [36] and this will probably be a rewarding exercise. For the moment, though, let us start the other way around and differentiate between the front-page issue clearly addressed in this film about stealing and the character/custom of the everydayness of stealing in Dutch society. For this purpose a particular controversy about a segment of P®IVÉ reported by an American weekly on the Internet, is remarkably revealing.

P®IVÉ is an episode film and it ups the ante in every subsequent episode in which examples of stealing are presented. The film starts with Honigmann's voice-over confession of childhood shoplifting. The next episodes are non-judgmental, fascinated explorations of the sensuous skills involved in a pick-pocketing act by two stage performers and the agile fingers of a street hustler. In every episode, the prize gets larger; Honigmann no longer minimizes the impact of theft. We change perspective: victims talk and perpetrators disappear. After this change of perspective, first there is the story of man violently robbed, twice in a row on the streets close to his home. Next is a woman's story of disappearing brothers and sisters in the 1970s South America. Mr. Jan Benjamins, third, appears to tell a similar story. Not a military junta but the Christian fundamentalists of an agrarian community in the Netherlands have stolen young Mr. Benjamins' older sister, although the theft in this case proves to have had an even greater, more devastating effect. In his sixties now, may-be his early seventies, Benjamins looks back on a traumatic experience in his youth. It is his own father beating to death his little sister. Honigmann makes clear that it was the ensuing communal silence in particular that has traumatically affected Mr. Benjamins. This fundamentalist community has not only stolen Mr. Benjamins' sister, Honigmann appears to argue, it has also stolen Mr. Benjamins' youth.

In P®IVÉ then, within just six brief episodes we have gone from fairly innocent to immensely guilt-ridden examples of theft.[37] Remarkably, Honigmann relativizes Mr. Benjamins' story by adding a final episode on a senior citizen's thrill of "stealing" a tram fare. Moreover, the intermissions between the episodes are stand-up routines by a comedian whom Honigmann allows to jokingly call God the biggest thief of all. This narrative embedding of Mr. Benjamins' episode has a double function. It builds up to a moral climax, topping all examples in the sphere of moral consequences of the act of stealing, but it also generates comic relief after serious dread. Hence, Honigmann's documentary, because of this structure, straightforwardly qualifies as an example of ethical exploration, almost as an obverse consequentialist treatise. Nevertheless, and despite the context of a documentary series on one of the most explicit examples of norms embodying values, [38] there are some details in Honigmann's documentary that emphasize the commonness of the good as belonging to the dynamics of shifting values and norms both limiting and potentially transgressive within the everyday.

One of the consequences of airing Mr. Benjamins' story on television could have been that the religious group to which Mr. Benjamins' family still belongs would become the subject of a criminal investigation. Apparently, these circumstances have urged Mr. Benjamins' family to contest Mr. Benjamins' allegations. Honigmann is reported to have said that she "would leave it to journalists to discover 'the truth' by exhuming the sister's cadaver; the film was about the farmer's truth and no one else's."[39] As an explanatory, but undeveloped suggestion the report adds that Honigmann calls the subjects of her documentaries "characters." The latter remark could tempt one to mistakenly presume that Honigmann, by calling her subjects *characters*, has projectively appropriated her subject's truth to fit her own. Honigmann's documentary truths would then be compared to the rightfully-questioned authenticity of certain realist art films that have their diegetic world populated by real persons, instead of star actors, in order to create true characters. On Honigmann's behalf, however, we should note that there is no contradiction in considering documentary subjects as characters and respecting these subjects' truths. Such is the result of acknowledging that a documentary character (as in *ethos*) may help us to creatively understand the habitual nature of cultural identity, not just the identity of the subjects in the film, but also and not least our own. For in this perspective and in the case of Honigmann's particular character in this segment of P®IVÉ, we should ask: what do the limitations and transgressions inherent in Mr. Benjamin's customs tell us about the everydayness of our own habits?

Honigmann has the camera close on Mr. Benjamins' hands when he tells her about the day he was visiting a friend for diner who casually had asked him how many brothers and sisters he had. Having a large family, quite common in orthodox religious families in the Netherlands, Mr. Benjamins tells Honigmann that at that particular diner party he started counting on his fingers, giving his fingers the names of his siblings. On camera, Mr. Benjamin again performs this act of counting and remarkably gets confused yet again. For that is what happened to him at the diner party: there were more names than sibling fingers. At that very moment, Mr. Benjamins realized that he once had another sister, that he grew up being silenced about her violent death, that he was led to believe that she had never existed. At that flash of insight, Mr. Benjamins explains: "I bellowed like a cow." The emotional outburst marked the beginning of a difficult journey: Mr. Benjamins' attempt to free himself from what he experienced as the suffocating, violent confines of his own community. Remarkably, the insight into the fact that he habitually failed to count his own sister among his siblings was not the result of an act of reason overcoming the habitual. It was the mutually interfering combination of at the same time counting on his fingers and casually telling about his siblings that interrupted the habitual and marked a moment of reflexive insight. From within the everyday, that is, not guided by an external moral compass, habitual everydayness was interrupted.

Something else becomes clear about Mr. Benjamins breaking through the confines of tradition inherent in his native community. Here, P®IVÉ again works like a phenomenology of the everyday. The film lets Mr. Benjamins tell us about the rules of the family: no speaking allowed, unless absolutely unavoidable, and even then preferably in monosyllabic words. Quoting from the bible, Mr. Benjamins still remembers how he was taught that not using the word of God in vain implied silencing children and silencing emotions. The film appears to explain that it is no wonder that Mr. Benjamins bellowed inarticulately at the very moment he missed his sister again. But what is most remarkable about Mr. Benjamins recounting of days he was not allowed to speak, is that we begin to realize that Mr. Benjamins' words throughout this episode do not belong to what could have been Mr. Benjamins' mother tongue. Indeed, the film shows that this man, whose youth was stolen, has never customarily learned how to speak in a language of his own. But Honigmann does not explicate it; she does not say it. It is because the film gets closest to the contemporary everydayness of Mr. Benjamins character, that it can be Mr. Benjamins himself who "tells" us about his lack of words.

We come to realize that the strangeness of his language is not attributable to a regional accent. In a sense, his accented speech more radically departs from any regional home dialect, for his language is not the language shared by a linguistic community, it rather is the language spoken by a man who has found quite another way to language, necessary for him to come to terms with, to be able to tell about the disappearance of, his sister. Mr. Benjamins' journey away from his own community, we understand now, must have implied the self-discipline of learning a language from a book, in all likelihood first and foremost from the bible. His accent is the accent of a non-native speaker who has found language to be a means of migration, and hence a means of transgression. Note though, that Honigmann's expertise as an exilic filmmaker does not result in an autobiographical sketch of her way of transgressing the habitual; however, she does find a way in which Mr. Benjamins can recreate his. The oddly biblical language in which Mr. Benjamins expresses the loss of his sister is a means of transgressing the community by way of what at first is not strange to the community. But even if biblical language as such cannot have been strange to the community, Mr. Benjamins' way of using it is. For anyone taught the lesson of not using the word of God in vain, the bible must have been an awe-inspiring book. For Mr. Benjamins it was the only language near enough for him to articulate his grief. From within the habitual everydayness of his own community, then, Mr. Benjamins has both experienced the interruption of the habitual and found a way to transgress the habitual towards a new linguistic practice with new habits of expression.

Honigmann no doubt has had her team of researchers investigate the religious group to which Mr. Benjamins once belonged. But it is only in and through her film, particularly in her personal and evocative camera work and simultaneous questioning resulting in the finger-counting scene that we witness the filmic act of researching the interruption and transgression of everydayness. Here, we begin to learn about the way out of the confines of everyday orthodoxy, as Honigmann's film comes closest to the very everydayness of a man who has broken with fundamentalism, not by way of a divination from outside, but rather by way of a new embodiment of the good in a new everyday practice. Honigmann's film, then, is about fundamentalism after all. And it could have been shaped according to the front-page dilemmas inherent in Holland's own contemporary morality. However, there is no formal indictment authorized by an accented filmmaker in Dutch society. Honigmann does not hold up an audiovisual mirror so much, through which we, the Dutch, could finally comprehend the double standards with which Muslim fundamentalism is generally abhorred and biblebelt orthodoxy absolved. Honigmann does not have such an explicit political agenda, even though P®IVÉ may be regarded, nevertheless, as an indirect political response to Dutch anxieties about Muslim fundamentalism.[40] Indeed, Honigmann follows through when it comes to appreciating the way in which a community's confines can be transgressed from within. A migrant herself, Honigmann appears particularly interested in the ways in which the aesthetics of the everyday reveal and conceal migrations from within the community. She is attentive to how Mr. Benjamins' biblical expressiveness can be a reference to what a community holds within itself as a perhaps rare occasion for change. In other words, Honigmann is not an investigative journalist unearthing a wrong that judiciary norms could be asked to correct; rather, Honigmann is a filmmaker and as such an investigator of the dynamics of the average everydayness that characterizes our Dutch identity. Characteristically, Honigmann's analysis would not dare to claim that we all agree about the highest values. It would emphasize the commonness in the common good and explore the ways in which the good is both obscured and continuously changed by the very everydayness of its manifestation.

Endnotes

1. Cavell, *Cities* 11.

2. Cavell, *Cities* 316.

3. Cavell, *Cities* 29.

4. *The World Viewed: Reflections on the Ontology of Film*, 1971; *Pursuits of Happiness: The Hollywood Comedy of Remarriage*, 1981; *Contesting Tears: The Hollywood Melodrama of the Unknown Woman*, 1996.

5. According to Cavell, the hypothetically concluding state of being human is best described by the moral perfectionism of Ralph Waldo Emerson (1803–1882): "there is no question of reaching a final state of the soul but only and endlessly taking the next step to what Emerson calls 'an unattained but attainable self' – a self that is always and never ours" (Cavell, *Cities* 13).

6. Bates 37.

7. Rothman 213.

8. Kracauer 304. Kracauer's theory of redemption is said to be related to Walter Benjamin's appreciation of the technology of film. Ben Highmore points out that both Kracauer and Benjamin were students of Georg Simmel (1858–1918) whom Highmore considers to be a founder of the tradition that "has often tried to register the everyday as the marvellous and the extraordinary (or at least to combine dialectically the everyday as both extraordinary and tedious)" (Highmore 17). Benjamin describes the dialectics of, on the one hand, the camera's intervention and surgeon-like penetration into everyday life "with its lowerings and liftings, its interruptions and isolations, its extensions and accelerations, its enlargements and reductions", and on the other hand, film's ability to mobilize absent-minded masses (Benjamin 217–251, 237 and 240–1 respectively). Kracauer emphasizes that films do not so much mechanically penetrate the everyday nor mobilize the masses, but rather virtually extend our everyday environment.

9. Ian Aitkin (2001) points out that Kracauer's theory of cinematic realism often was dismissed as "naïve," "conservative" and/or "ideological" particularly by Anglo-American critics. Aitkin's book in part is intended as an exoneration of European film realists, besides Kracauer notably John Grierson (1898–1972) and André Bazin (1919–1958). Remarkably, Kracauer's redemptive reality expresses a concern, Aitkin claims, about modern industrial society dominated by instrumental rationality. Kracaucer's expectations regarding film were expressed as an optimism not only about the film medium's capacity to first show the fragmentation and abstraction of modern life, but also about film's "ability to disclose the sensuous and ephemeral surface of reality, [offering] the possibility of transcending the abstraction inherent within modernity" (Aitkin 170). Kracauer is more like a Romantic thinker for whom the everyday transcends modernity. Cavell, not concerned with modernity in this way, is less inclined to embrace the redemptive qualities of everydayness.

10. Cavell, *Cities* 325.

11. Cavell, *Cities* 329.

12. Stanley Bates would point out that Cavell's reading of Plato here anticipates Cavell's understanding of Emersonian moral perfectionism: "What perfectionism wants is the possibility of self-transformation according to an ideal that is internal to the self's constitution rather than one that comes from without" (Bates 42).

13. Cavell, *Cities* 350.

14. Cavell, *Cities* 351.

15. Considering *Pursuits of Happiness: The Hollywood Comedy of Remarriage* (1981), one could argue that notwithstanding Cavell's personal interest in Hollywood classics like *It Happened One Night* (1934) and *The Philadelphia Story* (1940), it is Leo McCarey's *The Awful Truth* (1937) that he loves most.

16. Cavell, *Cities* 362. Cavell characterizes the relationship between Hildy and Walter, and all other re-marrying couples for that matter, as an Aristotelian friendship, described in the *Nicomachean Ethics*. Getting out of the cave of Plato apparently means getting into Aristotle's treatise on virtue.

17. "[T]he equal friendship of character ... is what Aristotle calls friendship for virtue, the highest form of friendship" (Cavell, *Cities* 363).

18. One could argue that Cavell here adds another chapter to an exploration already started in the 1970s. William Rothman points out that already in *The World Viewed* (1971), one of Cavell's "guiding intuitions is that American [films] of the 1930s and 1940s ... are about the human need for society and the equal need to escape it" (Rothman 208).

19. Cavell, *Cities* 366–367.

20. Willemen 1994b.

21. Willemen, 1994b: 177.

22. Willemen, 1994b: 201.

23. Willemen, 1994b: 199–200.

24. Willemen, 1994a: 212.

25. Willemen, 1994a: 213.

26. Willemen, 1994a: 213.

27. Willemen, 1994a: 216.

28. Willemen, 1994a: 213. Ella Shohat and Robert Stam use another Bakhtinian denomination for what Willemen calls "creative understanding." Shohat and Stam prefer "mutual illumination." They are less weary of the term "dialogue," as they explain that mutual illumination "takes place both 'within' and 'between' cultures and thus provides a model for dialogical cross-cultural study" (Shohat and Stam 241).

29. In Willemen's words: "the analyst's own socio-cultural formation is brought into focus as an historical construct, ... in need of transformation. The engagement with other cultural practices can (and in my view must) thus be geared towards the unblocking, or transformation, of aspects of the analyst's own cultural situation" (Willemen, 1994a: 216).

30. Given the need to understand alterity in a non-exotic way from within one's own cultural identity, I hesitate following Willemen in his description of the analyst's position. In keeping with Bakhtinian terminology, Willemen calls it "a double outsideness: the analyst must relate to his or her situation as an other" (1994a: 216). The analyst would then be outside his own community, just as he/she would be outside the other film culture. As should be clear from my analysis of Cavell's understanding of habit change in the everyday, I would support the description of reflexive, transgressive distance as necessary for the recognition of cultural identity, but I would want to avoid the connotation of moral guidance inherent in outside positions. Willemen would rightly warn against the danger of projective appropriations in Cavell. On the other hand, in a position of double outsideness, how do we avoid another act of ventriloquist identification?

31. Naficy 30.

32. Naficy 269.

33. Dutch public broadcasting organization IKON commissioned ten documentaries, one for each commandment. Ten prominent Dutch documentary filmmakers were asked to make a 50 minute documentary. The films were shown on public television in the winter of 2000–2001. Four out of the ten filmmakers would probably fit Naficy's category of exilic/diasporic filmmakers: Heddy Honigmann (1951) born in Peru, daughter of Holocaust survivors from Austria and Poland, Dutch citizen since 1978; Vuk Janic (1953), born and raised in Sarajevo, in Holland since 1994; Fatima Jebli Ouazzani (1959), born in Marocco, in Holland since 1970; Fiona Tan (1966), born in Indonesia, daughter of a Chinese father and an Anglo-Saxon mother, raised in Melbourne, Australia, in Holland since the late 1980s.

34. Naficy 269.

35. Naficy 271.

36. Naficy 271–279.

37. In an interview Honigmann explains: "I wanted to work towards more abstract forms of stealing. From candy, to the art of pick-pocketing, the life of a real criminal, to stealing love, or stealing the possibility to live a good life" (Doude van Troostwijk 10; my translation WS).

38. The materialization of values in the shape of a normative codex, here the *Ten Commandments*, can be recognized analogously in Rousseau's depiction of the principle of the people's sovereignty, holding that the expression of the general will of the people (*volonté générale*) is the law.

39. Scholtes 2002. Remarkably, Dutch newspapers have not reported on this "front-page moral issue." But even if Scholtes' representation of the controversy were contrived, the hypothesis would be no less relevant of a documentary filmmaker being interested in a truth that is not the truth of journalists.

40. In a 1995 interview on the occasion of her fiction film *Tot Ziens* (1995), in *De Groene Amsterdammer*, a Dutch current affairs weekly, Honigmann was asked about what seemed to be a dwindling interest in politics. Her first films, about Israeli oppression and about the nuclear arms race show a direct political commitment. Now Honigmann's films are less explicitly political. Honigmann replied: "When I made my first films, I thought I had to say things as clearly and directly as possible. ... I don't have that adolescent need anymore ... Poetry and Humor work much better. Moreover, my interest has shifted. Politics still interest me immeasurably, yet one way or another 'big politics' no longer fit my films" (Amsberg).

Works Cited

Aitkin, Ian. *European Film Theory and Cinema: a Critical Introduction*. Bloomington: Indiana UP, 2001.

Amsberg, Kiki and Aafke Steenhuis. "Tomeloos." *De Groene Amsterdammer*, 6 September 1995, viewed 15 December 2006, <http://www.groene.nl/1995/09_06/honig.html>.

Bates, Stanley. "Stanley Cavell and Ethics." *Stanley Cavell*. Ed. Richard Eldridge. Cambridge: Cambridge UP, 2003. 15–47.

Benjamin, Walter. "The Work of Art in the Age of Mechanical Reproduction." *Illuminations*. Ed. Hannah Arendt. New York: Schocken, 1983 (1968). 217–251.

Cavell, Stanley. *Cities of Words: Pedagogical Letters on a Register of the Moral Life*. Cambridge: Belknap, 2004.

———. "The Good of Film." *Cavell on Film*. Ed. William Rothman. Albany: SUNY Press, 2005. 333–348.

Doude van Troostwijk, Chris, Ed. *In het licht van de geboden: een werkboek bij de IKON-documentaire-serie De 10 Geboden*. Hilversum: IKON, 2001.

Highmore, Ben. *Everyday Life and Cultural Theory: an Introduction*. London: Routledge, 2002.

Kracauer, Siegfried. *Theory of Film: the Redemption of Physical Reality*. Princeton: Princeton UP, 1960.

Naficy, Hamid. *An Accented Cinema: Exilic and Diasporic Filmmaking*. Princeton: Princeton UP, 2001.

Rothman, William. "Cavell on Film, Television, and Oera." *Stanley Cavell*. Ed. Richard Eldridge. Cambridge: Cambridge UP, 2003. 206–238.

Scholtes, Peter. "Far Away, So Close." *City Pages*, vol. 23, no. 1119, 15 May 2002, Minneapolis/Saint Paul, viewed 15 December 2006, <www.citypages.com/databank/23/1119/article10390.asp>.

Shohat, Ella and Robert Stam. *Unthinking Eurocentrism: Multiculturalism and the Media*. London: Routledge, 1994.

Willemen, Paul. "The National." *Looks and Frictions: Essays in Cultural Studies and Film Theory*. Bloomington: Indiana UP, 1994a. 206–219.

———. "The Third Cinema Question." *Looks and Frictions: Essays in Cultural Studies and Film Theory.* Bloomington: Indiana UP, 1994b. 175–205.

Filmography

His Girl Friday, USA, 1940, 92 minutes, black and white. Produced by Columbia Pictures Corporation, producer: Howard Hawks. Written by Charles Lederer based on *The Front Page*, play by Ben Hecht and Charles MacArthur, directed by Howard Hawks.

P®ivé, The Netherlands, 2000, 50 minutes. Produced by Pieter Huystee Film & TV for IKON television, the Netherlands, directed by Heddy Honigmann.

IV. Relations, Conflations and Traumas

Thamyris/Intersecting No. 17 (2007) 179-190

Between Relation and the Bare Facts: The Migratory Imagination and Relationality

Isabel Hoving

Senses of Relatedness in Migrant Writing

As literary theorist Heike Paul (inspired by fellow literary theorist and cultural critic Susan Stanford Friedman) suggest, narratives of immigration can be seen as "scripts of relational positionality." Paul adopts the term to describe the different cultural perspectives interacting with each other in (women's) migrant writing. Could "relationality" be considered the decisive characteristic of a migratory aesthetics? The notion of relationality certainly has great potential, which since the last few decades has been explored within different disciplines, from the sciences to psychology and philosophy. Within the humanities, the concept takes pride of place in theories which might be considered of the more "anti-identity" approach (Deleuze), and moved from there to debates about migration. There, the concept helps us to move away from an easy essentialism that focuses on the migrant's identity as the exceptional problem to be solved, as if the problems of migration would lie in their problematic individual psychology. Instead, a relational approach might lead to the analysis of the political, economical, social and cultural dynamics that force people to migrate. The concept of Relation, developed in response to Deleuze's theories by Martinican writer, thinker and activist Edouard Glissant, as a complex effort at conceptualizing the dynamics of globalization and creolization, has become a key concept in both Francophone and Anglophone Caribbean studies and postcolonial theory and criticism. Glissant's poetics of Relation serves especially well as a frame for interpreting the imagination of space in migrant writing. Glissant's early evocations of relationality picture the cross-cultural world as a rhizomatic network of relations, in which the identity of every particular space, landscape, nation or individual is shaped by its cross-cultural and transnational relations to others, and therefore always in the process of transformation. Many migrant writers testify to a comparable imagination of global space as a layered, multiple, dynamic network. The spaces of the gardens described by Caribbean-American writer Jamaica Kincaid appear as the junctions in a political and economical network in which flowers, plants, and people are transported between various corners of the world, for reasons of profit. Surinamese-Dutch writer Ellen Ombre describes the layered spaces of the Dutch cityscapes, bursting with old and new references to the colonial exchanges between the Netherlands and its colonies, and to the actual power-invested relations between the multicultural Netherlands and the United States. Many other migrant writers join in this imagination of the world as interrelated. A new, transnational sense of (national, regional) space is created, to which migrants can relate as easily as natives. This new imagination takes its point of departure from the assumption that every location in the world is shaped by a global dynamics, operating in different domains, so that every location must be understood as the provisional effect of its relation with other locations, and with the global processes linking them. In this imagination, which captures the migrant experience of the world as a series of (accessible and inaccessible) transnational networks so well, relationality (as the anti-essentialist epistemological concept, explored in a range of disciplines) and interrelatedness (as the neutral term for the observation that specific life forms are interconnected in specific ways) are key-words.

The sense of space created in the literature of migration is often specific, though not always. Often, the texts focus on landscapes and the environment, rather than on abstract space. The abundant references to landscape, plants, flowers, gardens and plantations in migrant and postcolonial writing are particularly dense and significant instances, in which notions of political, economical, cultural and natural interrelatedness are explored. In this sense, migrant writing can well be read as environmental discourse. It ponders the social and cultural significations of changing national landscapes within an often destructive globalisation, and offers views of the dynamics of specific landscapes and townscapes, and the interaction between society and environment. On the other hand, environmental philosophers are also engaged in heated debates about the notion of relationality, in an effort to interpret the characteristics of the ecosystem, now that globalization represents such a threat. Their analyses imply social theories, and reflections on the relation between men and nature.

The omnipresence of the notion of relationality (in philosophy, literature, theology, science, and disciplines I have not mentioned yet, such as psychology) might encourage one to see a new direction for a series of theoretical practices. A critical move away from the Enlightenment fiction of autonomous, stable identity becomes visible, a move away from mechanitistic perceptions of nature and culture, towards a general theory of the world's relationality.

However, in spite of all its attractiveness, the notion of relationality is far from clear, and its productivity can be doubted. In this essay, I will argue that this term refers to very different, even conflicting models in migrant writing. For the sake of argument, I will differentiate three different positions towards relationality: a radical refusal of the view, and a focus on isolated, bare facts instead (sometimes in Kincaid); second, an interpretation of relationality as the convergence of political, social, economic and cultural forces in every location and event (in many migrant writers, including Kincaid, and in the early Glissant, who coined the concept Relation to capture his understanding of relationality); and, third, an interpretation of relationality as a non-specific transcendent force. To assess the relevance of the last two concepts of relationality to a migratory aesthetics, I will stage a discussion between three different perspectives: Glissant's poetics of Relation; recent environmental debates, which can be read as comments on basic assumptions in Glissant's work; and Peter Hallward's philosophical critique of Glissant's poetics. After that, I will come back to discuss the remarkable rejection of all relationality in certain moments in Kincaid's work, and evaluate their meaning for my discussion of migratory aesthetics.

Relationality as a Discourse of Resistance: A Debate between Poetics, Environmentalism, and Philosophy

In Glissant's early work, the intermingling of economics, politics, and the environment becomes highly visible. In his later work, notably *Poétique de la Relation (Poetics of Relation)*, Glissant, instead of continuing to explore the layered nature of particular landscapes, concentrates on the general principles of the dynamics of Relation. He then seeks to articulate a general poetics of the world's relationality. In doing so, he moves from an exploration of the density of the particular location to a consideration of, not the political, economic and cultural forces that have caused this density, but the dynamics governing those forces. Here he articulates a new approach to relationality, which has been both applauded by many, and criticized by some, for example by the philosopher Peter Hallward.

Instead of a discourse of identity that would help in coming to grips with the conditions of exile and dispossession, Glissant proposes a spatial discourse:

Rather than tear yourself apart between these impossible alternatives (alienated being, liberated being, being this, being that), summon forth landscapes, mix them together ..., imagine them, these landscapes, that blend into many ..." (*Tout-monde* 274, quoted in and transl. by Hallward 107).

Glissant's use of the term landscape (instead of space, etc.) is deliberate. Thus, he connects to a wider concern with the landscape, which is an urgent issue in the Caribbean. Chris Bongie, Elizabeth DeLoughrey, Dominique Licops, Timothy Reiss, and many others have analysed the Caribbean landscape (or the environment, or its flora) as the site where global processes of exploitation and creolization can be seen to converge in their most intense and violent ways, and which has called forth a long tradition of cultural and poetic identifications with the Caribbean land (Aimé Césaire is an oft-quoted example from the late-'30s). Glissant inscribes himself in that history when he explicitly proposes to summon up the landscapes, and mixes their complex social histories, and their complex environments. He does not stop here, though, but continues to articulate the general principles of these convergences. A comparison with environmentalist views might help in understanding the aims and effects of Glissant's approach. How do environmentalists react to his proposal to imagine the landscapes of the world as radically intermingled?

Glissant shares a few key-concepts with environmentalism. His poetics of Relation sees us all as intimately interrelated, participating in what Glissant calls the "tout-monde", the world-totality, or chaos-world. In the following quote, he links chaos to his own concept of Relation:

> *... the way Chaos itself goes around is the opposite of what is ordinarily understood by "chaotic" and it opens onto a new phenomenon: Relation, or totality in evolution, whose order is continually in flux and whose disorder one can imagine forever.* (*PR* 133)

The concept of chaos relates him to a recent group of environmentalists that has been inspired by chaos theory. This relatively new group of approaches in environmental philosophy, among which are Henry Allen Gleason's evolutionary ecology and individual proposals such as Alan Marshall's deconstructionist postmodern associationism, is now slowly moving centre-stage. These approaches are influenced by chaos-theory and postmodernism, and are organized around key-concepts such as dynamism, fragmentation, individualism and non-reductiveness. At first sight, there is great affinity between these approaches and Glissant's work. In contrast to Glissant's general poetics, however, I see in these environmentalist views a definite emphasis on specificity and concreteness. First, they insist on integrating pragmatic social and political analyses in their inquiry, and refuse speculative philosophies; second, (and this is a related point) they criticize reductive generalisations and universality, and insist on the concrete individuality, and untranslatable specificity of each environmental situation. Even if one may recognize elements from the early Glissant here, especially his insistence on the opacity and untranslatability of every location, it is also evident that the later Glissant has less affinity with this environmentalist reading of chaos theory: he then focuses on the *general* dynamics suggested by a non-specific reading of chaos theory.

The word "totality" in the quote points at a central paradox in Glissant's work: he aims at imagining a totality while opposing universalising notions, or, to put it in the terms of Natalie Melas: he wishes to articulate a "degeneralized universal" (135). Peter Hallward offers a less sympathetic analysis of this paradox. After stating that Glissant's critics agree that Glissant is hostile towards universalism and (especially Hegelian) totality (70), Hallward goes on to explain (sarcastically) that "Glissant is hostile to Hegel's 'totalising Reason' ... only to the degree that it is not totalising enough" (72). Referring to his opposition of the specific to the singular, Hallward argues that "[t]he essential thing to recognize is that Glissant's Relation is a properly *singular* concept" (122). From the perspective of singularity that Glissant adopts, the relations between locations do not spring from the specific nature of these locations. Instead, these locations would be mere expressions of an autonomous singular force. “Relation is a name for self-differentiating reality as such, it is not a ‘relationship’ *between* things”(122). In this remarkably sharp analysis, Hallward does not only argue that Glissant does not succeed in opposing universalism, but he also offers the terms that help to situate Glissant position within philosophical debates.

Thus, Hallward’s philosophical intervention supports the conclusions that sprang from the comparison between the environmentalists who are inspired by chaos theory and Glissant’s reading of chaos theory, namely, that Glissant is not very much interested in specificity and pragmatics. For their effort to understand the complex global dynamics that shape and change the environment, the environmentalists would find little of use in Glissant’s later work. Remarkably, their interest in the specific brings them closer to migrant writers such as Kincaid and Ombre.

Glissant’s work seems to show more affinity with earlier environmental discourses. This closeness is apparent in his use of terms like “totality,” his holism, and his insistence on the possibility to know this totality intuitively, from the inside. The “tout-monde” doesn’t ask for analysis but for awareness: “In spite of ourselves, a sort of ‘consciousness of consciousness’ opens us up and turns each of us into a disconcerted actor in the poetics of Relation” (*PR* 27).

The advocates of environmentalist philosophies such as deep ecology also insist on seeing the world as a “relational, total-field image” (Naess qtd. in Kirkman 21), “a web of interconnections that has its own internal unity, its own goals and interests” (Kirkman 8). Just as many organicist and holistic environmental philosophies, Glissant’s poetics of Relation responds often explicitly to Cartesian mechanicist discourse, and the critiques of mechanicism and dualism of the last three decades. These were articulated in disciplines as varied as science, ecology, and philosophy, in the wake of more general scientific revolutions at the beginning of the century that signified a break with Newtonian mechanicist science (Einstein’s theory of relativity, quantum physics, and big bang theory). In response, and through intense debates between ecologists and philosophers, organicist models were proposed, which assumed that living organisms, rather than being machines, were hierarchically organized wholes, which could not be reduced to the sum of its parts. In Europe and the United States, this approach was elaborated in theories which understood nature as a self-regulating, efficient system: climax theory and its successor systems ecology (Clements and Odum). This became the predominant view in the ’70s (Schouten, Keulartz, Marshall). It is a holistic, anti-mechanicist, organicist approach, though it did not break with dualism: in its most radical form, man is seen as exterior to nature, which is best left alone to develop to its greatest diversity.

The most ambitious environmental movement of the ’70s – the period in which Glissant had already established himself as a writer, poet and critic, though his influential essay *Le Discours Antillais* would only be published in 1981 – advocates a philosophical holism that emphatically strives towards an understanding of the world as a whole. This "deep ecology," a movement associated with Arne Naess, celebrated a philosophical holism that had elsewhere, in Germany and in the United States, lost much of its credibility because it appeared closely related to an undesired view of society: the submission of the individual to the state. Its very non-anthropocentrism attracts critique from socially committed ecologists.

Some of the comments from the opponents to deep ecology are particularly enlightening. Well-known ecologist and activist Vandana Shiva, for example, is deeply distrustful of unifying, totalizing discourses of the environment, and in a 1993 essay she argues why. Whereas in the '70s and '80s grass root movements addressed local environmental crisis, such as deforestation, which were identified as caused by multinational corporations and institutes, the '90s re-formulated these concerns as global environmental problems. A new agenda of global environmental problems appeared, reducing the many local environmental crises to only four (in the beginning of the '90s). The destruction of the ozone layer was one of these. The term "global" conceals the real causes of this problem, which is the production of CFC's by a small group of transnational industries. By redefining the problem as global, it now becomes the problem and responsibility of the millions of consumers of those environmentally destructive fridges and air conditioners – of which many live in the South. What is more, the producers themselves, who are the cause of the problem, are now called upon to provide a solution – that is, technological alternatives to the CFCs (Shiva 1993). Deep ecology does not seem to have much to offer environmental activists fighting this kind of global holism.

The comparison of Glissant's notion of relationality to the holism proposed by deep ecology yields useful insights into the ambivalence in Glissant's work. On the one hand, Glissant disagrees with the deep ecologists' binary opposition of generalized notions of culture to nature, and "man" to nature, in favour of notions that allow for a non-dualist, more political perspective (he proposes the word "surroundings" for the environment, *PR* 151). Here he seems to opt for another, non-dualist holism. That doesn't mean that his desire for totality is comparable to the political ecologists' much more critical view of totalising discourses. For on the other hand, there seems to be a definite affinity between his poetics and deep ecology's philosophy, especially where both are inscribing themselves in the phenomenological tradition. Deep ecologists argue that the experience of the world's organic interconnectedness is intuitive, and can be sensed "from within;" it is produced by "a perceptual immersion in the surrounding world" (Abrams qtd. in Kirkman 80). One recognizes the Heideggerian insight that this embodied experience would lead to an authentic way of being in the world, which could then serve as the foundation of an ethics (Kirkman 140). This approach is speculative, not empirical, and it can therefore not be refuted by empirical and scientific means. Yet, deep ecologists hold that this knowledge is scientifically sound. Glissant makes a comparable claim, as I will argue below. But this intuitive method is far removed from the strategies of a political ecologist such as Shiva. So seems Glissant's emphasis on language.

Just like Glissant, deep ecologist David Abram sees an intimate relation between the experience of nature as a "densely interconnected organic network" and language: "this dynamic, interconnected reality ... [lends] something of its structure to all our various languages" (qtd. in Kirkman 80). Glissant, too, uses the analogy with language (notably Creole language) to develop his theory of Relation, and he sees language – "la parole" – as the privileged way to inscribe oneself into the materiality of the world (*PR* 202). In Glissant's view, there is no gap between the landscape, or the world, and the text: "Then words, no one's fiefdom, meet up with the materiality of the world. Relation is spoken" (*PR* 202). As Jean-Paul Madou suggests, Glissant's text creates an almost tactile continuity between eye and world (75). The same dynamic, chaotic forces of Relation move text and world, and they are therefore linked metonymically.

This emphasis on language and poetry as the privileged means to "be in the world" need not be necessarily seen as a turning away from politics. It can also be read as a radical refusal of the all-invasive discourse of technology, which informs the discourse of global environmentalism criticized by Shiva and others. Only poetry would be able to evade the technological (and economic) endeavours to incorporate all possible alternative discourses on the environment, and erase their difference (Kirkman 140). This technological incorporation can be seen as a strategy of translation, as political ecologist and activist Larry Lohman has it: "[g]reen globalism appeals strongly to many Northern environmentalists ... because it tries to translate all important 'environmental' practices and insights into a common, comfortably modern vocabulary. This globalism ... satisfies a deep-felt Western ... need for containment and control" (159). This might imply that every specific, untranslatable language might counter that strategy of control. Glissant's insistence on the *opacity* of every specific location and moment in the world, and of its untranslatability, seems to spring from the same insight. However, as Hallward argues, Glissant's later work is less concerned with the specificity of languages and places, than with the general dynamics of creolization. His celebration of creolization as an autonomous force does little to oppose the universalism of globalism. The global market is perfectly at ease with notions of creolization.

This short comparison between deep ecologists, political ecologists and Glissant's poetics of Relation shows a telling ambivalence in Glissant's project. Hallward is right in suggesting that critics of postcoloniality and migration often read Glissant's work as a postcolonial project, aiming at a deconstruction of and liberation from (neo)colonialist discourses, and perhaps even the construction of a counter-discourse. However, the ethical dimension in Glissant's work is weaker than many of his critics might wish for. He takes his distance from the political environmentalists, who *do* demand an analysis of the specific nature of environmental disaster and global injustice, and an ethical stance against holistic discourses that veil particular responsibilities.

The problem lies especially in the ambivalent status of the knowledge produced in Glissant's work. If political ecologists suggest that specific knowledge is necessary to counter global discourses and take action, Glissant gives all priority to criticizing their assumption that such knowledge would be useful – though, on the other hand, he *does* claim to produce knowledge, stating that he wants to reconnect "with poetry's earlier ambition to establish itself as knowledge" (*PR* 138). However, he takes issue with the (deep ecologist's) claim that this knowledge might serve as the foundation for an ethics. He emphasises all the gaps in the chain poetry-knowledge-ethics-acting, without diminishing the importance of each element: "Let us not stop with this commonplace: that a poetics cannot guarantee us a concrete means of action. But a poetics, perhaps, does allow us to understand better our action in the world" (*PR* 199). As Nathalie Melas has emphasized, Glissant offers a poetics, and not an ethics of Relation. This in itself is clear. The confusion comes from his readers' understandable assumption that the knowledge produced by this poetics is the kind of knowledge that would be useful from the perspective of Glissant's own long-standing political engagement with the marginalized and the excluded. But the kind of knowledge Glissant offers appears to be of a much more abstract and general kind. As Hallward has it, "the *fact* of dispossession itself – has not changed ... Glissant's critique of dispossession risks conversion into an effective affirmation of dispossession (however 'positively' affected)" (120).

If one reads Glissant for his affinity with postcolonial projects of liberation, one might indeed feel uneasy with his insistence that his poetics doesn't offer a means to resist dispossession. But one can also recognize that Glissant presents a relevant argument against many present-day environmentalists (and other activists) who assume that the causes of the global environmental crisis lie in a destructive manner of thought, and that "good" thinking would lead to "good" practice. This assumption is also questioned by several critical environmentalist thinkers (Kirkman, Marshall).

Glissant's discourse of relationality, though articulated through a series of imaginations of multiple landscapes, yields a seductive but highly general, and, in Hallward's words, singular imagination of globalisation, with several gaps and paradoxes that are all too often overlooked or reasoned away. The ambivalent status of knowledge in Glissant's poetics is one of these problematic points (though it can be motivated), and so is Glissant's increasing lack of interest in the specific condition of the landscapes and societies he theorizes. This lack becomes problematic if one contrasts this attitude to the environmental activists and many migrant writers who do aim at such specificity, and for whom it is a political principle to resist universalizing discourses of whatever nature, and whose project Glissant often seems to share. The conflicts, however, often stem from the different needs and expectations between

Glissant and his readers, who feel perhaps most inspired by their political readings of his earlier, more specific work.

The recent studies of the often implicit social and political dimensions in radical ecological theories, such as Robert Kirkman's, prove that insights in one domain (such as the ecological notion of the relationality of all living beings, who participate in the same global network) can never be directly translated to another domain (such as global politics: even if this global discourse suggests the contrary, we are *not* all equally responsible for environmental destruction). In the same vein I would argue that one poetical insight – such as Relation – can never be a magical universal remedy against all natural, environmental, social and economical ills. Glissant's poetics may inspire, but the controversies surrounding his work suggest that a productive intervention in the processes of globalization has to be more specific and concrete.

Against Relation?

Glissant's extreme articulation of relationality as a singular force does not seem to address the migrants who are grappling with the specificities of their complex environment. The imagination of the specific multiplicity of the multicultural migrant societies I outlined in my first section, certainly does. However, there is also a last literary strategy I want to consider, a strategy as extreme as Glissant's, but completely opposite, as it focuses on the stark materiality of a particular object. Instead of imagining the totality of which it is a part, this imagination sees the object as detached from the many violent discourses from which it receives its usual meaning.

In one of Jamaica Kincaid's garden books, the narrator reports how, to her great joy and confusion, she encounters here

> *the most beautiful hollyhock I had ever seen. ... it was a most beautiful yellow, a clear yellow, as if it, the color yellow, were just born, delicate, at the very beginning of its history as 'yellow,' but when I looked at the label on which its identification was written my whole being was sent a-whir. It was not a hollyhock at all but* Gossypium, *and its common name is cotton. Cotton all by itself exists in perfection, with malice toward none; in the sharp, swift, even brutal dismissive words of the botanist Oakes Ames, it is reduced to an economic annual, but the tormented, malevolent role it has played in my ancestral history is not forgotten by me.* (110–11)

There is a curious tension here between two different views. On the one hand, the flower appears as the junction of the histories of colonialism, economic exploitation, destruction and murder; as such, this is a good example of a representation along the lines of the discourses of interelatedness. These memories, histories and discourses, triggered by the name *Gossypium*, are presented as real, immediate, and as actual as the flower before the narrator. "This is not a fiction; this all occurred to me while seeing this particular flower in bloom in Kew Gardens"(112). On the other hand, the flower's isolated presence seems to exist outside these discourses; its yellow colour is not part of history, but it has its own history, which it is only now starting. The two visions are never reconciled, but rather keep being juxtaposed.

One might recognize Kincaid's refusal of dominant discourses here as the desire to free a space outside of colonial and imperialist discourses, while acknowledging the powerful and very real effects of those histories and discourses. That is a continuous project throughout her writing: to find a material reality on which to base a sense of self, or a sense of space or history:

What to call the thing that happened to me and all who look like me? Should I call it history? If so, what should history mean to someone like me? Should it be an idea, should it be an open wound ... Is it a collection of facts, all true and precise details, and if so, when I come across these true and precise details, what should I do, how should I feel, where should I place myself? (114)

The narrator tries to find the meaning of history for those who are the descendants of slaves, by questioning the usual definitions of history – as an idea, as a sequence of events that happened once, and were then past. Instead, she proposes a concept of history as a non-causal collection of separate, specific facts. Here, she adopts the same look as when she watched the yellow hollyhock without knowing its name: a focus on the event or thing in its isolation, in its immediacy, in its materiality.

This strategy of fragmenting is not specific to Jamaica Kincaid's writing. Fragmentation, along with multiplicity, hybridity and creolization are phenomena emphasized by most theories of globalization and migration. The once coherent cultural and political systems, structures and discourses (such as the nation, discourses of history, colonial discourse) lose their relevance and coherence, while their parts may relate and interact in new ways with parts disengaged from other structures. Kincaid's art, however, is not aiming at interweaving the fragments, but of detaching these shards to an even higher degree, and to write about the bare fragments themselves.

Kincaid's refusal of causality mirrors the inability to recognize causal relations in schizophrenics, and the inability to relate to the external world of people who are deeply traumatized. Psychologist Judith Herman, sympathetic to the notion of relationality, suggests that the healing of trauma can only occur with the renewed capacity to relate to the world. Is Kincaid's representation of isolated fragments and facts an effort to linger in the space of colonial trauma? Are Kincaid's analyses of flowers as junctions of global processes the moments where she heals that condition, by embracing the discourse of relationality? One answer might be that Kincaid's focus on isolated facts and events is indeed mirroring the schizophrenia of the postcolonial condition, not the madness of migration (Hoving 211). The postcolonial Caribbean is still, Kincaid suggests, a space where people feel displaced, outside history, still unable to situate themselves inside or outside the dominant discourses that deny them full subjectivity. They are therefore unable to situate themselves within the larger world, and explain their situation. The holds of the reductive, confining colonialist discourses and the nationalist discourses continuing those are still strong. Kincaid's imagination of interrelatedness at other moments in her writing would then point at her capacity to situate herself within the more empowering discourses of migration, and analyse the global processes behind the exclusion and the injustice that become visible within such a more mobile context. If one accepts this answer, a migratory aesthetics would indeed be characterised by its success in interweaving and interconnecting the fragments disengaged from older structures and discourses, into a pattern woven from the active experience of the new global processes. Kincaid's focus on the ahistoricity of the fragment would represent an intermediate, (neo)colonial state, soon to be overcome.

But I am not so happy with such a hierarchical view. It seems to me that there is a range of semiotic strategies that are all part of migratory aesthetics. Many migrant writers (often women, and more perhaps than Peter Hallward thinks) *do* insist on imagining the specificity of the multiple landscapes of migrant trajectories and communities. On one extreme side of this range of writers, we find those who offer the general, singular poetics in which the specificity threatens to get lost, such as Glissant. But this tendency is balanced by those on the other side, such as Kincaid, who try to restore the materiality of the fragments and shards that have lost their meaning in the violence of globalisation. This focus on the isolated, individual, material entity that is placed outside discourse can well be seen as a necessary countermove to the flight into the imagination of totality. Migratory aesthetics cannot be identified with either strategy; it embraces all of these. As such, a migratory aesthetics should be seen as shaped by the tensions between the desire to know the world-wide movements of migration and creolisation, and the desire to renounce all knowledge altogether, and start anew with the bare materiality of an isolated, nameless yellow flower.

Works Cited

Glissant, Edouard. *Poétique de la Relation*. Paris: Gallimard, 1990.

———. Tout-monde. Paris: Gallimard, 1993.

Hallward, Peter. *Absolutely Postcolonial: Writing Between the Singular and the Specific*. Manchester and New York: Manchester U.P., 2001.

Herman, Judith Lewis. *Trauma and Recovery: From Domestic Abuse to Political Terror*. London: Pandora, 1994.

Hoving, Isabel. *In Praise of New Travellers: Reading Caribbean Migrant Women's Writing*. Stanford CA: Stanford UP, 2001.

Kincaid, Jamaica.*My Garden (Book)*. London: Vintage, 2000.

Kirkman, Robert. *Skeptical Environmentalism: the Limits of Philosophy and Science*. Bloomington: Indiana UP, 2002.

Lohman, Larry. "Resisting Green Globalism." *Sachs* 157–69.

Madou, Jean-Pol. *Edouard Glissant: De mémoire d'arbres*. Amsterdam and Atlanta: Rodopi, 1996.

Marshall, Alan. *The Unity of Nature: Wholeness and Disintegration in Ecology and Science*. London: Imperial College Press, 2002.

Melas, Natalie. "Re-imagining the Universal." *Unpacking Europe: Towards a Critical Reading*. Eds. Salah Hassan and Iftikhar Dadi. Rotterdam: Museum Boijmans Van Beuningen/NAi Publishers, 2001: 134–151.

Sachs, Wolfgang, Ed. *Global Ecology: A New Arena of Political Conflict*. London: Zed Books, 1993.

Shiva, Vandana. "The Greening of the Global Reach." *Sachs* 149–157.

Thamyris/Intersecting No. 17 (2007) 191-204

Running A(g)round: Migratory Aesthetics and the Politics of Translation[1]

Sudeep Dasgupta

Culture could provide a home for all those vagrant values which orthodox society has expelled as so much unproductive garbage: the deviant, the visionary, the erotic (Eagleton 98).

Interrogations

Migration as an adjectival term runs the risk of an unfortunate conflation: of identifying aesthetics as the unquestioned ground on which we then cultivate a new species of cultural terms: the migrant's subjectivity. Turning the terms around, aestheticising the migrant runs the other risk of evacuating the political. How should we read the relationship between both these terms? And what constitutes the political when it is wedged between "migratory" and "aesthetics"? My aim is to suggest ways of reading a particular film, Julian Schnabel's *Before Night Falls* (Fine Line, 2000), a film inspired by the life of the Cuban writer Reinaldo Arenas who died in New York in 1990. That interval between day and night, conceived of as a "loaming," already lends itself to a certain period of transition. Can we view the transition as a way of rethinking the political in aesthetics and migrancy? What Terry Eagleton in my epigraph calls "the vagrancy" of values housed in culture lends itself to a certain elective affinity with the question of migrancy. However, to leave this affinity between migrancy and aesthetics uninterrogated is to beg the question of a possible transition from the one to the other and back again. Interrogating this two-way movement might deliver a better understanding of how the political functions between notions of migrancy and aesthetics. How might interrogating the mode of this transition deliver an understanding of the political? If migrancy runs the risk of depoliticisation when conceived in narrowly aesthetic terms, or conversely, aesthetics "becomes political" only when migrant subjectivity is at issue, then maybe it is in the manner of the transition between the two that the political may be glimpsed. A caveat: questions of transition and migrancy do not secure an ontological place for a politics of culture; to assume such an essence is fraught with problems. It is not useful to ignore the subaltern or to hypostazise the transitory as the new subject of cultural change. Rather, if the political can be engaged with as the place of transition, it cannot ignore subalternity as the related underside to the discourse of migration and mobility.[2]

Migrancy is often the alibi for claims of the necessarily hybrid character of subjectivity and the conflation of the two is one way in which the specificity of certain forms of migrant subjectivity become erased and more globally homogenous notions of the nomad emerge. For example, the Deleuzian welcome granted to Documenta 11 at Kassel within the Indian art context is revealing.[3] The nomad gets aestheticised into the privileged mode of "being," thus erasing the messiness of history, cultural practices and their institutional validation from migratory aesthetics. Ranjit Hoskote argues "as a figure or trope, the nomad signifies the transgressive and emancipatory gesture ... it rejects borders, passports ... the zones it occupies are transient (28)."[4] This is a form of aestheticization coming from the "periphery" rather than the centre; the exigencies of how western aesthetics comes to migrate in other contexts is interesting from the perspective of a sociology of culture. My critique of the aestheticizaton of mobility and the migrant in western academic circles does not necessarily privilege a Third World space where such dangers are avoided. At a meta-level, aesthetic readings of the political and vice versa cannot be secured from a specific geographical or spatial vantage-point, be these sited in New York, Bombay or Havana. I am obliged then to signal briefly how the film reception also exemplifies the aestheticization of migrancy by coding it in interesting and interested ways.

In Transition: The Politics of Migration

A specific form of migrant subjectivity circulates in and around the text in question. *Before Night Falls* was published posthumously after the death from AIDS of the Cuban emigré Renaldo Arenas in New York in 1990. Based on the autobiography, the film was made by acclaimed painter Julian Schnabel whose last project *Basquiat* marked his first foray into film. The autobiography had already received much attention in the circles of the New York art scene in the early 1990s, and thus Schnabel's translation of the book can be situated in the context of a cultural sphere in which artists "from elsewhere" such as Basquiat and Arenas circulated.[5] "New York" functions like Eagleton's "culture" as the final resting-place for migrant artists. But in what ways do the "vagrant values" of visionary poetics and erotic politics get coded within this home? In the closing of this argument it would take some conceit to mark out a geographical space as the safe-haven in which the politics of migrant aesthetics can be protected. Rather, the coding of the value of transiency, deviancy and the erotic within and outside the film enables a rethinking of the political between migrancy and aesthetics.

There are important shifts at the level of the cultural coding of authorship here; these pass from Arenas' hands into that of Schnabel and then onto the reviewers.

This migrancy of textualization at the double level of form and authorship is, despite "Death of the Author" talk, important since specificity is crucial to thinking migrant aesthetics in a sedimented and nuanced rather than a free-floating and generic sense.[6] I first read the memoir when it was named *The New York Times* Best Book of the Year in 1993. The resonance of the book was closely tied to the art scene there around which Arenas had been an uncomfortable, interesting outsider (denied access to healthcare he died of AIDS three years after it was diagnosed). In terms of the passage from book to film, this literature to cinema passage was thus circuited already through a particular frame – that of a homosexual Cuban emigré, an outsider within his own country, finding refuge in New York and making it posthumously (again) to the silver-screen in a Fine Line (Time-Warner) production authored by Schnabel. This is a form of migrancy or movement at an intermedial level which, I will insist, results less from the tenuous hold of the signifier on the signified. Rather, this transition relies on the conflictual and relational trajectories of specific migrant subjectivities; it does so more than on the politics of cultural production of the other.

Its maker, Schnabel, further framed the film. Thus if Arenas' autobiography resonates as a public text from imprisonment in Cuba to "liberation" in the U.S., Schnabel's does so as well, though in a different way. His resonance is not just as a famous New York painter but as one who also migrated from painting to film. His first film explored another famous dead artist – Jean-Michel Basquiat. The death of the author critique is thus slightly misplaced here, for if migrancy whether in the art world or outside it is to be figured in all its density, authorship secures it an authority that can neither be dismissed nor uncritically celebrated. To hypostasise Arenas' autobiography into the "condition of immigritude" would be an aestheticization of politics, as much as to forget the coding of Schnabel's retelling of Arenas' story would be to forget the politics of aesthetics. My argument about the migratory aesthetics of authorship is thus not a revamping of the pathos of a dead artist dressed up as an unacknowledged genius but an insistence on the material specificity of migrancy in its differentiated experientiality and its relation to aesthetics.

Travelling Stories: Skipping From Shot to Shot – Sexuality, Politics and Mobility

The diegetic analysis of the film requires an analysis that jumps across it, taking a foothold on crucial moments which help filter some sense of its relevance for a discussion of migratory aesthetics. In this regard, the reading which follows, and the film as it emerges is not an *analyse a thèse*. Rather than an instantiation of "dramatizations of *a priori* ideas" (Bazin 96), both my argument and the film that emerges through it could be seen as a migration across selected and interested moments (in Arenas' life as depicted in *Before Night Falls* and my reading of it). A close-reading here minimally implies at least two things to me: a sustained engagement with every possible detail of the film that might be of relevance to my argument is neither possible nor desirable given that any such claim to comprehensiveness betrays the essentially fragmented character of an incomplete document (Arenas' life, the film, my analysis). However, comprehensiveness need not imply a disinterest in totality, since my reading of specific fragments in the text, and its relationship to extra-diegetic elements of social discourse, will attempt to think about and see questions of aesthetics and migration in a relational manner, as metaphors and metonymies of a larger social and political landscape. Neither interested in universalistic claims of migrancy (or aesthetics), nor politics, the reading that follows tracks specific dissonances and incommensurabilities as they refer to larger issues within which they are emplaced.

In a different, often polemic exchange with Guido Aristarco, Bazin defends non-dogmatic realist film (his understanding of neo-realism) metaphorically by comparing it to skipping on rocks in order to cross a ford: Such films rely less on the perfect dimensions of bricks which form a bridge than the found quality, size and location of the rocks in a stream which one uses to cross it. Bazin goes on: "I use them to cross the river. If the service which they have rendered is the same as that of the bridge, it is because I have brought my share of ingenuity to bear on their chance arrangement; I have added the motion which ... gives them their provisional meaning and utility" (Bazin 99). The analysis of the film that follows is thus the construction, through time and space, of the chance arrangement of shots and sequences that help me make the transition from migration to aesthetics through the political. The arrangement here is not just by chance, neither simply given, but also re-arranged and filtered through the specific questions a discussion of migratory aesthetics brings up. In that sense, both the film and my reading of it is the inscription or register of the meanings of movement in time and space; not only the creation of meaning through time and space but also the meaning *of the movement* in time and space, for both the analysis and the film gather meanings in their movement, or their migration, chronotopically.

The film opens within a matrix of gendered and sexual conflict, his mother running through the forests of *Oriente province* with the three-year old Arenas in her arms, returning to her grandmother's house in 1943, a failure. Arenas' schoolteacher visits the young boy's home announcing to his grandfather "Mr. Fuentes ... Reinaldo has a special gift, a sensitivity for poetry." An awkward silence follows, interrupted by the cautious glance of the child towards the head of the table where his grandfather is seated. Erupting into rage, the latter walks out of the house where he chops down the tree on which Arenas has carved "Christmas." It is also the period when the child watches the nude bodies of men swimming in the river from the bank, across from which his mother will scream abuse at the man who had absconded after fathering him. This matrix of multiple conflicts leads to migrancy; the family leaves for Holguin, his birthplace. No single cause can be attributed to the vagrancy of the family: the story begins between different relations: "the room full of unhappy women" bossed over by the grandmother, "the only woman who peed standing up and talked to God at the same time" and the symbolic violence of the male head of the extended family, his grandfather Fuentes; the fleeting presence of the absent father and the abandoned young mother; the enforced masculinity of hard labour and the poetic "sensitivities" of the sexually suspect grandson.

Yet as we will see later, this movement will get coded in interesting ways by viewers of the film for their own monocular interests, either within the grand narrative trajectories of U.S.-based socialist politics (which admits no criticism of Castro) or the equally American Horatio Alger narrative of personal empowerment, in this version through escape from Communist homophobia to Free World "success." While Arenas is defiant about his sexuality, it is important not to overlook that his desire to write and be published is what lands him in trouble with the State.[7] This is important because as we see later in reviews of the film, either from the socialist or "cultural" field, this fact gets systematically overlooked. Once more the complexity of this migration gets reduced in interested ways – so that a justifiable critique of homophobia flattens out Arenas' experiential and artistic experience in Cuba to the interested readings of a political kind.

Visually the lushness of Cuba, what one could call the visual poetry of Schnabel's Arenas in Cuba, is captured through music and the use of colour, all of this is circuited partly through the discourse of the painter's artistic genius.[8] What interests me more, however, is how this aural/visual experience keeps breaking up, within the frame and across it. So first Cuba: the film is structured like a circle moving out of the pit in the mud where the young Arenas plays in the dramatic opening sequences and returns to that same pit and the same opening sequence after his death in New York. In narrative terms, it is not a *bildungsroman* structure, a Horatio Alger story of rags to riches, or imprisonment to freedom, that holds the film together. Neither is it a rendition of the singular event of the *arrivé*, the sexual foreigner in one land who finds a home in the U.S.[9] Both the *telos* of a final homecoming and the radical openness of an arrivant's contingent wanderings are not discernible – rather it is desire, akin to Julia Kristeva's (1984) early materialist reading of the abiding tension between the symbolic and the semiotic, which structures and destabilizes the film.[10] Desire for artistic expression, political empowerment, sexual freedom and the material survival of the body are the many, often irreconcilable motors which drive the Arenas family in the film simultaneously in different directions.[11]

Visually and aurally, multiple contradictions interrupt any temptations toward unified and singular conclusions – the beauty of the Cuban landscape, marked in the opening with the staccato sounds of rain drops "reverberating like gunfire on the zinc roof;" the use of colour and black and white for documentary and filmed material; the celebratory acknowledgement of Arenas' budding artistic talent immediately followed by the secrecy required to survive under a regime of censorship.

This dissonance is captured within the home of Cuba in a nightclub scene where Arenas and his sexual and material mentor, Pepe (Andrea di Stefano), spend an evening. The subjective experience of Arenas' homoeroticism is guided aurally through a seemingly stereotypical visual lushness. This is not to fall into the paradoxical realist critique of realism argument that structures much contemporary visual analysis – that is, arguments where dissonance at level of form are directly read, in unmediated form, as representations of a fragmented subject. As his friend and occasional lover embraces a woman on a circular stage below the seated Arenas and a band occupies the background of the frame, the musical accompaniment to the visual frame of lush tropical sensuality goes awry. Rather, the camera goes awry because as we register that the music we hear is not being played by the band we see, our gaze is redirected away from the dance-floor to the face of a young man standing by the bar. The disjunction between the visualization of the band and the soundtrack's registering an "elsewhere" is slowly revealed through the wandering of the camera, and implicitly Arenas' gaze towards the man at the bar.

The visual and aural clues direct us, not to the clichéd eroticization of a tropical nightclub but to the musical rendering of the erotic gaze of Arenas within the screen. This shift from a gaze offered to us of a scene to the gaze within the screen/scene of the protagonist is choreographed through a dissonance at two levels. On one level, it is the non-synchronicity of the image (the big band) with the sound (Arenas' subjective position); at another, it is the movement from a seemingly clichéd rendering of lush nightlife to the erotic desire of Arenas for the stranger. This movement is underlined in the scene which follows where the camera lens literally becomes Arenas, their kiss not seen from a distance, of two men embracing, but the lens coming closer and closer to the young man's face till we realize it is rendering not our image of the two men, but Arenas' image of the stranger as his face blurs when they kiss. I signal this episode for a couple of reasons: to point out both the visual/aural dissonance, and the corresponding shift in the rendering of Cuba, especially one that is familiar to us from Bacardi commercials and other clichés of sultry coastal eroticism, to a personal, non-clichéd rendering of homo-erotic desire that becomes subjective to the point of erasing the protagonist's position by making him the camera itself. The traditional close-up's function of plunging into the psychological depth of the visualized character is reoriented as the visual and aural cross each other – the dragging, hypnotic music reveals the play of desire in Arenas while the visual image renders in increasing intimacy the object of his absent gaze and lips. One hears the subject while observing then merging into the object of its desire.

The wandering camera and dissonant soundtrack puts the spectator itself into the kiss, as recipient and initiator of it, rather than as a dispassionate observer from a distance. Further, both a diegetic and an extra-textual reading of the scene delivers multiple interruptions. The diegetic shift in perspective interrupts a visualization of friendship between the protagonists into desire between Arenas and a stranger while simultaneously shifting our focus from an externally-placed perspective on a social scene into an intensely personal development of desire between two strangers.

External to the film, this dissonance disallows any rendering of a simplistic move from one homogenized and clichéd rendering of Cuba, to an equally homogenized and clichéd rendering of the U.S., in particular of New York.

When Arenas finally manages to leave Cuba, under the infamous Castro-U.S. agreement to ship 10,000 Cubans in the 1980 Mariel "riffraff" boat lift, there is a dramatic shift in the use of colour. The first scene in New York is of Arenas and his friend Lazaro on the top of a car, seen from a bird's eye view as they smile, then from their perspective up at the strip of sky between the steel and glass lighted canyons of skyscrapers as powdery snow falls onto them. The visual dissonance between Cuba and the U.S. (the exodus is shown in vivid blues while the New York scene is grey) is matched by the music. The hypnotic drag of Ennio Morricone's "Surrounding the Casbah" written for Pontecorvo's *Battle of Algiers* accompanies Arenas' journey across the narrow strip of water that separates Cuba from Florida. Our first glimpse of the U.S. though is New York, as Lebanese singer Fairuz's "Mariyam," from the Voix de l'Orient recording sessions in Arabic, accompanies our view of Arenas as he gazes skyward up through the Manhattan skyline from the top of a driving car.[12] The darkness is followed by a watery grey light, which suffuses the screen, as Arenas is shown talking through a camera to us during an interview. In a voice-over Arenas comments: both the communist and capitalist systems "give you a kick in the ass. The difference is that in the communist system you have to applaud, while in the capitalist system you can scream (And I came here to scream)."[13] The irony of this statement is matched by the visual rendering of New York – in its grey, coldness, its impersonality registers Arenas' loneliness, his social circle in Cuba shrunken here to Lazaro (Olivier Martinez), punctuated by the occasional sympathetic remark by his African-American nurse as he is wheeled out of the hospital after another attack triggered by his HIV infection. Arenas is dying, and since he is without a passport he has no right to healthcare – "The Justice Department has classified me as 'stateless.' That means from a legal point of view I don't exist. I live up in the air and I don't belong to any country." The last scene in the flat he shares with Lazaro is visually powerful in its banal rendition of assisted suicide without any musical accompaniment. After swallowing an overdose of sleeping pills brought in an "I Love New York" carrier-bag, Lazaro reads aloud Arenas' "The Lover Sea" before smothering him with the same bag. Arenas struggles, then falls silent and immobile, our last image of him is a close up of his face covered by the "I Love New York" of the plastic bag.[14]

Contradictory Conclusions

The world of art is that of … estrangement … it contradicts (Marcuse 10).

I am not religious, I am homosexual and at the same time anti-Castro.
I meet all the conditions of never publishing a single novel.[15]

The reading of the film in the preceding section must hop over some further rocks and migrate briefly to the different receptions of the film. Winner of the Jury Prize at Venice, and garnering nominations at both the Golden Globe and Oscars, the film received accolades for the director Schnabel, its star Bardem and was generally well-received. The official website by Fine Line includes a synopsis written by the acclaimed director of *Kiss of the Spiderwoman*, Hector Babenco, which explicitly connects Schnabel's own ethnicity to Arenas' life and its rendition in film – "What is so interesting to me is that a Jew [Schnabel] who lives in New York – a man who is almost the paradigm of the "successful artist," and not a guy who grew up in Colombia or Brazil or Havana – arrives and tells us the story we were never able to tell."[16] The "we" in question are Latin Americans like Babenco and Arenas. For Babenco, there seems to be a structural affinity between Schnabel's insider (New York artist)/outsider ("Jew") status and his ability to create "the best Latin American movie ever made about the subject of freedom." The implicit assumption that Schnabel's incomplete (non-)belonging to a particular scene, whether artistic or political, enables him to make the best Latin American film, might inadvertently say more about the modes of economic and cultural valorisation of the migrancy of texts (Arenas' memoir) than any ontological claim of exilic authorship (Schnabel's film).

Politics, in particular an anti-Castro stance, is explicitly made in the packaging of the film. Included in the DVD is an interview Arenas gave French television in which he attacks Castro. Arenas' own denunciation in his memoirs of the ultra-*machiste* and right-wing Cuban community in the U.S. is lost in the film. The Cuban-exile community in Miami disapproved of his homosexuality (that and the fact he died of AIDS were left out of several obituaries). This coding of the cultural value of the film as an interested political tract continues in other arenas. In an interview, given, to the *Boston Herald* in 2001, the Spanish star of the film Javier Bardem comments "It's [the film's] not a problem of Cuba. … It's human beings. We don't like differences in each other. The colour of the skin or you speak another language. It's like [the pope] saying we have to condemn homosexuality. You cannot do such things." Bardem's universalist statement is prefaced by the interviewer Stephen Shaefer in the particularistic tone of its own location – "Although probably the most anti-Castro movie ever made, 'Before Night Falls' isn't seen by its star Javier Bardem as a political film." If for Bardem the film reveals a problem common to all, and thus not relating specifically to the theme of either migrancy or aesthetics in particular, his interlocutors feel obliged to frame the film as both explicitly political and "anti-Castro." Condensed in this one paragraph one can glimpse the tension between universalist claims and particular interests that interpret the film in seemingly incommensurable ways. Admittedly, the thrust of my argument is to counteract Bardem's desire to expand the specificity of Arenas' experiences to a general human condition. To follow the actor's argument would be to make migrancy just another sub-set of a broader set of either humanist or artistic concerns I cautioned against in the introduction. By a different token however, one cannot accept Shaefer's desire to see the film as "probably the most anti-Castro film ever made" without succumbing to a particularist argument that masquerades as the End of History and capitalist triumphalism.[17]

In a scathing 12,000 word review titled "The Sexual Politics of Renaldo Arenas: Fact, Fiction and the Real Record of the Cuban Revolution," Jon Hillson frames the film as the latest in a long line of attacks on Cuba from the "promiscuous" homosexual right, beginning with Tomas Gutierrez Alea's *Strawberry and Chocolate*.[18] While admittedly a far more weighty, and fact-strewn engagement with both Arenas' work and the Cuban Revolution, that Arenas' shifting politics (both in Cuba and the U.S.) is reduced to a *sexual* politics is significant. Hillson suggests that Arenas' homosexuality determines his politics which he then explicitly moralizes in terms of familiar clichés of bourgeois degeneracy. A discussion of Arenas' sexuality is opened in a section titled "Promiscuity vs. Self-Worth," where he proclaims "Arenas' sexual credo was the opposite of the central element the revolution sought to inculcate in the free women and men who discovered their talents and capacities in responding to complicated challenges, such as self-worth. Human sexual liberation, freed from the fetters of repressive norms, requires such a dignified starting point as negation of the alienating and abusive fetishism that defines sex and sexuality." Rather than engage in a tempting polemic with this moralizing and factually incorrect representation of the Cuban revolution, its leaders and the lives of other revolutionaries such as Trotsky, Mao, Luxembourg and indeed Marx,[19] the question of self-worth calls attention to the manner in which the "value" of Arenas' resistance to both Castro, the Cuban exile community in Miami, and the U.S., and his self-worth, travels. Signifier of the human condition (Bardem), "Latin American" fighter for freedom of expression (Babenco), worthless homosexual rightist (Hillson), Arenas' life and memoirs, as well as Schnabel's film, reveals not so much the floating, utterly contingent values that reside in "culture." Rather, it exemplifies a glimpsing of the political between the aesthetic and the migrant. It is in the transition from one to the other that the incommensurabilities in the film gather outside it and circulate in different directions. The text itself, originating in Arenas' memoir, then celluloid, hyper-text and reviews around the world, migrates.[20] The politics of the film's diegetic form and content circulates through contradictions, estranging us from a familiar or homely reading, proliferating localised and interested readings.

The inescapable dialectic between the symbolic power of social discourse and the semiotic destabilization of subjective stasis results in a subject-in-process, for Kristeva. The juridical understanding of such a term lends itself, I would argue, not just to Arenas' traumatic series of incarcerations within Cuba, but equally to his precarious status as a "nobody" within the U.S., denied access to health-care among other rights of domicile based on citizenship. Kristeva's reading of a subject-in-process thus broaches the legal implications of migrant subjectivity, which gets aesthetically reconfigured in incommensurable ways in the film. Narratively, Arenas' death cannot be separated from the continual reach of another nation-state's statute books once he has left his land of origin. The aural-visual language of the film further complicates a clear break from imprisonment to freedom. For Kristeva (1980), the materiality in question is that of the mark on the page, and the phoneme, exemplified in the modernist poetry and literature of Artaud, Mallarmé, Joyce and others.[21] My argument attends to what Christian Metz termed "film language" and moves beyond it to the discursive reception and circulation of the text in question. At issue in my analysis has been both the specific concatenation of image and sound in Schnabel's film, and the ways in which it has circulated and received attention. The contradictions Arenas sees in himself – homosexual, anti-Castro, non-religious – will paradoxically, despite his own estimations, result in numerous of his novels being published, some to great acclaim. Might the *non*-contradictions between his contradictory character and his later publishing success say something about how a certain non-belongingness, "up in the air, not belonging to any country" is getting valorised in our historical moment?

Can one talk about a migratory aesthetics in the ontological sense of its political value, even if one recognizes its variegated styles? I don't think so. Rather one might ask how a close reading of an intensely personal story, told in the first person, migrates through multiples voices and across multiple spaces – and what that reveals about the ways we situate the migrant, enclose him within our own theoretical protocols and make him the subject of aesthetic reflection. I am suggesting that the migrant and the vagrant values of the visionary, the erotic and the deviant have multiple homes. These are both incommensurable in themselves and as they are coded artistically, politically and socially. Culture is both homely and *unheimlich* in the sense of *Heimat* as ground or home.[22] The inextricable relationship between aesthetics, politics and sexuality can, when thought through the specificity of Arenas' life and the film, reveal how the "migrant" circulates. Further, the importance of the specificity of Arenas' subjectivity, as well as the choreography of image and sound underline a dissonance which must be understood as not occurring in the same way and to the same people.

To come full circle then to the beginning and ending. The camera rests in silence on Arenas' head smothered by the pillow and the "I Love New York" plastic bag. If we might be tempted to view the ending of his life on screen as pathos, the misunderstood perpetually homeless and hopeless migrant, our attention is jolted by a sudden movement as the camera moves rapidly along the ground and descends into the pit it had crawled out of at the opening of the film: the child Arenas, playing naked in the mud, turns toward the lens, and us, and freezes in mid-movement. Arenas' (Bardem's) voice-over begins to narrate "The Lover Sea," the poem Lazaro began to recite to the dying Arenas. The extract scrolls up the screen. It begins:

I am that angry and lonely child of always, that throws you that insult of that angry child of always. And warns you: if hypocritically you pat me on the head I would take that opportunity to steal your wallet.

Endnotes

1. "Untranslatable heterogeneities" done violence by an architectonics of Reason that grounds, less itself, than other heterogeneities, but running them aground. Derrida's focus here in this maritime metaphor (Derrida, *Rogues* 122) is of migratoriness. My focus will be precisely where migratoriness does run aground, not so much in itself only, but in the ways it is received and translated. The migrant often literally runs aground, in the heat-seeking sensors, the airless compartments of vehicles that run them around. That there is a topography of migration that is linked to the topography of Reason as in the Kantian architectonic is Derrida's point in "The World of the Enlightenment to Come" (Derrida, *Rogues*).

2. This ignorance has been called attention to and engaged in G. C. Spivak (1999). The title of her book *The Critique of Postcolonial Reason* suggests a development and critique of Kant's three Critiques and thus lends itself to an analysis of the relay between aesthetics and politics. For a recent critique from a feminist perspective of the over-valuation of migrancy and nomadism, see Wuthnow (2002).

3. See <http://www.r2webnet.nl/Kassel/kassel.htm> for a comprehensive view of the event.

4. See also Honrou (2002).

5. This is not to collapse the differences between the two: Basquiat's work was undertaken primarily in New York; Arenas' notoriety as a novelist had begun while he was still in Cuba via the publication of his first book in Paris.

6. See Moya (1997). Moya, for the purpose of this essay, does not engage with the specificity of the representational dimensions of migrant experience; she turns to social and demographic factors which while not unimportant limit the scope of her intervention by ignoring the specificity of modes of representation (the focus on form for example in aesthetics).

7. *Le monde hallucinant* (Paris: Editions Du Seuil, 1968), English translation by Gordon Brotherston published as *Hallucinations: Being an Account of the Life and Adventures of Friar Servando Teresa de Mier* (New York: Harper & Row, 1971).

8. The film is reminiscent in this respect, yet departs from the now-canonical Soy Cuba whose poetic visual and aural quality, without commentary, is shot in black and white. The importance of dance and music in the film is revisited in *Before Night Falls* though from a much more intense mobile and subjective set of shifting perspectives.

9. The arrivant has been receiving increasing focus as a trope and figure through which migration, hospitality and politics can be thought through. For example "Awaiting without horizon of the wait, awaiting what one does not expect yet or any longer, hospitality without reserve, welcoming salutation accorded in advance to the absolute surprise of the arrivant from whom or from which one will not ask anything in return and who or which will not be asked to commit to the domestic contracts of any welcoming power (family, state, nation, territory, native soil or blood, language, culture in general, even humanity), just opening which renounces any right to property, any right in general, messianic opening to what is coming, that is, to the event that cannot be awaited as such, or recognized in advance therefore, to the event as the foreigner itself, to her or to him for whom one must leave an empty place, always, in memory of the hope—and this is the very place of spectrality" (Derrida, *Spectres* 65). My reading of the film will mark a distance from this characterization. The "memory of hope" in Arenas' case resides precisely in being able to partake of the ambivalent privileges of the state he left and one which will not recognize him, renouncing him.

10. See Julia Kristeva (1984).

11. The terms "drive" and "desire" are used in a loosely psychoanalytic sense: it is the encounter with the Other of the subject in the sense of a demand which "produces the drive plus a remainder which remains implicit, that is, desire". See Marie-Hélène Brousse (109). On

the dissimulation of desire in its articulation in language, see Jacques Lacan (1997); on a theory of subjective destitution, see Lacan (1997), "The subversion of the subject and the dialectic of desire in the Freudian unconscious."

12. The soundtrack, composed by Carter Burwell, is accompanied by signature contributions from Lou Reed and Laurie Anderson.

13. Left out of the film.

14. The slogan "I Love New York" with the red heart-shape, is the registered trademark and service mark of the New York State Department of Economic Development.

15. Arenas in an interview redramatized in the film.

16. Online at <http://gfn.com/archives/story.phtml?sid=8289>.

17. Derrida's measured ambivalence to Fukuyama's "End of History" argument is undermined by its own demand for a non-demanding call to the Other (the arrivant) by the State. This radical openness that remembers the hope and annuls the content of Marx fails to acknowledge that the call, indeed demand, of the Other (the foreigner) for the benefits of state protection, when not heeded, lead in Arenas' case to death by denial. Kristeva thinks the performative subject-in-process installed in the act of the demand from the Other and thus acknowledges this tension in terms of a futurity that is dialectical rather than radically open (rootless).

18. <http://www.blythe.org/arenas-e3.html>. The biographic detail on Hillson describes him, among other things, as "a Los Angeles union and political activist, was involved in the defence of the Cuban revolution for more than 30 years" and having written "a 1998 front-page feature article on Cuba's fight against AIDS and its work in sexual education for La Opinión, the largest U.S. Spanish-language daily."

19. The explicitly political and erotic poetry of Catholic Marxist revolutionary Ernesto Cardenal immediately comes to mind as a counter-example to Hillson's moralizing description of "dignified" modes of sexual behaviour in a revolutionary Latin American context.

20. The politics of art in relation to technology and history is broached in Walter Benjamin (1977). For a discussion of his argument, see Paul Crowther (1993).

21. See Kristeva (1980) " Giotto's Joy," 210–236, which extends the analysis to painting.

22. This ambivalence in culture is registered between at least two texts of Walter Benjamin – "The Author as Producer," reprinted in Walter Benjamin (1999) and "The Work of Art in the Age of Mechanical Reproduction" (1968). "Any human movement, whether it springs from an intellectual or even a natural impulse, is impeded in its unfolding by the boundless resistance of the outside world. Few things will further the ominous spread of rambling as much as the strangulation of freedom of residence, and never has freedom of movement stood in greater disproportion to the abundance of means of travel" (Benjamin, *One Way Street* 75).

Works Cited

Arenas, Reinaldo. *Hallucinations: Being an Account of the Life and Adventures of Friar Servando Teresa de Mier.* Trans. Gordon Brotherston. New York: Harper & Row, 1971.

Bazin, Andre. "In Defence of Rossellini: A letter to Guido Aristarco, editor-in-chief of CINEMA NUOVO". *What is Cinema? Volume II.* Berkeley: University of California Press, 1971. 93–101.

Benjamin, Walter. "The Work of Art in the Age of Mechanical Reproduction". *Illuminations: Essays and Reflections.* New York: Schocken Books, 1968. 211–252.

———. *Understanding Brecht.* London: New Left Books, 1977.

———. "One-Way Street". *Reflections: Essays, Aphorisms, Autobiographical Writings.* New York, Schocken, 1986. 75.

———. "The Author as Producer". *Selected Writings, Vol. II.* Cambridge and London: Harvard University Press, 1999. 768–782.

Brousse, Marie- Hélène. "The Drive (II)". *Reading Seminar XI: Lacan's Four Fundamental Concepts of Psychoanalysis.* Eds. Richard Feldstein, Bruce Fink and Maire Jaanus. Albany: SUNY Press, 1995. 109–118.

Crowther, Paul. *Critical Aesthetics and Postmodernism.* Oxford: Clarendon Press, 1993.

Derrida, Jacques. *Rogues: Two Essays on Reason.* Trans. Pascale-Anne Brault and Michael Naas. Stanford: Stanford University Press, 2005.

———. *Specters of Marx: The State of the Debt, the Work of Mourning, & the New International, London*: Routledge 1994.

Eagleton, Terry. *After Theory.* New York: Basic Books, 2003.

Hou Honrou. "Some Notes on Nomadism." *Art India* 7.4 (2002): 26.

Hoskote, Ranjit. "The Nomad Position." *Art India* 7.4 (2002): 28.

Kristeva, Julia. *Revolution in Poetic Language.* New York: Columbia University Press, 1984.

———. "Word, Dialogue, Language." *Desire in Language: A Semiotic Approach to Literature and Art* New York: Columbia University Press, 1980. 64–89.

———. "Giotto's Joy". *Desire in Language: A Semiotic Approach to Literature and Art.* New York: Columbia University Press, 1980. 210–236.

Lacan, Jacques. "The direction of the treatment and the principles of its power". *Écrits: A Selection.* New York: Norton, 1977. 226–280

———. "The subversion of the subject and the dialectic of desire in the Freudian unconscious", *Écrits: A Selection.* New York: Norton, 1977. 292–325.

Marcuse, Herbert. *The Aesthetic Dimension: Toward a Critique of Marxist Aesthetics.* Boston: Beacon, 1978.

Moya, Paula. "Postmodernism, 'Realism' and the Politics of Identity: Cherríe Moraga and Chicana Feminism". *Feminist Genealogies, Colonial Legacies, Democratic Futures.* Eds. M. Jacqui Alexander and Chandra Talpade Mohanty. New York: Routledge, 1997. 125–50.

Spivak, Gayatri Chakravorty. *Critique of Postcolonial Reason: Towards a History of the Vanishing Present.* Cambridge, Mass.: Harvard University Press, 1999.

Wuthnow, Julie. "On Deleuze and the Postcolonial: On Nomads and Indigenous Politics". *Feminist Theory* 3.2 (2002): 183–200.

Thamyris/Intersecting No. 17 (2007) 205-228

Daydreaming Before History: The Last Works of Sigmund Freud and Charlotte Salomon

Griselda Pollock

I. Derrida and Said

With the all too recent deaths of both Edward Said in 2003 and Jacques Derrida in 2004, and the irreparable losses our intellectual communities have sustained as a result of their archiving, I am calling on both as my mourning for intellectual fathers, amongst whom I also place Sigmund Freud. Through the perversity of the interlocking histories of the twentieth century, all three found themselves dying as migrants, displaced from their place of birth, the culture of their familial homes. I want to identify a shared aesthetic in these migratory thinkers about the dynamics of culture, dissemination, and the worlded text. These non-trivial effects of their diverse migration constitute not merely the politics of their thought, but a possible aesthetic of deracinated intellectual identities.

Derrida and Said meet across the renewed interest during the 1990s in Freud's last and most difficult text, *Der Mann Moses und die Monotheistishe Religion* published in Amsterdam in 1939, and as *Moses and Monotheism* in New York and London in the same year.[1] In 1991, historian Josef Hayim Yerushalmi published Freud's *Moses: Judaism Terminable and Interminable*. Reviewing Freud's highly contentious argument that Moses was an Egyptian whom his Hebrew followers murdered, Yerushalmi's book is an investigation into Freud's thesis about cultural memory and tradition.

What readers of Moses and Monotheism have generally failed to recognise – perhaps because they have been too preoccupied with the more sensational aspects of Moses the Egyptian and his murder by the Jews – is that the true axis of the book, especially the all important Part III, is the problem of tradition, not merely its origins, but above all its dynamics.[2]

The book's deeper purpose was Yerushalmi's desire to understand Freud's own relationship to Jewish tradition: "The difficulty of interpreting Moses and Monotheism is directly related to the difficulty in grasping the nature of Freud's Jewish identity."[3] This led to two interesting moves. The first is the publication and analysis of a "canonical text" by Freud's father, Jacob Freud's inscription in Hebrew on the flyleaf of the Philippsohn illustrated Hebrew Bible he had given his son on his bar mitzvah at the age of thirteen, but which he re-presented to him, newly rebound in leather, on his thirty-fifth birthday 1891.[4] The paternal invocation of Freud's disavowed knowledge of Hebrew haunts Yerushalmi who concludes his erudite study of Freud's texts with a monologue addressed to the dead author: "Dear and most highly esteemed Professor Freud."[5] The ghost of this dead "father" is invoked by this device to confirm once and for all the Jewishness of psychoanalysis.

It was this monologue and its compulsive quality to know for sure "from the horse's mouth" that Derrida took as his text at the 1994 Colloquium: "Memory: The Question of Archives" later published as *Mal d'Archive /Archive Fever*.[6] The untranslatable title suggests a cultural affliction: the psychopathology of memory as Freud's lesson.

Yerushalmi's invented monologue with Freud is a conversation with a spectre, or like Hamlet, with a dead father in a line of dead fathers who, in being thus addressed, acquire the authority that is being created and interrogated in the same performative movement. This is the double space of the archive. Derrida argues that without this possibility of our phantasmatic investment in and memory of the dead others that are the archive in which we imagine "they speak," there would be neither history, nor tradition nor culture.[7] Culture becomes a sublimated hero-worship, and following Freud's thesis, it is, therefore, a conflicted enactment of both devotion and guilt-ridden murder. Interrogating tradition as a necessary haunting of the present by what is past but what is only belatedly animated as memory is, of course, the anamnesic core of psychoanalysis itself that tries to bring us face to face with the always determining complex of archaic sexual desires and aggressive impulses forged in infancy that create what we might call the psyche as archive, always containing the spectres with whom we are in permanent, phantasmatic conversation and interrogation.[7]

Derrida has learnt Freud's lessons better than Yerushalmi. The latter desires his spectral Freud to confirm his identity by affirming Jewishness. In effect, deconstruction works as the literary methodologisation of psychoanalysis. Through his own reading, Derrida reveals how historian Yerushalmi has failed to integrate into his historical method Freud's monitory lessons. Yerushalmi wants to offer a psychological history of Freud and his relation to his father, but without reference to psychoanalysis: that is, without Freud's teaching on the unconscious, the return of the repressed:

To want to speak about psychoanalysis, to claim to do the history of psychoanalysis from a purely apsychoanalytical point of view, purified of all psychoanalysis, to the point of believing one could erase the traces of any Freudian impression, is like claiming the right to speak without knowing what one is speaking about, without even wanting to hear anything about it. This structure is not only valid for the history of psychoanalysis, it is valid for all the so-called human and social sciences, but it receives a singular inflection here ... [8]

The subtitle of *Mal d'Archive* is *a Freudian impression*. Derrida plays with this term, as is his wont, throughout the book, catching the perfectly psychoanalytical dialectic between something that leaves a mere impression like the writing on the superficially erased wax block of the child's toy – what Freud called the mystic writing pad, a pressure that leaves a memory-trace or affect and, on the other hand, something that is an impression, an imprint, a text which must be read for both what it says and what is concealed beyond knowing – a condition that causes the effect of the *mal d'archive*, the fever of knowing, the burning passion for the haunting past, the promise of a secret forever hidden. We are both sick of, and made ill by, memory and its feints.[9] Derrida's book ends with some speculations on what can never be archived: the secrets concealed beyond even the intention to conceal – which makes a mockery of the historian and the archaeologist who seek secrets, which by definition can have no archive. Derrida does not pose the question of Freud's secrets to Freud biographically, deluded as was Yerushalmi, but only of Freud, and hence of all of us caught in this game; afflicted by the *mal d'archive*. The archive is thus the textualisation of cultural memory populated by our own ghostly projections and phantasies, the encryption of both a conscious record and an unconscious impression. Using psychoanalysis deconstructively as a reading process balances delicately between an anti-biographical attention to constitutional predicaments of all subjects determined by language and its otherness, and a sense of the subjectivised particularity of each utterance or text marked precisely as such by that which is secreted within it. If the aesthetic is a form of knowing that is not quite cognition and a form of sensing that is not merely perceptual, but, as the French verb *sentir* retains, is also tinged with affects, perhaps we might think the space between history, memory and subjectivity through the aesthetic "impression."

In 2003 Edward Said lectured at the Freud Museum on Freud's *Moses and Monotheism* under the title *Freud and the Non-European*.[10] As literary and post-colonial critic, Said studied writer Freud's "late style" evidenced in the Moses book. He drew contemporary relevance out of the contradictions and unevenness that disfigure Freud's Moses text as it struggles with ethnicities, cultural memories and identities. Freud's text interests Said for the opposite reasons to Yerushalmi, as one would expect. Said endorses Freud's continuing struggles against the secret fixity of ethnic, national or cultural identity by his shocking conviction that Judaism was created by the African monotheist: "If Moses was an Egyptian ... " being Freud's key thesis.

Said also showed, however, that the historically and culturally situated Freud could not escape his own inner necessity to reclaim the Europeanness of the Jewish people – he names them a remnant of Mediterranean peoples – faced as he was at the time of writing with an anti-Semitism that sought to render Jewish Europeans alien not only from the German nation but foreign to humanity itself.[11] None the less, Freud's possibility for post-European insight, according to Said, was to think this problem of the radical instability of identity resulting from the legend of the foreigner at the origin of a tradition, inside which so many have suffered as forced exiles, as not a mere plea for "tolerance and compassion." Said endorses Freud's insistence on the problem of traumatically created alienation at the heart of cultural identity as a "troubling, disabling, destabilizing, secular wound" – "the essence of the cosmopolitan, from which there can be no recovery, no state of resolved Stoic calm, and no utopian reconciliation even within itself."[12] Said used Freud's thinking about the ambivalence of identity as a means to imagine "a condition of a politics of Diaspora life" in which two currently warring peoples of Israel and Palestine are imagined as parts in a bi-national state rather than as "antagonists of each other's history and underlying reality."[12] Said's strong sense of worlded creative practice and politically engaged intellectual practice, therefore, claimed Freud as a mediating figure for a contemporary crisis of racialised violence and ethnic conflict giving back a contemporary politics to the aesthetics of his late style.

I want now to difference this archive. I want to bring the ageing Freud, writing his last book into a frame with a young woman painting her first big work. The possibility for this spectral conversation – pace Yerushalmi's archival fantasy – lies neither in art history's protocols nor in those of psychoanalysis. Drawing on both Said's historical location of the text and Derrida's analytical readings of its own undoings, I am searching for a way to address migratory aesthetics through my current preoccupation with trauma and cultural memory, which begins with a study of an Amsterdam archive where the work of the German-Jewish exiled and murdered Charlotte Salomon (1917–1943) is kept through the accidents of history.

II. Deprivatising Charlotte

In 1963, the first selections of a massive, single art work dating from 1942, comprising 784 paintings and textual overlays and titled *Leben? Oder Theater?* was published under the title *Charlotte: A Diary in Pictures by Charlotte Salomon*.[13] Ladened with its initiating post Eichmann-trial moment of Holocaust memory, this vast art work was corralled in 1963 into a gendered and familiarising frame that invites comparison with the other work that had since the mid-1950s become the key icon of Holocaust commemoration: *The Diary of Anna Frank*, first published in Dutch in 1947, translated into English and other European languages in 1952, made into a Broadway play in 1956 and a Hollywood film in 1959.

The first page of *Leben? Oder Theater?*, however, clearly defines its own genre: a Singspiel (musical play or operetta) and identifies its author by an entwined pair of initials, CS, that formed a play on the shape of the swastika. The work is, therefore, not a diary in form, genre or intention. Partaking in a Weimar legacy of theatricality, the playbill cover is followed by a cast list: the same three colours are now draped as proscenium curtains announcing a three-coloured operetta reminiscent of Brecht's staged and then filmed *Drei-Groschen Oper / Three-Penny Opera* (Pabst, 1931), complete with names that caricature real persons from the Berlin Jewish community including CS – who appears as Charlotte Kann, i.e. Charlotte [is] Able, an elderly couple Knarre: the Groaners, diva stepmother, Paulinka Bimbam, Dr Singsang, conductor and founder of the Kulturbund and Amadeus Daberlohn, i.e. a penniless Mozart, a traumatised survivor of the WWI trenches who finds salvation in a Nietszchean philosophy of sexuality, creativity and the singing voice.

The first and only public combination of the artist's name and artistic profession during her lifetime comes not from an art historical but a genocidal archive. It is the typed list for Transport 60, 7 October 1943 from Drancy that arrived in Auschwitz 10 October 1943. She is listed as "Nagler, Charlotte" following her marriage in 1943 to fellow refugee Alexander Nagler. In a document in which designating a profession is a strategy to offer a possibly life-saving skill, many of the women, especially the elderly ones are listed "ohne" – without. Their birthdates and lack of skills are death warrants. There are tailors, bookkeepers, students, shopkeepers, jewellers and lawyers. Charlotte Nagler is identified as the only Zeichnerin: graphic artist. Despite such a claim for a useful skill, the 26 year-old artist, was sent to the gas chamber on her arrival in Auschwitz on 10 October 1943. This was because she was five months pregnant, a gendered potentiality proscribed by the terms of Final Solution of the Jewish Question minuted in January 1942 that sought to eradicate "the germ cell of a new Jewish revival." Mary Felstiner writes: "Genocide is the act of putting women and children first. Of all the deceptions a death camp settled on, this one went down the deepest. This was the hard core of the Holocaust."[14]

The initial framing of the murdered, pregnant "Zeichnerin" Charlotte Nagler's work as a girl's diary in pictures, therefore, does considerable violence to the Nachleben of the work of a young artist whose self-defined professional creativity was so brutally pre-empted by fascist murder. Unlike the compulsive post-war desire to find relief and even redemption in the testimonies of witnesses to the Holocaust by elevating them to monuments of human hope, our mourning for these lost generations of artists or writers must not use their surviving work to fetishise our own response to the horror of their annihilation.

Leben? Oder Theater? is not a diary which is by definition a contemporary recording of life as it is being lived and narrated at the end of the day. *Leben? Oder Theater?* records nothing of the life of Charlotte Salomon between July 1941 when she began the work and the moment in July 1942 when, after a year's gap, she returned to what she had painted a year earlier and revised it, selected some paintings, mutilating others by taping strips of paper over eyes and mouths of figures, ordered, numbered the selection and added a series of introductory and concluding pages of painted script which she dated "in year One of the new salvation" and signed with the term Der Verfasser given in the masculine gender. German distinguishes between Verfasser meaning author in terms of a scientific text and Dichter which would indicate the author of a creative or poetic work. What makes this text so different from diaries, or even autobiographical reminiscences which allow of retrospect and a variety of strategies, is above all the peculiar temporal structure of the work framed, a year after the paintings flowed from her hand, for its anticipated publics by two sets of texts that address readers.

Let us study now the complementary set of final and introductory text pages. The final set are preceded by fourteen paintings that provide the immediate historical context for the work's beginnings. The issue is the inception of the project not the beginning of the events the project "narrates."

1. Sparsely painted with a splash of dripping paint, the paper is marked by simple crosses whose slight distortions suggest a fleet of aeroplanes: from the leading five brown shapes emerge – bombers are shitting bombs that rain down the painting fixed in time by the encircled words Mai 1940 (written in French, therefore), the date of the German invasion that found Hitler in Paris on 23 June 1940 after France's rapid capitulation.
2. A painting of an official notice in French from late June 1940 demanding that all foreign women refugees submit to round up and deportation. (This order had been first directed at all foreign men in May 1940: Walter Benjamin was rounded up from Paris and imprisoned; his sister's exertions rescued him).
3. The next painting covers a gap – the gap, the secret of this work, according to Felstiner.[15] The space of the concentration camp at Gurs is never represented, falling under a spontaneous but determining *Bilderverbot*. It is this never pictorially archived absence around which the mass of image making builds as commemorative disavowal. The horror, mud, rats, hunger, filth of the camp at Gurs however, leaves it stain on the characters by displacement onto colour.
4. Released because of the age of the elderly grandfather Groan for whom Charlotte Able is given a licence to care, they have to find a way back across France when they are finally given permission to travel on 12 July 1940. First, they find refuge with thousands of other refugees in a railway car – its shit colours seeping into the people barely marked out from their ghastly environment by shaky outlines.
5. The reverse of this painting is built on a wildly brushed ground that does not create realistic space but binds the two characters in a tense bond that is also a yearning for distance. A mattress, an old man in a short nightshirt stands in a pool of words that end in the chilling phrase: I am always for what is natural. Pressed into the lower edge of the painting, kneeling before her empty suitcase, a young girl sends a stream of words back across the painted space : Don't torment me; You know – I know exactly – what I have to do. (JHM 4195v)

Lightened by the cleansing use of the white ground of her paper, brushing in colour with energetic violence, the painter represents vignettes from the traumatic return on foot through a beautiful landscape from the Pyrennees to the south coast. Traumatic it was not only because of the attempted incest implied in the painting but by an attempted rape by another desolated refugee. This sequence ends with a painting in which the girl Charlotte is seen packing, speaking to herself:

> *A little love,*
> *a few laws,*
> *a young girl,*
> *a big bed,*
> *after so much pain*
> *and so many dead*
> *That's life and those its joys*
> *A little culture*
> *A few laws*
> *And (written on the girl's body) inside a vacuum*
> *That's what's left,*
> *That's all that's left*
> *Of Human beings of this time* (JHM 4290r)

On the verso a painting confronts the young girl and the menacing grandfather again, painted in the dismal fascist-stained shades of browns and greens. Their words flow around them marking the failure of contact and communication between the two figures. The grandfather rises up from the lower right to enclose or rather imprison the girl pressed to the back of the page/space.

She says:

You know Grosspapa, I have the feeling that the whole world has to be put together again.

He says:

Go ahead and take your own life so all this babble can stop!

[So shocking were these words that they were airbrushed out of the 1963 publication]

It is at this point that we encounter eight pages of hand-painted text that state how all this took place in July 1940. But, one year later, it all became so desperate that "she" (recall the use of the masculine pronoun in the later written opening pages) wondered if she should commit suicide. Another's generosity provided a room of her own. Floods of memories returned, of love, of faces revisualised and philosophies of self-creation after a kind of death reheard and rehearsed "She remembered his book ... – mit wachgeträumten Augen – with daydreaming eyes – she saw the sea and all its beauty and she knew she had to leave the human plane and out of the depths create her world anew." There follows the final painting and its overlay: And from that came Leben oder Theater??? – three interrogatives hussled together replace the careful placement of two after the core nouns of the title. *Leben? Oder Theater?* The body that was before a vacuum is now filled with this work on which the words are directly painted, without any interrogatives.

Thus the paintings and the textual narrative addressed to a solicited reader explains the genesis of the very work at whose conclusion we have only just arrived to discover its moment of beginning: a woman painting beside the sea. The text explains the project that flowed from the decision to begin to paint the work that now ends, but was constructed by the artist's secondary revision to arrive/conclude at its own beginning.

The moment shown in the final painting of the modern young woman in a bathing suit taking up a paintbrush beside the blue Mediterranean, who is about to lay down the first marks of her painted world of memories, is but the start of an aesthetic quest. The making will perform its primary analysis of a motley group of human beings, several childhoods, many deaths, some love and a distanced self-analysis. It is undertaken on the verge of catastrophe and psychic disintegration. The multi-channelled song, spoken and visualised play will stage memories, invented and recreated, in order to set up a question that opposes not only life to theatricality – hear the play in schauspiel, but also life to death. Having performed the work of memory, the artist will transform it into an aesthetic archive, structuring its form to hide as well as discover meanings some of which, captured by the act of painting, remain unrecognised or unnoticed to the painter herself.

Following Paula Lindberg's affirmation in the 1963 film that, in painting, Charlotte Salomon looked death in the eye, this work becomes less a compensatory monument to the human spirit than a dialectical philosophical enquiry into the relays between a traumatic historical situation of migratory exile and endangered life and the psychologically traumatic personal conditions under which a woman should decide her own fate: to live in some real understanding of the meaning of such a life or to choose to die because, in understanding such human life, it became unliveable. Hinged between the impact of external events of history and knowledge of many family suicides, between dangerous external forces and shattered internal worlds, between progressive aspects of modernity that offered new possibilities for a young female Jewish subject and those that put her very survival in question, *Leben? Oder Theater?* demands to be approached in a wider frame than either art history, Holocaust studies or studies of the autobiographical or life-narrative – although all are in play in its complex forms and processes. As an aesthetic practice, it poses a question of what is a marked but radically deterritorialised, dislocated, disarticulated life. It also asks: what makes it possible to choose life over death in circumstances so overwhelmingly traumatic as those that afflicted the historical twenty-four year old refugee in July 1941 when the work was begun?

Departure Berlin 1939: The Exile of Subjectivity

Leben? Oder Theater? is in three unequal parts, labelled prelude, main part and epilogue. The huge main part of 469 paintings deals with a triangular drama of love and art in Berlin between 1933 and 1938. Introducing the irruption of external historical events at the end of the 1930s, a new section in the main part starts with the most violent pogrom in modern European history unleashed on the German-Jewish community between 9–11 November 1938 as a result of which the artist's father was arrested and sent to Sachsenhausen where, within a few months, he nearly died from starvation and hard labour. It was clearly time to escape and Charlotte Salomon was sent off on the pretext of a holiday weekend to visit her grandparents who had found refuge in the South of France.

Throughout the work, Charlotte Salomon signifies the invasion of Nazism by colour: mixing her three colours, she creates a fecal brown that stains the very space they enter or suffuse. By packing her page with bodies and visual colour-noise, she creates a sense of the violent occupation of public spaces by militarised masses. The artist Gustav Metzger has recently given interviews about his memories as a small boy in Nüremburg in the 1930s. He too remarked on the powerful impression made on him by the streets of his childhood being constantly filled with paramilitary parades and political marches: noise, massed male bodies, the repeated spectacle and menace of violent crowds politicised the "spaces of modernity." Salomon catches the acoustic quality of fascist display in the scale of letters she paints onto her images. She also identifies the phenomenon Adorno would later discuss: the loss of individuality in the mass identification of a populace with the ideology, its uniforms, its leader whose word is visually shouted to a willing pack whose singular contours are no longer discernible in the economic strokes that constitute the forest of aroused followers.

The main sections ends in Chapter Four: Departure. In radical contrast to the terrifying riot of Kristallnacht, the silent room in which the girl is seen packing her world into a single suitcase produces the effect of a terrible desolation. It visually anticipates the condition of exile in which the encompassing space of home is forever suspended; even at this moment its familiarity is waning into uncanniness. The yawning suitcase becomes the bare container of remnants that will never reconstitute anything but a lamentable trace commemorating what was left behind by also insisting on dislocated transitoriness.

There are two versions of this scene of the girl confronting her suitcase, which show different decors and create different emotional tenors. It is significant that both were included in the final selection. From internal evidence, the first version is a displaced memory for the room and its bedding belong to the moment in St. Jean de Cap Ferrat when the work was being made in 1941. The room with lemon yellow walls, carpet and a tightly made couch-bed smacks of Berlin Hochbürgertum and is a painted reconstruction of a former redecoration of the Wielandstrasse apartment in 1930. The coloration belongs with the mournful sequence of drained colour with reddened outlines in which the girl revisits the rooms in the apartment on Wielandstrasse – to receive a portrait of her father from the doctor at his desk, to stand alone in the once musically filled salon and to say farewell to the maid. In a very cinematic interlude the farewell party go to station by smart red car painted racing comic-style through Berlin streets. Then, standing on the platform, the artist adds the sinister touch of a Nazi already in the carriage, standing directly behind the departing girl. The farewell scenes are long and drawn out; every dreaded step towards departure is painfully delayed to convey the dragging dread of separation.

As the train eventually speeds indifferently away from Berlin, we see the remaining trio on the platform waving. Closer analysis of the streaks of paint that form the speeding train, reveals a figure almost falling out of the window in its desperate lunge to maintain contact. The next frame moves the viewer inside a compartment, where a single figure edgily pressed close to the window, looks out, looks back, and turns contemplative of all that is now lost.

In our historical accounts of these "escapes" from Nazi Germany, we are rarely called upon to pause and feel the enormity of those moments of mechanical movement when those who were being transported, hopefully to safety, had to face the real possibility of never again seeing any of those waving on the platform, or ever coming back home. Time alone builds departure into separation; yet the dread of it seeps into our anticipation, calling forth the shapeless weight of anxiety. In a recent documentary on the Kindertransport, a father is simply unable to let his child go. Reaching into the carriage, he literally dragged her back out of the window. In other testimonies, children, now elderly people bluntly recall, the moment as "the last time I saw my mother."[16] I ask myself, could I have ever done this – what would be the psychological cost of deciding to save one's child's life at the risk of possibly bereaving them forever by that necessary kindness?

The painter's deliberate prolongation of the images of departure, therefore, alerts me to emotions that were invested in this event: not a departure so much as a sending away, the first ever separation, the first ever solitary journey across a now dangerous Europe, sudden exile from everything ever known: a linguistic world, a Jewish world, worlds of music, art, cinema, and theatre. Did it feel like the very end of the world? Is that what that moment of the final painting suggests with its solitary figure in a posture of thought? What happened between the desperate straining of the figure almost out of the window in the painting of the departing train – terrible, heartbreaking sobs or the stilling chill of emotions frozen by unknown terror?

This painting uses a novel cinematic device. After dramatic action, a stilled shot calls upon the viewer to pause on the actor's face whose inner world of turmoil or silent grief cannot be shown except by the duration of the suspended face before the viewer's halted gaze. The Berlin world closes over her departure: the final scene returns to the platform and shows the alternative parental pair commenting on the courageous quality of the girl's mien while leaving. It bodes well. She might make it.

But in opening that space to a question, the painter has hoped that someone there still remembered her and worried at the very least.

These images stage the memory of those days, giving them not merely a documentary form of chronicle or reportage. The extended sequencing, the contrasting placements of figures in space, of positioning of the viewer, the alternation between an inner soliloquy and an external third person narrative are all aesthetic devices drawn from a range of contemporary and Baroque (her father collected Baroque paintings) visualities that build a visual scaffold for a set of affects projected: the momentary halting of historical stories about flight and emigration to catch the heavy emotional freight in a series of cinematic pictures. These recall Benjamin's aphorism: Language teaches us that memory is not an instrument for exploring the past, but its theatre.[17] This is a very psychoanalytical proposition on anamnesis. Memory is akin to what Sarah Kofman names an originary repetition.[18] Memory is always a restaging of a past that had no body and no signification until thus given an aesthetic form that structured pain into representation that is, therefore, both secondary and poetic. Memories both demand and create narrative, but in being stagings, repetitions of lived rehearsals, they are shaped by both conscious and unconscious logics that are mutually impressed in displaced repetitions.

To de-personalise *Leben? Oder Theater?*, freeing it from the imposed privatisation of the feminised, diaristic framing, I read the work as "a theoretical object".[19] I listen analytically to both its logics at play in sequencing, emphasis, colour, silence, and the range of visual and textual modes knowingly deployed from modernist painting, popular art forms, cinema and theatre itself. If Salomon's project is an historically situated and analytical work on memory, trauma and culture, could I propose a preposterous conversation with another theorist of memory, another Jewish exile: Sigmund Freud.

III. Privatising Sigmund

Vienna, 1938

Under menacing political conditions, in May 1938, a young Viennese amateur photographer Edmund Engelman was commissioned to take a series of what would become historic photographs of the work and dwelling space of Sigmund Freud and his family at Berggasse 19, Vienna, as they prepared to escape Vienna a few months after the Anschluss in March of that year brought the National Socialists to power in an Austria swallowed up into the Third Reich. Sneaking around the rooms according to a timetable designed to avoid infringing the doctor's privacy or work routines, Engelman wandered photographically through the unpopulated but densely furnished rooms to produce a photographic archive of the space in which psychoanalysis was created. Rooms filled with antiquities, lined with books and orchestrated with hangings of highly significant images have been read by George Dimock as "an art installation that stages the history and theory of psychoanalysis itself."[20]

One day, changing patterns of a lifetime as he anxiously awaited his flight in conditions of increasing danger and perpetual uncertainty, Freud was unexpectedly working at his desk when Engelman came to photograph his study. Once personally known to Freud, he was then asked to take the passport photographs necessary for the exit visas of Sigmund, Marthe and Anna Freud. Amidst the vast photographic archive, Freud's image becomes iconic. It is perhaps the most naked photograph taken of the elderly Freud catching an uncharacteristic fragility so different from the well-posed images of the intellectual in his lair. Without his signature spectacles, the photograph registers inadvertently something more of the stress of this moment for the old man as his created world of books and antiquities was about to be packed up so that he could escape with his life from a situation of violent threat in which his publications had been burned, his psychoanalytical associations had been banned, his publishing house closed, his journal, *Imago*, suspended and the very survival of psychoanalysis itself seemed at risk.

Before his encounter, Engelman had photographed Freud's desk from the place in which Freud would normally sit in his specially designed chair as he prepared to start his daily writing. Freud did not write alone. Lined up as an audience, or as interlocutors from other cultures, or as reminders of an irreducible alterity in human cultures' many imaginaries, the array of figurines from the pagan cultures of Egypt, China and the Greco-Roman world confronted the Enlightenment scholar, the Viennese-Jewish doctor as he opened the file containing the drafts of his last major manuscript. It is generally believed that this file contains the text of the third of three essays on Moses and Monotheism. Writing in 2005, I cannot but note the return of the repressed: the other *Drei Abhandlungen* appeared in 1905 – as Freud's most audacious and resisted theorisation of sexuality.

I would like to discern in the eerie effects of Freud's full but empty rooms captured by Engelman in an uncanny echo of Charlotte Salomon's paintings of a melancholy ramble through soon-to-be left familiar spaces, and in the manuscript that rests for eternity on that desk, a site of migratory aesthetics structured by trauma.

In "Freud's Study of Moses as a Daydream: A Biographical Essay", psychoanalyst and editor of Freud's German manuscripts, Ilse Grubrich Simitis treated Freud's last great text as both a daydream in the face of traumatic history and a final self-analysis.[21] She suggests that the text is itself impressed into its peculiar shape by unconscious memories aggravated by a real historical crisis in Freud's life: imminent forced migration into exile. Haunted by agonies of cancer, fear of old age and terror at the deadly political pressures of fascism, Freud's last years during the 1930s were filled by a compulsion to write a fanciful, fantastic but also, according to many scholars autobiographical text: another form of the theatre of memory, a conversation with the archives.[22] A work about cultural trauma, it is itself marked by that trauma that, none the less, it cannot articulate. The traumatic is registered, according to Simitis, in the text's atypically ugly, unaesthetic, form.

IV. Freud's Daydreaming, Vienna 1934–38

According to Ilse Grubrich-Simitis, Freud's written texts are normally beautiful objects, both as manuscript artefacts and as intellectual architectures. The Moses manuscripts break this rule. Jagged, uneven, badly structured, repetitious, uncertain, the last book is deeply impressed by the old man's anxiety about the *Nachleben* of psychoanalysis; the story of Moses' murder and the eventual vindication of his teaching has obvious parallels. If it is a daydream, it is about survival. Writing so obliquely about the most archaic world beyond archaeological history is a permitted play in the face of a treacherous reality of terminal disease and political barbarism that performs a regression of the most dangerous, because politicised and collectivised, kind.

Yerushalmi stressed Freud's thesis about the dynamics of tradition rooted in a cultural narrative based on migration and faithfully maintained in the process of deterritorialisation, denationalisation and diaspora. Freud's work on the Jewish heritage might easily be misread to support the current abuses of religious traditions that fixate on cultural narratives of origin as legitimations for fundamentalist regressions and defensive fixities of identity. Following Said's reading, Freud's migration aesthetics seem to me to be profoundly engaged with the way a dynamics of cultural memory is also a politics of cultural memory. So is there a politics of the daydream?

V. Daydreams

In *Interpretation of Dreams*, Freud states,

> *Like dreams, they [daydreams] are wish fulfilments; like dreams, they are based to a great extent on impressions of infantile experiences; like dreams they benefit by a certain degree of relaxation of censorship. If we examine their structure, we shall perceive the way in which wishful purpose that is at work in their production has mixed up the material of which they rebuilt, has rearranged it, and has formed it into a new whole.*[23]

The pivotal work of Freud on aesthetics is his 1907 study of Wilhelm Jensen's novella *Gradiva*. The significance of this work about a relief is impressed into the archive Engelman documented in the placing of the relief associated with this novella at the foot of the analytical couch.[24] The *Gradiva* novella involves delusive, compulsive amnesia, fetishism and a cult of the dead in lieu of living eroticism. On the other hand, it also revolves around the curative work of a woman (analyst) who becomes the living figure of movement. She is named life – Zoë. She is also Gradiva, the Latin version of the fictional Zoë's surname: Bertgang, meaning a lively tread. She is therefore, a figure countering masculine neurotic arrest by the dynamics of analysis, following Derrida, anticipating a psychoanalytical understanding.

Freud published "Creative Writers and Daydreaming" in 1908. The text explores the analogies between infant play and adult fictions that involve aesthetic restagings of infant phantasising. These negotiate the gulf between private phantasies and the public who must be both bribed by the famous surplus of aesthetic pleasure, aesthetic foreplay as Freud calls it, and then helped to enjoy the work into which this forepleasure lures us so as to work through the resolution of tensions constitutionally, rather than biographically, shared with the authors, whose wishes have been smuggled into, and are equally articulated in, the work of art. Freud declares that: "The opposite of play is not what is serious, but what is real."[25] What distinguishes imaginative and emotionally invested play from delusion is that capacity to hold onto the distinction between play and reality, using the former to negotiate the latter rather than to lose sight of it completely in delusion as happened to the archaeologist Norbert Hanold, in the Gradiva story. German as well as English preserves this connection between children's play and theatrical plays in the words Trauerspiel, Lustspiel, Schauspiel – and of course Singspiel – the genre selected by Charlotte Salomon for her exploration of *Leben? Oder Theater?* – Leben? oder Schauspiel? Living or Playing? set as a singspiel, a musical play. Pushing this connection I suggest that CS's work, therefore, was a daydream of a creative artist that plays, therefore, between permitted fantasy, creativity, the imaginary and its known other, social reality, which the subject wishes to be cast from but not to forget.

Freud characterises daydreams as always impelled by a wish, hence arising from dissatisfaction. But they also carry a date-mark, an impression of time, arising from a moment in the present. The structure of the daydream strings together three temporalities: a triggered memory of the past, the irritating present and a prospective future. Creative writing, argues Freud, bears similar characteristics of being inspired by an event that evokes an older, childhood memory, through which is brought forth, fictionally, the new staging of possible difference from the unsatisfactory present. Some of the material hence arises in the particular history of the writing subject; but, in some cases, writers take over ready-made material in the form of legends, myths and older histories that must already offer personal resonance in so far as they appeal to the writer. Here Freud already begins to hypothesise about cultural memory; he suggests that "myths, for instance, are distorted vestiges of the wishful phantasies of whole nations, the secular dreams of youthful humanity."[26] Cultural memory – transmitted in the cultural archive that is both the texts and the spectres by which we/they are haunted – is a textual encryption of structural human dissatisfactions, wishes and wishful resolutions from moments when the intensities associated with the formative psychic processes in individual histories were culturally more manifest in symbolic-aesthetic forms of ritual, story-telling and performance. They lent their impression to the shared rituals, narratives and image systems that, *pace* Warburg, persist like the *pathos formel*, as bearers of since lost or overlaid archaic histories relaying their charge between stages of human culture that are repeated and, in Freudian terms, originated, therefore, in the stages of individual enculturation.

The Moses studies were date stamped. They were written between 1934 and 1939. These dates mark the period that I have begun to theorise in my work of

Charlotte Salomon as "before Auschwitz." Because of the unimaginable horror that was perpetrated after December 1941, the traumatic impact of what it was like to live through the preceding decade inevitably wanes. My Adornian reversal, however, allows us to theorise a traumatic pre-epoch, 1933–41, in which the daily increment of persecutory racial violence and terrorising violation radically destablised initially Germany's then Austria's and finally Europe's Jewish subjects in ways which collectivised them as repudiated others while marking this trauma individually on each subject according to their singular psychological, social and situated history. Freud's trauma was not the same as Walter Benjamin's or Charlotte Salomon's. The point is to register that such historical disturbances were psychically traumatic and then to plot the role of play, the aesthetic, in negotiating its effects into memory or rather, into the archive of culture through texts that remember rather than are mere deposits of memory.

The horror felt before the triumphant assumption of political power by fascist regimes across Europe must have been particularly acute for intellectuals like Freud, radically secular followers of Enlightenment ideologies of progress and freedom of thought. Writing to Arnold Zweig just after Hitler's seizure of power, Freud states that "everything around me is gloomy, stifling to the point of choking. Fury is mounting and gnawing away at the core. If only one could do something liberating."[27] Was writing about Moses a defence or a wish? In what ways does that address its relation to trauma as both its topic and its own repressed?

The overt content of Freud's book on the origins of religion and specifically the meaning of Moses is the proposition that an ethical monotheism, Judaism, was a) created by an exiled Egyptian follower of Akhenaten; b) that the people upon whom he tried to imposed his religion rebelled and murdered him; c) that the Mosaic tradition survived with a remnant, the Levites; d) that a memory trace of the murder survived in oral rather than official tradition; e) that varied hybrid compromises followed the murder; f) that eventually the trauma of the repressed murder returned in the distorted form of an elevating and resilient acceptance of the rigours of the once repudiated Mosaic system as the defining character of a collective identity. Mosaic monotheism then provided those who embraced it with an unshakeable self-respect based on the grandeur of the One, the deity that had "chosen them" and on the ethical elevation and intellectual uplift provided by the aniconic call for social justice and righteousness in place of gratification of instinctual, infantile pleasures. The core problem of tradition, Freud reveals, is not persistence since time can only weaken the grip of the original. The challenge is to theorise both the "gap" between the murderous event as a violent acting out of violent emotions and its re-inscription in a distorted form through this concept of a return of the repressed – a presence of repressed materials that will unconsciously shape, impress, even the mode of amnesia. Religion, then, or what Freud saw it as: cultural tradition that marks the interface of individual and social identity, is not the cause, so much as the site of this symptomology, a field where a psychoanalyst can read both aspects of the historical constitution of human subjectivity and our recurring attachments to those repressed foundational fantasies that only our repetition activates as foundations.

What makes Freud's argument psychoanalytical is the attention to three core mechanisms: trauma, latency and return of the repressed. Many cultural theorists express dissatisfaction with the current use of psychoanalytically based trauma theories in cultural studies. They cannot see how we can move from individual psychological mechanisms of psychic registration and repetition to thinking about similar formations in group experience. This is precisely what Freud addressed in this final text. Freud suggests that if the individual subject is an archaeological palimpsest of his/her own formation that is itself shaped not only by contingent biographical events but by constitutional factors such as language, so too we might allow ourselves to consider human history as such a sedimentation of its own formations which relay between contingency of history and structural predispositions that make society/culture possible – such as shared systems from ritual to language. These are traumatically impressed and subject to returns of repressed materials, unarchived secrets, that allow us to discern patterns in their repetitions even if we do not yet have a theory of the mechanisms of transgenerational transmission.

Freud hints that it is precisely where those general elements of a human social formation are psychologically significant and emotionally charged for each individual subject qua human that the strings of cultural memory link individuals into group formations in a kind of mirroring exchange that is not identity but re-enacted identification. This is, therefore, not the collective unconscious in any way. Freud offers a real if still flawed attempt to theorise precisely how the dynamics of culture, of the archive as depository and haunted house, catch us individually, but also generationally and in groups, within traditions that persist only through that animation provided by actual peoples' emotional/psychological repeating investments, charged up in each case by their own traumatic surpluses from the crucible of singular and structural infantile experience. The relevance of this investigation to the moment that witnessed the mass mobilisations of fascism needs little underlining.

The key concept is trauma: that is, "early impressions experienced early and forgotten later to which we attach great importance in the aetiology of neuroses." Trauma can either be positive – impelling us to repeat its originary situations in the search for repeated gratifications or negative, causing us to bury all traces. The power of the cultural bond that makes the Jewish people a people, providing the cultural cement, is not mere persistence and social repetition – the Halbwachs thesis on collective memory that inevitably becomes an alibi for nationalism.[28] Nor is it phylogentically based: an alibi for essentialism and racism. Tradition has its power from the rupture created by the negotiation of conflict, the effect of the rebellion and its aftermath of guilt. This gap is the now much abused concept in trauma theory of latency.[29]

Jan Assman, who has taken up the challenge of this question of cultural memory, notably through his studies of the Moses question in Egyptian history, remarks:

Freud's great discovery and lasting contribution to this discourse is the role he attributed to the dynamics of memory and the return of the repressed ... one should acknowledge that the concepts of latency and the return of the repressed are indispensable for any adequate theory of cultural memory. They need, however, to be redefined in cultural terms. Freud reminded us of the fact that there is no such a thing as "cultural forgetting" or even "cultural repression". Since Freud, no theory of cultural can afford not to take these concepts into consideration.[30]

In a book that fascinatingly juxtaposes the first and last of Freud's major writings, Grubrich-Simitis' "Freud's Study of Moses as a Daydream" was combined with a later article on the earliest of Freud's published psychoanalytical studies, "Studies in Hysteria," of 1895. Grubrich-Simitis argues that there is a thread which ties the early to the late Freud: they represent two completely different stages in the development of the psychoanalytical concept of trauma.[31] In the early trauma theory, neuroses are predicated on an event, an external shock such as parental seduction or witnessing the primal scene whose effects are registered in delayed fashion because of their prematurity and the intervention of primal repression. This clearly happens and does generate the after-effects of trauma. With the beginnings of Freud's own analysis, however, in the later 1890s, Freud also theorised a complex internal world of the subject shaped by drive theory. Unlike the trauma theory with its exceptionality of external events, drive theory addresses "the psychogenesis of everyone"[32] by plotting out the impressing structure of the drives that form a register of infantile psychic experiences that become the unconscious matrix of adult psychological life. Ilse Grubrich-Simitis speculates that late Freud was seeking to reconcile these different theories. Could he think through both the impact of a real, external historical trauma, posited by the anthropology of religion, and one visibly being enacted in a contemporary political situation, that might also explain, psychologically, the force of cultural patterns in which what must be analysed as a means of liberating us from their current danger is the structure that keeps initiating a return of the murderous repressed against a specific teaching: the Mosaic now embodied in those designated as Jews?

So by plotting out the histories of Egyptian Aten monotheism, Judaism, Greek religion and Christianity with its still vivid pagan underbelly, Freud was struggling with a way of interrupting the current ideologies of anti-Semitism that threatened his and others' lives on the basis of a genocidal paranoia about the Jewish people that had rhetorically already called for their extinction. He had to offer a psychoanalytical interpretation of the deep, constitutional structure of human culture, taking varied historical forms, encoded as religious tradition which remained dynamic and ever more potently mobilised in politically appropriated forms such as fascism. In modern times the structure had migrated into secular, political ideologies emotively more effective by virtue of that migration. It provided the drive-based force exploited and harnessed by the political aesthetic of Nazism, what Benjamin termed the aestheticisation of politics, that in the 1930s claimed the passionate attachment of German masses to a fascist demagogue through the orchestration of spectacle, emotion, anxieties, paranoias and longings for reconsolidation of threatened boundaries and destabilised, injured narcissicisms.

Freud, it might be said, is precisely trying to work out a non-fascist response to the conditions of psychic disintegration aggravated en masse in periods of profound political and economic destabilisation: very pertinent to current political problematics of defensive fundamentalisms and xenophobic anti-immigration conservatisms in Europe. Instead of essentialising collective memory, Freud wants to explain the phenomenon of massification of singular psychic crises. In passing, I should mention that this political, leftist reading is otherwise supported by a direct aesthetic translation of Freud's text by a Mexican Marxist-feminist artist: Frida Kahlo who painted her metaphoric vision of new life inspired by reading Freud's *Moses and Monotheism* in 1945 in a truly transcultural modernist political archive (Moses, 1945, Private collection).

The invisible other of Freud's Moses text, therefore, the counter-image that is its haunting spectre are, like the work of Charlotte Salomon's nightmarish daydream, the Nuremburg Rallies and the iconisation of a Führer, in whose fascist excesses of aesthetic manipulation of anxiety, paranoia and narcissistic mortification, we can see the dangerous opposite of the aniconic vision of an ethical monotheism Freud deduces idealistically from his depiction of the religion offered to the world by Moses the Egyptian. Religions draw their power from the "acting out" rather than from a therapeutic, dynamic remembering of primal impulses that are murderous. Idealisation of the father is shattered by some discovery of his failures. Recall Freud's disappointment at Jacob Freud's submission to the anti-Semite who knocked his hat off. To compensate and shield the boy child's narcissism that was once enhanced by the idealised but now dethroned father, a hero figure is phantasied as identification. Onto the hero is projected traces of the powerful feelings for the father and the child's own (reparative) phantasies of omnipotence. Psychoanalytically, fascism both punished the failed fathers of traditional Germany's old and new cultural establishment and offered the comfort of an even more omnipotent and authoritarian ego-ideal disguised in the form of the hero, following the classic legend of the lowly soldier elevated to absolute power (the very opposite of the Moses legend). Writing in 1951 on the mass psychological base of fascism, Theodor Adorno drew on Freud to show how group processes repeat individual conflicts and provide the permitted space for a release of individuals from unconscious repressions that are part of the civilising process. Thus mass movements are not made up of primitive men; they are formed by people who are allowed to display primitive, that is archaic impulses "contrary to their normal rational behaviour." The move from violent emotions to violent actions in fascist politics is not so much imaginary as prehistoric. The actualised destructiveness of fascism is itself testament to such a primordial violence which now emerges in rebellion against civilisation in a manner that Adorno argues is not simply the recurrence of the archaic but is its reproduction in and by civilisation/culture itself.[33]

Reading Freud psychoanalytically, Grubich-Simitis argues that Freud was haunted by his own archaic, murderous wishes towards the sibling, Julius, who supplanted him at the mother's breast, an intense and dangerous wish that appeared to have been realised when the baby died early, casting his mother into profound grief. Freud transposed this discovered force in his own psychic life to a larger picture, deriving its power not from historical documentation but from the symptomology of culture as repetition, in the form of the social as a form of amnesiac memory – the return of the repressed wishes that stem from the crucible of human experience, the pre-verbal hence traumatic intensities of infancy, with all their rivalries, hierarchies, devotions, narcissism, libidinal investments: drive theory.

Freud's image of Mosaic monotheism is not the product of his ambivalent Jewish identity. He portrays it as the humanising discovery of unpleasant truths about what is necessary for social existence: rules, prohibitions, subjection of the pleasure principle to the reality principle, internalisation of a super-ego, and sublimation – the domination – of *Sinnlichkeit* by *Geistigkeit*. Sensuality or indulgence in immediate gratification is opposed to something that lies between the English words spirituality (too religious) and intellectuality (too cerebral). It is the adult capacity for reasoned rather than rationalist judgement and self-management with an eye towards self-elevation beyond immediate and bodily pleasures. *Geistigkeit* is not a natural given of rational man – the broken reed of Enlightenment modernity; it is an always fragile victory willed only by self-understanding and acknowledgement of guilt for the dangerous power of our counter-impulses generated in the powerful moments when we are written into human becoming by the force of drives. For Freud, psychoanalysis must replace religion as the mode of cultural memory in order to make each individual responsible for the psychic freight he/she invests in the social whole which can work for progress, *fortschritten in die Geistigkeit*, or which can fall into regressions into asocial, unethical but mass submission to the infantile drives solicited and culturally enacted by fascism's success.

So the Jewish people defined by Freud becomes the paradoxical example of growing up. First comes a rebellion of childish violence resisting the imposed authority of the adult, the Father, the rule of culture that decrees the incest taboo and makes possible the sublimations on which adult and social creativity are built. That is the first stage which creates the conditions for the coming into being. The guilt associated with the uncognised return of the repressed – the murderous revolt – forms the psychological motor for the assumption, as a dynamic rather than residual tradition, of the very discipline that was initially rejected. This assumption transforms the very terms of subjective experience with a positive and enhanced sense of self that unfortunately attracts the violence of those unprepared to take the same step. In fact, the core of Freud's thesis is precisely an argument that cultural memory acquires its potency from the gap – the mark of the traumatic past and the delayed reaction to the trauma out of which a cultural form is made as fidelity to the demanding vision of a human sociality built on a justice that disciplines us against the violence of narcissistic infantile wishes to kill, to have, to disregard others for the sake of immediate pleasures. Far from specifying a genetic or phylogenetic inheritance of any sort, Freud is theorising a possible response from within the very out-group currently turned on by the fascist masses that might counter the latter's current rebellion against Enlightenment generalisation – i.e. departicularisation – of Mosaic human ethical sociality which aspired to make religion redundant in the name of social abstractions such as ethics, justice and realism.[34]

Playing between the social realm of political terror and Freud's self-analysis of the early traumas of the arrival and death of his mother's second child, Grubrich-Simitis addresses what Freud could not acknowledge, what his self-analysis began to reveal as he struggled with the traumatic anxieties generated by the rise of fascism. The insistently Oedipal story of rebellious sons and overwhelming father-worship screened the force of earlier traumatic impressions that involved experiences of isolation, loss, discontinuity and instability in the mother/child bond. It was loss of the archaic mother that was reactivated for Freud by the loss of home and birthplace to become the overpowering traumatic repetition. Grubrich-Simitis suggests that these inchoate and disintegrating anxieties were released in the octogenarian by the terrors of Nazism and the imperative to flee, jaggedly inscribing their pain into the compulsively re-written text that served as a daydream escape into a vision of a world in which the outcome of a paternal murder – his own professional assassination hidden in the Moses legend – was the gain of a victory of ethical social justice, a means to enhance sociality by a renunciation of the instincts which is the project of psychoanalysis.

If Freud is correct that the Moses murder was passed on both through fragmentary survivals in oral tradition that insinuated themselves as traces even in canonical biblical texts and through unconscious traces that pressed negatively on the texts as repressions, and if Freud is correct in suggesting that that which acquires the compulsive power as religion is both secondary repetition and repression of a primal murder, where, we must ask, are the traces of that which even these stories screen and render secret? Where are the traces except in their almost total repression of the other powerful archaic presence: the Mother, the transformational subjectivising figure of early post-natal becomings?

In his text, Freud does briefly insert a matriarchal phase between the primal horde (where the sons rebel and kill their overweening father, whom they later resurrect through the totem they ritualistically consume in annual festivals) and the revival of worship of the father god. Even in its brevity Freud intimates that the mother-child bond is also capable of giving rise to an ethics or a structure of sociality but its power he radically eviscerates by allowing it only a transitional place in his psychoanalytical anthropology. This hardly remembered and theoretically proscribed repression opens the space for feminist cultural analysis as my political daydream in a newly fascist and dangerous world that is trying to cast feminism back into a historical waste bin (as another brief moment between two kinds of phallocentrism). Kristeva and others have dared to suggest in the study of the sacred and the feminine, the complete repression of the maternal puts our very survival at risk from the murderously rebellious and damaged sons. Kristeva defines maternity as that structure which transforms the violence of eroticism – the son's and daughter's passions – into the tenderness that allows the other to live. Kristeva claims:

Outside motherhood, no situations exist in human experience that so radically and so simply bring us face to face with that emergence of the other. I like to think that in our human adventure, we can encounter "the other" - sometimes, rarely - if, and only if, we, men and women, are capable of that maternal experience, which defers eroticism into tenderness and makes an "object" an "other me".[35]

Derrida read Freud's text for our suffering from memory that we, none the less, need in order to have any sense of identity. Said read Freud's text for the possibility of an unfixing and relativisation of shared identities. Grubrich-Simitis reads Freud's texts for the imprint of his deepest traumatic determinations that involved the desolation of the distance from his mother. It is here that Charlotte Salomon's partnership with Freud in creating a theatre of memory in the conditions of deadly fascism breaks off to suggest its deepest particularity – its address of questions of life, love, and loss to the three women whose suicidal memories she dared to stage but withstand. I have elsewhere positioned her work as a fantasia on feminine melancholia and hysteria. I have named it an invented theatre of memory. Here, I have treated it as a worlded text, in Said's sense, as a feminine negotiation of a Derridian mal d'archive, compelling, but without delusion, the suicided spectres to whom she addressed her questions of living and dying to speak their truth. Above all, I have explored it as a Freudian daydream in the face of and against fascism that, threatening to make life a theatre, made it deadly.

Unlike Freud, who ultimately chose to die, Charlotte Salomon found hope by having done or by doing her work. In making of aesthetics a means of migration from deadly melancholy and trauma to creative life, she signed herself an artist, even on her transport to her fascist-determined/demanded death in Auschwitz, on October 1943.

Endnotes

1. Sigmund Freud, "Moses and Monotheism: Three Essays" [Der Mann Moses and die Monotheistische Religion: Drei Abhandlungen] Amsterdam, Verlag Albert de Lange, 1939; London: Hogarth Press and Institute for Psychoanalysis, 1939; New York: Knopf, 1939, trans. Katharine Jones. In the Standard Edition Vol. 23, 1–137, the translation is by James Strachey. The first draft of the book was completed in 1934. The prefaces explain the conditions of his hesitation in bringing it into public view.

2. Yosef Hayim Yerushalmi, *Freud's Moses: Judaism Terminable and Interminable*, New Haven and London: Yale University Press, 1991, 29.

3. Ibid, 8.

4. The creation of Hebrew/German editions of the Hebrew Bible that incorporates the five books of Moses known as Torah and bound in a Chumash with the two other parts that constitute the Jewish Tanach, namely the Prophets Nevi'im and the Writings Ketuvim is already a historically intriguing sign of the intersection of Jewish culture and modernity. That the "Bible" should furthermore be illustrated indicates the Reform and hence modernising intellectual trend within German Judaism. In terms of Jewish identity, the question of the Reform or Orthodox affiliations of the Freud family are culturally highly significant. The clue lies in the cultural politics of the illustrated, anthropologically and art historically advanced Philippsohn Bible itself that placed the ancient Hebrew texts against illustrations from contemporary archaeological and art historical research into the cultures of the ancient world.

5. Ibid, 82. "Monologue with Freud" is 82–100.

6. Jacques Derrida, *Archive Fever: A Freudian Impression* [Mal'D'Archive; une impression freudienne] trans. Eric Prenowitz, Baltimore: Johns Hopkins University Press, 1995 and Chicago: University of Chicago Press, 1996.

7. "There would be neither history nor culture without that possibility." Ibid, 62.

8. Ibid, 54–55.

9. Sigmund Freud, "A Note upon 'The Mystic Writing Pad' [Wunderblock]", [1924/5], trans. James Strachey, *On Metapsychology*, Vol. 11, The Pelican Freud Library, Harmondsworth: Penguin Books, 1984, 427–434.

10. Edward Said, *Freud and the Non-European*, London, Verso, 2003.

11. Ibid, 54.

12. Ibid, 55.

13. The very first exhibition of this work had taken place in 1961 at the Fodor Museum, Amsterdam accompanied by a short leaflet written by her father.

14. Mary Lowenthal Felstiner, *To Paint her Life: Charlotte Salomon in the Nazi Era*, New York: Harper Collins, 1994, 208. Anyone writing on Salomon is enormously indebted to the scholarly dedication and diligence of Mary Felstiner.

15. Felstiner argues that "If CS's paintings looked unswervingly at private history, this was because they took shape after Gurs." (Felstiner 121) I would put even more emphasis on the remarkable absence of any representation of the concentration camp at Gurs amidst such an outflow of visual representation which I suggest is the structuring absence.

16. *Into the Arms of Strangers: Stories of the Kindertransport*, (Mark Jonathan Harris, USA, 2000).

17. Walter Benjamin, "A Berlin Chronicle," *One Way Street*, trans. Edmund Jephcott and Kingsly Shorter, London: Verso, 1979, 314.

18. Sarah Kofman, *The Childhood of Art*, trans. Winifred Woodhull, New York: Columbia University Press, 1988, 217. "Repetition is second and originary – the text of art repeats the text of life which is itself repetition." Through lengthy quotation, Kofman tracks Freud's own thesis of the death of the author in which "... the work proceeds as it can, and often presents itself to the author as something independent, even alien."

19. Mieke Bal, *Louise Bourgeois's Spider: The Architecture of Art-Writing*, Chicago; University of Chicago Press, 2001.

20. George Dimock, "The Pictures Over Freud's Couch," in Mieke Bal, *The Point of Theory: The Practices of Cultural Analysis*, Amsterdam: University of Amsterdam Press, 1993, 239.

21. Ilse Grubrich-Simitis, *Early Freud and Late Freud Reading Anew Studies on Hysteria and Moses and Monotheism*, trans. Philip Slotkin, London and New York: Routledge, 1997, 53–89.

22. The final part of the Moses book has two prefatory notes, one written in Vienna, before the Anschluss in March. "We are living in a specially remarkable period. We find to our astonishment that progress has allied itself with barbarism." In London, in June 1938 Freud's second preface confirms the radical change of just a few months which led a man persecuted for his race to find himself now "a welcome guest in lovely, free, magnanimous England ... There are no external obstacles remaining, or at least none to be frightened of." Freud, *Moses and Monotheism*, op. cit., 298.

23. Sigmund Freud, *The Interpretation of Dreams* [1900] Pelican Freud Library, Vol. 4, Harmondsworth: Penguin Books, 1976, 631–2.

24. The claim is made by Sarah Kofman, op. cit, 198. See also my extended reading in "The Image in Psychoanalysis and the Archaeological Metaphor: Thinking Art with a Feminist Gait ..." in *Psychoanalysis and the Image*, Ed. Griselda Pollock, Boston and Oxford: Blackwell's, 2005.

25. Sigmund Freud, "The Creative Writer and Daydreams, Art and Literature," Pelican Freud Library, Vol. 14, Harmondsworth: Penguin Books, 1985, 132.

26. Ibid, 140.

27. Cited in Grubrich-Simitis, 82.

28. Maurice Halbwachs, *On Collective Memory*, Edited and trans. Lewis A. Coser, Chicago: University of Chicago Press, 1992.

29. So the temporality of trauma is about to become clearer:
"It may happen that someone gets away, apparently unharmed, from the post where he has suffered a shocking accident, for instance a train collision. In the course of the following weeks, however, he develops a series of grave psychical and motor symptoms, which can only be ascribed to his shock or whatever else happened at the time of the accident. He has developed a 'traumatic neurosis' This appears quite incomprehensible and is therefore a novel fact. The time that elapsed between the accident and the first appearance of the symptoms is called the 'incubation period,' a transparent allusion to the pathology of infectious disease. As an afterthought we observe, that in spite of the fundamental difference between the two cases – the problem of traumatic neurosis and that of Jewish monotheism – there is a correspondence in one point. It is the feature we might term latency." Freud, Moses and Monotheism, 309.

30. Jan Assmann, *Moses the Egyptian: The Memory of Egypt in Western Monotheism*, Cambridge MA; Harvard University Press, 1997, 215.

31. Grubich-Simitis, 10.

32. Ibid, 63.

33. Theodor Adorno, "Freudian Theory and the Pattern of Fascist Propaganda,"[1951] *The Esssential Frankfurt School Reader*, ed. Andrew Arato and Eike Gebbhardt, New York:Urizen Book, 1978, 118–137.

34. My reading of Freud's purposes in this book have been inspired by Richard J. Bernstein's brilliant reading, *Freud and the Legacy of Moses*, Cambridge and New York; Cambridge University Press, 1998. He makes the strongest case against the accusation of Lamarkianism in Freud's notion of culture and tradition, 46 ff.

35. Cathérine Clément and Julia Kristeva, *The Feminine and the Sacred* , trans. Jane Marie Todd, New York: Columbia University Press, 2001, 57.

Works Cited

Adorno, Theodor. "Freudian Theory and the Pattern of Fascist Propaganda." [1951] *The Essential Frankfurt School Reader*. Ed. Andrew Arato and Eike Gebbhardt. New York: Urizen Books, 1978.

Assmann, Jan. *Moses the Egyptian: The Memory of Egypt in Western Monotheism*. Cambridge MA; Harvard University Press, 1997.

Bal, Mieke. *Louise Bourgeois's Spider: The Architecture of Art-Writing*. Chicago: University of Chicago Press, 2001.

Benjamin, Walter. "A Berlin Chronicle." *One Way Street*. Trans. Edmund Jephcott and Kingsley Shorter. London: Verso, 1979.

Bernstein, Richard J. *Freud and the Legacy of Moses*. Cambridge and New York; Cambridge University Press, 1998.

Clément, Cathérine and Kristeva, Julia. *The Feminine and the Sacred*. Trans. Jane Marie Todd, New York: Columbia University Press, 2001.

Derrida, Jacques. *Archive Fever: A Freudian Impression [Mal'D'Archive; une impression freudienne]*. Trans. Eric Prenowitz, Baltimore: Johns Hopkins University Press, 1995.

Dimock, George. "The Pictures Over Freud's Couch," in Mieke Bal, *The Point of Theory: The Practices of Cultural Analysis*. Amsterdam: University of Amsterdam Press, 1993.

Felstiner, Mary Lowenthal. *To Paint her Life: Charlotte Salomon in the Nazi Era*, New York: Harper Collins, 1994.

Freud, Sigmund. "Moses and Monotheism: Three Essays" [1939]. Penguin Freud Library, Vol. 13, *The Origins of Religion*. Harmondsworth: Penguin Books, 1985. 237–386.

———. *The Interpretation of Dreams* [1900]. Penguin Freud Library, Vol. 4. Harmondsworth: Penguin Books, 1976.

———. "A Note upon 'The Mystic Writing Pad' [Wunderblock]" [1924/5]. Trans. James Strachey. The Penguin Freud Library, *On Metapsychology*, Vol.11, Harmondsworth: Penguin Books, 1984. 427–434.

———. "The Creative Writer and Daydreams." Penguin Freud Library, Vol. 14, *Art and Literature*, Harmondsworth: Penguin Books, 1985. 129–142.

Grubrich-Simitis, Ilse. *Early Freud and Late Freud: Reading Anew* Studies on Hysteria *and* Moses and Monotheism. Trans. Philip Slotkin. London and New York: Routledge, 1997.

Halbwachs, Maurice. *On Collective Memory*. Edited and trans. Lewis A. Coser, Chicago: University of Chicago Press, 1992.

Harris, Mark Jonathan, dir. *Into the Arms of Strangers: Stories of the Kindertransport*. USA, 2000.

Kofman, Sarah. *The Childhood of Art*. Trans Winifred Woodhull, New York: Columbia University Press, 1988.

Pollock, Griselda, "The Image in Psychoanalysis and the Archaeological Metaphor: Thinking Art with a Feminist Gait." In *Psychoanalysis and the Image*, Ed. Griselda Pollock, Boston and Oxford: Blackwell's, 2006.

Said, Edward. *Freud and the Non-European*. London, Verso, 2003.

Yerushalmi, Yosef Hayim. *Freud's Moses: Judaism Terminable and Interminable*. New Haven and London: Yale University Press, 1991.

Contributors

Mieke Bal, a well-known cultural critic and theorist, holds the position of Royal Dutch Academy of Sciences Professor (KNAW). She is also Professor of the Theory of Literature in the Faculty of Humanities at the University of Amsterdam. Her many books include *A Mieke Bal Reader* (The University of Chicago Press, 2006), *Travelling Concepts in the Humanities: A Rough Guide* (University of Toronto Press, 2002) and *Narratology: Introduction to the Theory of Narrative* (University of Toronto Press, 1997). She is also a video artist.

Sudeep Dasgupta is Assistant Professor in the Department of Media and Culture at the University of Amsterdam. His current research and teaching interests include: aesthetics and migrant subjectivity, art history and contemporary visual analysis, and the relevance of postcolonial theory for media studies. He is editor of *Constellations of the Transnational: Modernity, Culture, Critique* (Rodopi: Amsterdam, 2006, forthcoming) and recent publications include: "Visual Culture and the Place of Modernity." In *Internationalizing Cultural Studies*, edited by Ackbar Abbas and John Erni. London: Blackwell, 2004; "Gods in the Marketplace: Refin(d)ing the Public under the Aura of the Religious." In *Religion, Media and the Public Sphere*, edited by Birgit Meyer and Annelies Moors. Bloomington and Indianapolis: Indiana University Press, 2006, and "Suspending the Body: Biopower and the Contradictions of Family Values in *Les Terres Froides*, in *Shooting the Family: Transnational Media and Intercultural Values*, edited by Wim Staat and Patricia Pisters, Amsterdam: Amsterdam UP, 2005.

Sam Durrant is a lecturer in Postcolonial Literature at the School of English, University of Leeds. He is the author of *Postcolonial Narrative and the Work of Mourning: J.M. Coetzee, Wilson Harris and Toni Morrison* (State University of New York Press 2004, paperback 2006) and several articles on Morrison, Harris, Coetzee and South African literature. He is currently working on a monograph provisionally entitled *The Mimesis of Mourning in Postapartheid Literature*.

Graham Huggan teaches and researches in comparative postcolonial studies at the University of Leeds. The author of *Territorial Disputes* (1994) and the *Postcolonial Exotic* (2001), he has just completed two books, one on contemporary travel writing and the other on Australian literature. He is currently working on two further book-length projects, one on modes of interdisciplinarity in postcolonial studies and the other, co-written with Helen Tiffin, on postcolonialism, animals and the environment.

Catherine M. Lord is a university lecturer in Media and Culture at the University of Amsterdam. She has a special interest in the relation between artistic practice and the practice of theory. In 1999, she published *The Intimacy of Influence: Narrative and Theoretical Fictions between the Works of George Eliot, Virginia Woolf and Jeanette Winterson*. She has published articles that contain her own fiction and poetry, and is currently publishing short stories which experiment with the themes and concepts underpinning essays. In 2006 she premiered her short fiction film, *She's Back Again*, in Amsterdam and New York. She is in preproduction for a play about the dialogue between psychoanalysis and contemporary British Culture. Lord's work increasingly focuses on the relationship between identity, globalisation and the growing crisis in the environment.

Lily Markiewicz uses time, lens and digital technologies to evoke a sense of ambiguity and uncertainty. Her works are designed with inherent spatial and sensory qualities that implicate the viewer in subtle ways. She exhibits regularly both in the UK and abroad and lectures at the University of the Arts, London (Camberwell), and Birkbeck College.

Sarah de Mul is finishing her PhD project at the University of Amsterdam. She has published and taught about feminist postcolonial studies in relation to contemporary literatures in Dutch and English. Her dissertation is entitled *Yesterday Does Not Go By: The Return to the Colonial Past in Women's Travel Writing and the Contingencies of Dutch and British Cultures of Remembrance*.

Griselda Pollock is Professor of Social and Critical Histories of Art and Director of Centre for Cultural Analysis, Theory and History at the University of Leeds. Committed to feminist studies and author of over 20 books, she is currently focussing on psychoanalysis and aesthetics, and issues of trauma, art and catastrophe. Recent books include edited collections *Psychoanalysis and the Image* (2006), *Encountering Eva Hesse* (2006) and *Museums after Modernism* (2007). Forthcoming are monographs *Encounters in the Virtual Feminist Museum: Time, Space and the Archive*, (2007) and *Theatre of Memory: Charlotte Salomon's Leben? oder Theater?* (2007), as well as articles on the death of Anna Frank in *Mortality* and on Charlotte Salomon in *Art History*.

Ihab Saloul studied English Literature (BA) at Birzeit University in Palestine, and English Literature (MA) and Cultural Analysis (Mphil) at the University of Amsterdam, the Netherlands. Currently, he is a PhD candidate at the Amsterdam School for Cultural Analysis (ASCA) and preparing a dissertation on contemporary Palestinian identity with special reference to the concept of catastrophe (*al-nakba*, 1948).

Joy Smith is a Ph.D. candidate at the Amsterdam School for Cultural Analysis, University of Amsterdam. She is writing a dissertation on Dutch-Caribbean women's literature and narrative identity theory. Mieke Bal is her advisor. She holds master's degrees in Philosophy and Cultural Analysis, with honours, from the University of Amsterdam, and in Cultural Anthropology from the New School for Social Research, New York.

Wim Staat is an assistant professor of Film and Visual Culture in the Media Studies Department at the University of Amsterdam. His research and teaching interests are: theories of audiovisual and political representation, cultural identity, ethics and film. He is co-editor (with Patricia Pisters) of *Shooting the Family: Transnational Media and Intercultural Values* (2005).

Judith Tucker is a painter and currently lecturer in the School of Design at the University of Leeds. She exhibits regularly both in the UK and abroad and has recently held an AHRC Fellowship in the Creative and Performing Arts. She is co-convenor of LAND2, a network of artists associated with higher education who are concerned with radical approaches to landscape, with a particular focus on memory, place and identity.

Index